MAN OF ARAN

by
PAT MULLEN

1970

The M.I.T. Press
Cambridge, Massachusetts, and London, England

Original edition copyright © 1935
by E. P. Dutton & Co., Inc., New York.

First M.I.T. Press paperback edition, March 1970

SBN 262 13063 7 (hardcover)
SBN 262 63027 3 (paperback)

Library of Congress catalog card number: 77-103890

CONTENTS

5

CONTENTS

ACKNOWLEDGEMENT

Many thanks are due to the Gaumont-British Picture Corporation for permission to use these pictures, and for other very willing help.

MAN OF ARAN

CHAPTER I

Early Years—School—The Family—Folk-tales—
Seaweed and Kelp—The task of making Land—
A lasting Memory

*

My earliest recollections need not go any further
back than the time when I was about five years
old and when, after running about the road all
the evening, I came in with dirty bare feet to fall asleep
by the turf fire in the chimney corner—that is if I got a
chance to have the corner. There were many of us in those
days and one couldn't expect to have the favourite seats
all the time.

The reason I remember those times so well is that my
mother always made us wash our feet in a tub of luke-
warm potato water before sending us to bed. Potato water
was used because we always had potatoes for supper and
the water was still warm at bedtime; oftentimes there
would not be fire enough to boil another pot of water.
For my own part I hated having to wash my feet; they
were nearly always cut on the stony roads and I dreaded
being shaken up out of a sound sleep to get into a tub to
do it, so that after a time, though wide awake enough,
I would pretend to be asleep. My mother believing me to

11

be very tired would lift me out of the corner, stand me in the water and while keeping one arm round me to prevent me from falling, would wash my feet with her other hand. She caught me tricking her many times, because when turning me around she sometimes took her arm away for a second and I, fearing the sudden fall to the floor when off my balance, would open my eyes and grab her with both hands. For these tricks of mine I always got a scolding but with a smile breaking in at the end.

I was sent to school when I was about six. My father and mother were good scholars, as scholars went in Aran, and all through the years of our growing up they managed, no matter how hard the economic pinch, to send us all to school long enough so that we could go up before the inspector each year for examination. This meant that one had to have one's name on the roll book for so many days in each year before being allowed to go up for examination in order to pass into a higher class.

All the work on the land, then as now, has been done by spade labour, and I was learning to use a spade when I was eight years old.

My father was a great worker, he always had a hand in everything that a shilling could be got out of; he fished in his canoe and worked on his garden, and of course he made kelp. I will speak of kelp later. Buying lambs in Aran and selling them in County Clare was another job at which he used to try his hand in order to make a little profit; he also bought cattle and ponies with the same object in view. The ponies used to fetch a good price in those days; he used to sell them to gipsies on the mainland. Yes, my father though not a big man was as good a worker as ever stood in shoes, and in driving us to work as we grew up he was as ruthless as the devil. Rain or sun, storm or calm, it was always the same with him—work, with seaweed taking first place in his thoughts.

During those early years of mine my mother also worked on the shore filling baskets with seaweed and lifting them on to my father's back, he to carry them high up on the beach where the seaweed was spread out to dry.

As we grew stronger my mother stayed at home to look after the house, getting meals ready and patching up our clothes, and attending also to the never-ending job of knitting stockings.

Johnny was the eldest of our family and he had to work the hardest of us all in order to help rear the others; he never grew very big, though he was very hardy. I have often thought his growth had been stunted by trying to do a man's work when only nine years of age; he died in America. Next came my sister Mary, a dark and very curly-haired girl—she used to be called in her very young days Curly Peep. She was always very nice to me, and all through our lives we remained good friends; she did her share of the work both inside the house and out. Her job in the spring of the year was always that of sticking the potato seeds into the ground with a trowel; later on I too did some of this work. After some years she went away to America, where she still lives.

Martin came next, he who died young because of the evil eye, as I tell later.

I was next in line and I often wondered why I was always my mother's favourite; it might be that she saw I was the one with the least sense, but the true reason will never be known now. Peter came after me, a fine hardy lad who feared nothing—he too is still alive in America.

Joe was next; he was a fine fair-haired boy and turned out to be a great worker; he also went to America where he still resides. Jim was next to Joe. I remember him well, he was surely the finest child in our family, curly-haired and with large black eyes; but unhappily he died young, and on looking back now I believe it was of sunstroke, but the doctor at that time, so people say, really killed him by slapping on his little chest a red-hot mustard plaster on a hot summer's day, believing of course that the child was suffering from some other ailment.

Bartly and Tom were two very fine friendly boys, but I knew them only slightly because they were very young when I went away. They died from the after-effects of influenza or from consumption—it does not matter what they died of, now that they are dead. Winnie was the youngest and turned out to be a very fine girl; she stayed in Aran and got married. She was alive when I came home from America but died shortly after my mother passed away.

There were eleven of us altogether, and my father and mother made our family thirteen, an unlucky number I have often thought as most of them are now dead.

*   *   *

Fish was very plentiful, and I remember once how my father and two other men who were with him in a canoe divided some money they had received for a catch of fish. They went off to O'Brien's public house to have a few drinks. I was eight years old at the time and I went with them; they sat on a form and I sat on top of a porter barrel. As they drank, they every once in a while gave me half a tumbler full of porter, and after a short time I got very drunk and fell off the barrel on to the floor. I was a little bit, but not very much, ashamed next morning when my mother scolded me for getting drunk. Times have changed somewhat since then, for in those days it wasn't considered any disgrace to be drunk.

Folklore tales would be told as we sat around our winter fire, tales of our grandfathers and great-grand-fathers, of how they went to fairs on the mainland, how they played cards and fought, of how they danced and drank their jugs of punch. Nothing very harmful in such stories if one never left Aran but, to one going out to face the world raw and young, I don't think such ideas were very helpful.

In our house at this time there were three books, which my father, being a great reader, read many times over to us and to a few chosen neighbours who used to come in to listen to the stories and also to learn from him about the world. He was in Manchester once (he went there to keep an eye on a salesman who had the selling of some wagons of pigs that my father had sent over), so he knew some-thing about the outside world. But I know now that if he had been blindfolded all the way to Manchester and back he would know about the world anyway, because what he didn't learn he would invent, and it was just as well because either way it was strange news and kept every-body interested and happy! The names of the three old books were: *The Story of Ireland, The Rye House Plot,* and *Don Zalva the Brave.* I had a thirst for reading and when I was able to read, I went through those three old books many times. Later sometime we got the *Arabian Nights Entertainments,* but no book ever thrilled me more, or indeed as much, as our own folklore tales as told by my

Uncle Jim, tales of *The Fionna, Fion-Ossian, Oscar and Diarmuid, Ghoul MacMorna, Conan Maol,* and hosts of those mighty men. The men of Aran in those days read little fiction. They lived in their stories, and their eyes flashed with fire or grew dim with emotion as a tale reached great heights of courage or sank down to sadness. *The Sons of Usna and Cuchulain,* those heroes too came in and performed their deeds of valour and chivalry as we sat and listened by our winter fire.

In the mornings though, things were different. The greater the storm and the higher the sea the more seaweed and searods (the searod is the stem on which certain kinds of seaweed grow and from which the best iodine is extracted) were driven ashore, and at one, two, three or four o'clock in the morning as the tide approached high water mark, my eldest brother and I were routed out of bed by my father, and we all three would hurry down to the shore. Sometimes, but not often, others would be there ahead of us, it being a case of every family for itself. At such times my father was like a tiger. He yelled at us and cursed us up and down the shore as we gathered the seaweed in the tide and filled our baskets, which he would carry up the beach and then come running back again for more. On a pitch-dark night he would hurry just as much as in broad daylight and would never let us rest until we had gathered more seaweed than anyone else. I tried to carry my first basket of seaweed when I was fourteen. I wasn't strong enough and it brought me down, but I was growing strong quickly and a few months later I managed to carry my first basket, and I was very proud.

Seaweed has always been one of the biggest things in the lives of the Aran Islanders, consequently when the

great storms filled the shores with seaweed, which was
torn from the bottom of the sea by the great waves, all
families spent most of their time on the shore gathering it.
Seaweed was considered the greatest source of income.
Some of it, when dry, was shipped to the mainland where
it was sold and used for manure; we also manured our
own crops with it. But more than anything else it was
used for making kelp. This is how kelp was made. The
best seaweed (all the long clean stuff) was dried on walls
and on the beach from August till June or July of the
following year. The seaweed collected in the autumn or
winter was built up into big stacks and covered with
briars and ferns; these stacks stood all through the winter
months. When the May crop of seaweed had been dried,
every family made its kilns and got ready for the burning which in those days was one of the biggest events of
the year. First a kiln was made of stones about twelve
inches high and about six inches thick, for a distance of
eighteen or twenty feet; two lines of these stones were
placed three or four feet apart with stones to close the
ends. Into this, briars or small pieces of turf were placed
and on top a layer of very dry seaweed. Then the whole
thing was set on fire and the burning began. The fire was
usually started in the morning and continued on through
the night, oftentimes until late the next evening. It took
three or four men to keep the fires going, and two or
three young men or grown-up boys to haul the seaweed
from the stacks to the kilns. As the seaweed burned it
turned into a fairly soft ash, and as this ash increased in
bulk iron rakes were used to soften it further by driving
them back and forth through it, so that later on when the
cooling process took place it would stick together into

hard solid blocks. As the kelp increased in the kiln this raking became terribly heavy work. I have often stood by a kelp fire throwing on seaweed and raking it with iron rakes between times for thirty-six hours without ever a sit down except to eat a meal. We believed in those days that the harder the blocks were made by intensive raking, the better the stuff would be, and consequently the more iodine content and the better price for us. We were all wrong, for we found out later on that the seaweed should just be burned into ash, and that way it is of far superior quality. But whether good kelp or bad, in those old days the maker was entirely at the mercy of the buyer, and when the price, as I remember it, was five pounds a ton for kelp—that is the burned substance—it meant that we had to collect about twenty-five or thirty tons of wet seaweed in order to get one ton of kelp! The first on the market usually got a fair price. Then would come one big day when hundreds of tons would be up for testing, nearly all the kelp from Connemara and the three islands of Aran. Black looks from the buyer, and then the test, by pouring some drops of vitriol on a small piece of kelp. Next thing the bargaining, "One shilling a hundredweight," and so on; this would go on all day. And this is all we got after the toil and the heartbreaking work all the year round.

At the kilns, nearly always, would be a master burner who would get five shillings for his skill and knowledge in the making of good kelp. Some of these men, like many others who make or mix medicine of one kind and another, used to resort to trickery to boost their reputations. I remember one who claimed that by sticking one end of the iron rake into the kiln and putting his ear to the other end, he could hear the drops of iodine falling out of the burning seaweed. I have seen him at it, and I well remember the wise look on his face as he put his ear to the iron and held up one hand to command absolute silence so that he could hear the drops falling! Kelp was burned in the month of June, about the hottest time of the year. The money received for kelp, when put together with a few shillings earned here and there, meant life.

One year when the weather was very calm and hot, we started work at the kiln at seven in the morning, and at about eight o'clock in the evening of the following day, when we were giving the kiln the final and most important raking, my elder brother fainted from the excessive heat and the long hours of work. We dragged him down the beach to a pool of salt water and began to throw it on his face to bring him to, when suddenly my father, who had stayed at the kiln, yelled out:

"Come on up and leave him there to the devil. Our kelp is getting cold and it won't stick together unless we hurry and give it more raking."

We did come up, a neighbour and I, and left my brother there on the shore. However, he came to before we had finished our work. Hard, yes, but the struggle for life was harder still.

*   *   *

I was by now well able to handle a spade, that is turn the sods with the spade properly. Each sod of new ground had to be cut so that it was three-cornered. They went further that way and covered the seeds better. I was also allowed to follow a donkey. Following a donkey meant being able to keep a load of seaweed straight on its back without letting it tip over, until the desired spot was reached where the seaweed was to be thrown; also to be able to loosen the ropes on the baskets made for hauling sand, in order to let a basket drop without the straddle turning over and falling to the ground. My elder brother had of course passed this stage a couple of years before me.

My father and mother now began to talk more and more seriously of making land out of a very bad stretch of what had always been a waste of rock, on which nothing grew except, here and there, a white thorn bush that had found root in the deep fissures.

"Our help is growing," they would say when talking to the neighbours, "and we may as well start any day now, because every stone that's cleared away and every load of sand that's hauled will sooner or later amount to something."

Our neighbours talked in wondering tones to one another, asking what had come over Johnny Mullen, or how had he become so foolish as to entertain the idea that he could hope to make land out of this stretch of rock. And the reason why they wondered was this. There was no sand near by except private sand that nobody was allowed to touch, and the only sand to be had was a mile away and was covered by the tide for six hours out of every twelve. Also this sand was what we called dead sand, very fine, without life and with no heart in it to produce a crop of potatoes or grow any grass worth while. In such sand a potato seed rarely produced more than two medium-sized potatoes, even with a heavy seaweed manure on top, whereas coarse sand, with a fair mixture of seaweed, brought in a good return if the year was moist and favourable. The coarse sand also grew grass while the dead sand only grew moss. A little mixture of clay helped both of these sands considerably, but even so the dead sand could never be made to pay for the labour of bringing it from the shore and hauling it long distances.

Quite near to this waste stretch of ours was a beach called Corra Strand, a place where a considerable amount of good sand had collected thirty years before this. The high spring tides at this spot always covered the top of the beach and had formed a lake there, where row-boats and curraghs used to be hauled up to shelter and to safety from the heaviest winter storms. In this little lake were a few small rocky islands each about a hundred yards long and about fifty yards wide. These islands had an owner of course. In the summer time a few blades of grass grew on them and three or four sheep could be fed there for a couple of weeks in the year. In Aran at that time was a Protestant minister named Kilbride. A great scholar, we had always heard, and a man who helped the Antiquarian Society a lot in their work on the ancient ruins of Aran.

Kilbride conceived the idea of drying up the Corra Lake and turning it into a little farm of from about twenty-five to thirty acres. As a first step he managed to get the owner of the little islands a reduction in rent for the rest of his property, and then by giving a couple of pounds for luck, he became the owner of them.

Aran men never want to part with a sod or a rock of their few acres, but at this time they were very poor and had very little say about any of the laws that were in force. Kilbride could have taken these islands at this time, had he so wished, and have given no compensation whatever to the owner. And if the owner had objected to the selling, he would have got a notice to quit his little holding entirely. Such things had been done many times before, but not by Kilbride. Anyway, before he took the notion in his head to dry the lake, all the sand that the tide threw up on the beach had been eagerly gathered night and day, and of course the biggest family collected the most sand.

Kilbride went ahead with his work. He began by hiring men for tenpence or a shilling a day, and women for about sixpence or eightpence, to dig the mud at low tides, in the dry summer weather, and to pile it up on the islands; then he had stones hauled from the adjoining crags and filled in the places where the mud had been dug from, until they were level with the islands. A layer of stones, broken small, was spread on top and then the mud placed over all, which, when mixed with seaweed, made a fine rich soil. Finally, after some years of work, the farm was made. A few drains ran through it to the shore, at which end they were covered by iron plates backed by heavy stones. These were removed every day at half ebb tide, when the water ran from the drains into the sea, till half flood time came, when the iron plates were put up again to cover the openings and to prevent the tide from getting in as it grew higher and flooding the land. A wild, powerful workman was always employed to do this work, and to look after the farm.

Kilbride had also constructed a road along the top of the beach, where before there had only been a rough stony path that had to be put into some kind of shape after every spring tide. A strong stone wall about five feet thick protected the ten-foot-wide road. This wall was well built—the long, heavy stones being placed side by side on edge, with the ends facing the shore. Layer on layer of these had been sunk deep in the beach till they came up and made a wall about four feet higher than the road. However, the people of Kilronan village were due for a surprise, because as soon as the farm and the road were finished, Kilbride claimed all the sand that the tide threw up on the beach, his reason for this being that if the sand was taken away, it would endanger his property. There was a great deal of truth in this, but the people could not see why they should be deprived of a right they had always possessed. However, they soon quietened down, because a few who had tried to take the sand away had been summoned to court and heavily fined.

For a number of years after this the sand had been accumulating on the shore, and when the wind blew strong from the south-east the sand was often blown over the shore thereby blocking the road. Even then no man was allowed to touch it and Kilbride's workman would come and shovel it inside, where there had formed in the course of years a great high bank of sand overgrown with stringy coarse grass, all of which served as a strong backing for the wall if the sea ever broke over the road, which indeed it did sometimes during the winter months.

While this arrangement was satisfactory for Kilbride, *we* had to live too. Our family was increasing and we had to make more gardens, and for years nobody had dared to take any sand from this beach. My father was possessed of more than the average share of brains, and now that there were two of us able to follow the donkeys, he had thought out a plan to outdo the minister—though it was not until we had cleared most of the rocks off the place where we intended to make the land that he and my mother let us into the secret. There was also another drawback; for in spite of being near the shore, we had no sea-weed-right in this particular one, and the nearest place we could get seaweed was at a spot that was very difficult to get at, a place where the shore sloped down in ledges from five to six feet high and where a man must go almost up to his waist in the sea before he could reach the rich sea-weed with his knife.

Neither horse nor donkey could travel on this shore on account of the ledges, and there was no way of getting down to, or up from it except by scaling a forty foot cliff for three-quarters of its height, the rest of the distance being covered by walking down a great slanting boulder that the sea had undermined—it formed part of the cliff at one time, but had fallen away. A deep fissure lay between this slanting boulder and the cliff, across which a man or woman carrying up a basket of seaweed had to jump and then catch a foothold on a three-inch-wide bit of out-cropping rock on the cliff; then from that point to the top had to be negotiated carefully, either by finding a scant foothold with the pampootie (cow-hide shoe) or by reaching up hand over hand for a grip. Only men and women who carried their baskets on the left shoulder could work there because one had to climb with the right side to the cliff, so that a person carrying a basket on the right shoulder would be unable to keep a foot- or hand-hold, and would have slipped and fallen on the sharp rocks below. Very few women were ever able to negotiate this difficult passage. Only three women that I ever knew in the two villages could do it, and my mother was one of them. The other two were Kate Shaun Maura and Una Burke. But even so seaweed could be had some-how, somewhere, if only there was soil enough to put it on, and as I have already said, my father was planning on making more land. In fact he had made up his mind.

We had to clear about an acre and a half of rock and also level it. My father hired a man for a shilling a day and his meals, and they both set to work smashing the great shales of limestone and throwing them together in great heaps. Later on we all, including my mother, helping as best we could, built the stones into great double walls, about nine feet high and three or four feet thick. Neighbours of ours used to stroll in and watch us working, and they never failed to ask my father where he was going to get the soil to cover the place when it was cleared.

He always answered them in a half careless, tired, hopeless kind of way, as if he fully realized that they knew what they were talking about and that it was indeed a hopeless case, by saying:

"Oh, well, the boys are growing up and sure they may be able to find a load of sand now and again somewhere when they have nothing else to do, even if they have to go to the cockle strand to get it."

He used to add that the cockle strand sand was dead, but just the same anything was better than nothing. Then after some more talking, the neighbours went on their way, wondering what had come over a smart man like my father, that he could go and lose his wits so. However, to cut a long story short, the waste stretch of rock was finally cleared and the acre and a half made into five little patches enclosed by great stone walls, and in the gap which led out on to the road and the shore, we piled thorn bushes ten feet high. Another winter was coming on, and when we hadn't much to do my father, when the tide favoured, put me following the donkey, putting up sand by the roadside from the Cockle Strand.

Later on, when the heap grew big, we hitched the donkey to the little cart and slowly, but surely, a cartload of sand would appear here and there on all of the five little patches of ground. We scraped up from under the foot of the hills in the road an odd shovelful of poor clay and powdery stone, which the rains had brought down, and with this we covered the fissures. The dead sand was only a blind of course, and winter now being on us with its long and—when the moon was full—bright nights, we sat one night around our turf fire and held our final council of war; and there we laid our plans for taking five or six hundred tons of sand from Corra Strand without being found out.

The first thing was to pick a moonlight night when the tide favoured and when there was a stir, but not too big a stir in the sea, just a sea small enough so that no searods would be torn from the bottom of the ocean and cast in on the shore; because if the sea ran high many people from the village would be awake all night gathering searods, and we were surely bound to be seen. On the other hand, the sea had to be big enough so that it stirred and dragged the sand back and forth along the beach in order to wash out any signs and depressions left by us when working there. Also the night on which we worked must have a high-water tide a couple of hours before daylight, otherwise all our plans would have been of no use, because if the high tide came any later than that, somebody from the village was sure to be moving about, and sooner or later the traces of our marauding would have given us away. However, our plans were well laid, and we picked the night to make our first big haul.

As the evening came on, all signs were favourable. The moon was nearing its full, and a small stir was in the sea. My brother and I had borrowed, here and there from houses far apart, three shovels. If we borrowed these from neighbours who lived close together, they were liable to get talking, and the borrowing might come out and rouse suspicion. We rambled carelessly amongst the fields along the shore also, and laid an eye here and there on the straddles and baskets of our neighbours' donkeys; and kept in our minds the ones that would suit us best. These straddles and baskets were seldom taken home. They were usually left inside a high wall in a sheltered spot. This was done for the sake of handiness, because one had only to get a donkey in a field or boreen and go direct to the shore where straddle and baskets were waiting, instead of getting the donkey, and having to go back again home for them. One kind of basket was used for seaweed, whilst another was used for sand or clay. The latter ones were also used for seaweed which rotted in the winter time and became like heavy dung.

Having located the straddles and baskets, we then knocked about the boreens over a wide area; donkeys often rambled around, sometimes two or three together, and we wanted to be sure to know exactly where they were when we wanted them, because we intended to borrow three of these without their owners' knowledge. Any neighbour will lend his donkey if asked for it on Aran, provided he is not using it himself, but for us to ask our neighbours for the loan of donkeys was out of the question for very obvious reasons.

And now everything being ready, we waited for the hour. When it came on to ten o'clock that night, my mother draped a heavy shawl over the kitchen window to prevent the candlelight from being seen outside. This was done to show that Johnny Mullen and his virtuous family had retired to bed early, after having said the rosary very piously! All Aran Island families used to say it in those days, and most of them do to-day.

As it came about half-past eleven we drank a cup of tea hurriedly as we sat around a small fire, speaking in whispers. Then my brother and I sneaked out of the back door; one of us went up through the village and the other went down the road. This was done to make sure that no light shone in any house, a sure sign that all our neighbours were safely in bed. All the lights were out, and back we ran and away we went—four of us—my father, mother, brother and I.

My brother and I ran on ahead and collected three donkeys, put straddles and baskets on them and then drove them to where we were going to work. Our own donkey had been placed conveniently in one of the little enclosures that we intended making into a garden, and we soon had him ready too.

We got our shovels, took the thorn bushes out of the gap in the wall, drove down on the forbidden strand till we were well below high-water mark. Then, filled with excitement and a fury for work, we began. Never in my life have I worked harder, and I can say the same for the rest of our family. Each one of us had a donkey to load, but this plan was soon changed, for we found it worked better to have two donkeys dumping the sand inside on the land whilst the other two donkeys were being loaded on the strand.

I drove two donkeys and my brother the other two;

my father and mother worked furiously taking the top off the strand and throwing it into heaps in order to have it ready for us if all the donkeys were away from the strand at one time. This was the best way, for one could not go too deep in any one place in case the high tide did not do its work thoroughly, thereby leaving a depression which could be seen the following day. So we took off only about six or eight inches. Our donkeys were driven across the beach, always below high-water mark, until they came opposite the path that led up to the road.

In a hoarse low voice my father kept telling us to hurry, and at about five o'clock in the morning we thought it time to hurry away from the strand. We finished up by filling the gap with the thorny bushes. My mother hurried home in order to get some hot tea ready for us, while my brother and I drove the three donkeys down to where we had found the straddles and baskets, which we carefully rinsed in the sea to wash off all traces of sand, then we put them behind the high sheltering walls, placing them in exactly the same position as we had found them. Then we drove the donkeys into the boreens (narrow byroads). My father in the meantime had taken a shovel and, back-tracking all the way from high-water mark till he crossed the road and came to the gap in our wall, he covered up very carefully all traces and tracks of our work and our donkeys.

We then hurried home, drank our tea and had a slice of bread, and went to bed happy.

Next morning my father sent my brother and me down to the garden, as we now began to call the patch where we had put the sand. There we threw a light covering of dead sand on top of the good stuff, then we carelessly walked down the road by the shore and cast a sideways glance at the strand. Our work had been well done. The strand was level and nobody could tell that one hundred and twenty donkey loads of sand—about fourteen tons—had left it during the night.

Some few days after this, I again went hauling the dead sand at Cockle Strand, and my father went around with the same woebegone face, looking for sympathy.

Many nights through the long winter we attacked the Corra Strand, and always with great success, until finally a lot of stones began to make their appearance rising up through the sand. We began to get nervous and began to pray for an easterly wind, because always when the wind blew from the east it caused some kind of an undertow that dragged out a great deal of sand and left the stones exposed where before the sand had covered them. With a few days of easterly wind nobody would be in the least suspicious.

People began to say to one another that the Corra Strand seemed to be getting lower, but while this talk was only just beginning, fortunately for us, came the easterly wind. More and more stones became exposed, and it was taken for granted that the sea had swept the sand away.

After a few days the wind swung around to the west and the sand was thrown in once again, and even if some stones were still to be seen, everybody expected that sooner or later the sand would cover them again. These people of course had their own work to attend to, and the slightly changed appearance of the strand was soon forgotten. However, we worked and covered our tracks all through the winter and well into the spring, though the working hours during the early spring were few owing to the short nights.

In April my father rowed his curragh to Straw Island, about two miles distant, and there at low tide he cut seaweed and loaded his curragh down to the water's edge with it, he then rowed back and we threw it out on the strand. We then carried it up to our gardens, as we did several other curragh loads of seaweed, and then at last we planted three of the five little gardens. They gave a very fair return of potatoes, plenty to give our growing family enough strength to continue with renewed courage and hope the never-ending fight for existence of the Aran Island people.

All these five little gardens are now, through endless improvements, very rich and can grow all kinds of vegetables and root crops as well; and when in grass they can be mown for hay if the summer happens to be showery.

The farm that Kilbride made was not injured by our taking the sand away from the Corra Strand. It is still in good shape and the sea has never broken across the road to it.

*   *   *

I wore petticoats till I was thirteen; the last one was of heavy grey flannel and built on economic lines, having three welts or hems, each between two and three inches deep. Every year a welt would be loosed out so that the petticoat kept pace with my growth. About that time an incident happened to me in school which has forever stayed in my memory and has most of the time hurt me.

The memory of an old child is long, as they say on Aran. One morning in the month of March my father had gone to the shore long before daylight. He had gathered some seaweed for manure. But before it could be spread on the garden the potato seeds had to be stuck in the ground. I was hurried out of bed; the donkey carried a load of potato seeds, and I had to go and stick them in the ground before school time. The morning was cold and my fingers got numbed as I pushed down the seeds with a trowel. When I came home I knew I was late for school and said so. But my mother having other cares, I suppose, hurried me out, saying:

"You aren't late, it's only letting on you are, run away now."

I did run, all the way up the road, on over the hill to the school. I went in and the schoolmaster immediately came up and asked me why I was late. I told him the truth, but he didn't believe me, and gave me twelve heavy slaps on the hand with a heavy cane. This unfair beating I have never forgotten. I cried, yes, and more than that. But I will leave it and say no more about it, only that while willing to admit that this man believed he was acting in the right way, yet my thoughts when they stray back to the days of my youth grow bitter when I think of them. I left school when I was fifteen, and all or most of what I had learned I soon forgot. At sixteen I was pretty strong for my age.

CHAPTER II

Fishing Boats from Arklow—America—Dislike of
Routine—Accidents—Call back to Aran—Ghosts

★

One day in early spring, there came sailing down
Gregory's Sound the first of the fine fleet of fishing boats that had sailed from Arklow (Co. Wick-
low), and all the way around the south coast of Ireland,
then up the west coast, to begin spring mackerel fishing
in the waters around Aran—boats with beautiful names
and manned by hardy men: *Mystical Rose, St. Veronica,*
The True Light, The Frigate Bird, The Rover's Bride, and so
on. How the sight of those boats used to thrill us. It was
the beginning of better days for Aran. The first of the
great boom fishing years, and since then, until very lately,
kelpmaking fell away and nothing much was thought of a
kelpmaker.

Nowadays we catch only mackerel or herring; there
are practically no other fish because foreign trawlers have
swept them away and also ruined the spawning grounds.
Big fish like ling, cod, haddock or hake and bream also
and pollock we rarely fish for, for they are not to be had
in sufficient quantities—it wouldn't pay curraghmen to
spend much of their time fishing them.

Aran men, up to the coming of the Arklow men, had

never done any spring mackerel fishing. Now they began
to get boats. The Congested Districts Board helped them
and sent Arklow men to instruct them in the work of
handling nets and boats. Every young man who had the
chance became a fisherman, and inside of a couple of
years Aran men captained their own boats and no longer
needed instructors. They sailed the seas on the roughest
days as well as any man, no matter where he came from.

My father of course went fishing. It wouldn't seem
right without him. My eldest brother went to sea soon
after, but I was kept on the shore. I had become too good
a hand at seaweed, and my father would never give up
kelpmaking. A Norwegian steamer arrived in Aran with
a load of ice. Two old dismantled ships were towed in by
a tug and were anchored in Killeany Bay and then
loaded up with ice. The fishing boats sailed in from sea,
moved up alongside the old ships, and delivered their
catch of fish, where it was iced and then shipped by sea
around the coast to England and also to Galway, then by
rail to Dublin. The Aran men who manned those ice ships
were called "bummers" by the fishermen, a name used to
belittle them, as much as to say they were not good enough
men to go to sea.

At seventeen I was nearly six feet tall and was getting
a little bit independent, so that my first step towards the
sea was to work in the hulks. Was I able to work there?
Oh, yes. Work had been driven into my bones for years,
and I remember one day while stowing ice it blew a whole
gale of wind and the sea was soon running very high.
Smith, the fish buyer, wanted to be rowed ashore, and
asked for two volunteers. One man stepped up, but only
one, when my uncle, who happened to be paymaster and

who was also going ashore, asked me; he leant over the
hatch and shouted down into the hold where I was working:

"Pat, what do you say, will you come up and take an
oar?"

I did, and a hard pull it was, so hard that my uncle got
up out of the stern of the small boat and passed me up, in
order to help the other man who was failing. When we
stepped out on the pier Smith tapped me on the shoulder,
saying with a smile:

"Why, you could row all day. Both of you go up to
Mac's public house and drink what you want in my
name. Then, if you think it is fit to go out again, get a
basket of bread and take it out to the men."

We each drank a couple of pints of porter, and much
against the advice of some fishermen we got the bread
and went out again. We didn't need to row, as the wind
was blowing astern. As we flew past the Norwegian a
sailor threw us a rope. I grabbed it and quickly took a
bight under the forethwart. The small boat swung about,
shipped a sea, and the basket of bread was ruined, but we
managed to get aboard safely; I must pass over many
other little incidents, and I only mention this one to show
that at the time I was very strong, and strength has always
been the greatest virtue in Aran. A strong man is always a
man while he holds his strength, a sickly man on Aran
never was, or will be, considered a man.

* * *

Some time later my sister got her passage for America.
We had talked about it often. She was a true comrade.
And once when I happened to have earned eight pounds

35

when working for my uncle, I offered it to her and asked her to pay her passage with it. But she wouldn't take it, knowing what I'd have to face at home when the time came for me to turn in my money and I wouldn't have any. However, she got her passage from friends and sailed away.

America! How I used to sit by the sea and watch the sun sink in the western ocean, beyond which that great country lay! How I used to dream of that great land, of its freedom, its liberty and its wealth! Alas for the foolish dreams of youth. But that is how it should be, because youth will always be dreaming.

My sister earned and saved some money. She paid for my eldest brother's passage to America, and he went on his way. When I was nineteen she paid mine and, six feet tall, fourteen stone in weight, and as ignorant of the affairs of this world as if I had just flopped down out of the moon, I too began to get ready to go in search of my fortune, as if I knew what good fortune was! My mother always wept quietly at our going away but she never made any fuss about it. On the other hand my father always got terribly excited, praising us highly and bemoaning his loss. He said, on the day that I left Aran, that I was the best son he had ever reared.

The steamer for America was one of the last of the old Allan Line boats; it wasn't due to leave Galway for a few days. My father took a notion that he'd like to have another look at me before I sailed away forever. So he went across to Cashla Bay in a sail boat and made his way from there to Galway. He put up at Mrs. Feeney's, hired a fiddler and put in half a barrel of porter, all to help give me one last good night before I went. Then he began to

AMERICA

look for me. After a long search I was found in a public
house much frequented by Naval Reserve men. A big
man was stripped to his shirt; in his hand he held a pound
note and he was betting it against any man in the house
that there was no man there who could lift a half barrel
of porter and stand it on its end on top of the counter. A
half barrel of porter weighed about sixteen stone. My
father walked in, looked around, and took in the whole
scene. There wasn't anybody who would take the bet.
But my father suddenly shoved his hand inside his vest
pocket, pulled out a purse which had many turns of
string tied around it, and said:

"I will cover your pound." He turned to me: "Step
out there, son, and take hold of that barrel."

I did, and just as I took a turn out of it, the big man put
his pound in his pocket, picked up his coat and hurried
out of the door. That night in Feeney's was a big night.

Next day I, with a lot of others, went on board the
Corean, and after a fourteen days passage landed in
America on the fifth of May, nineteen hundred and five.

My sister met me on my arrival. She was much excited
and happiness shone all over her face. She had her plans all
made as to what line of work I should follow. Her idea
was that after I had got used to my new life I might with
her help get a job doing gardening work, which would
keep me out in the open air where I would of course be
far happier than indoors. She worked for a family down
on the North shore and here too she hoped to help me get
employment. After allowing me to spend a week in the
city to see my brother John and some cousins and friends
of ours from Aran who had crossed over ahead of me, my
sister came and took me away with her. Had I gone alone

37

with her things might have been different, but a cousin of mine who had come to America when very young came with us. This cousin of mine was used to city ways and later on I went back with him to the city, a happening that did not help me at all because I was entirely too raw a product to be brought too suddenly into the hard-drinking, gambling, devil-may-care life of the majority of young Irishmen from the western seaboard of Connaught, some of whom had settled around where my brother stayed.

But I suppose that what's to be will be. However, be that as it may, my sister took me down to the North shore where she introduced me to the lady of the house where she worked. This lady was very kind, because she came out into her kitchen to see me; and she couldn't have seen very much wrong with me, because she told my sister that she would ring up a contractor and get me a job, and then after some months, when the rough edges had been knocked off me, she would send me somewhere where I could learn to drive a motor car; after that she would employ me herself. All of which was very kind and decent of her. But it was not to be.

My cousin took me away to the city; and then began that kind of half roving life that went on until I settled down and got married.

I used to work in the city in the winter if I could manage to get any, but I would go away again in the spring back to the country, with the first melting of the snow.

I was not built for America anyhow—either that, or America wasn't built for me. I was always very impatient of any kind of control unless that control was tempered with kindness. If asked to do a job of work in a kind voice by a boss, I'd work as hard or much harder than most men, but being ordered to do it in a dominating tone of voice I just couldn't work. I became as headstrong and as stubborn as a mule, and on the slightest provocation I'd leave the job even if I knew that at the time I stood a poor chance of getting another job elsewhere. I will give just one instance of this kind of thing. I had been working in a place for a couple of weeks where marble was being cut; times were not extra good, and I had been rambling around for some weeks before I went to work there, and consequently I was broke. From the marble works I could, by hurrying, reach the house where I boarded in ten minutes, ten minutes more to eat my dinner, and then ten more to get back to the job where we clocked in as we went in at the door. Half an hour for dinner; it was long enough for me, though I always hated any store or shop of any kind where one had to clock in.

One day as I hurried to my dinner I met Johnny Quinn; he was an old friend of mine and had been to my lodgings, looking for me. Quinn was a master mariner and he was bound on a trip to a South American port to sail back from there a ship that had been bought by some firm of shippers in Boston or New York, I forget which now. Quinn had come to have a parting drink and a shake hands with me; we had a drink together hurriedly and it turned out to be the last one, because on his way back from South America he was shot dead in Tampico, Mexico. We shook hands, and then I hurried back to my job at the marble works. I punched the damn clock and went in to work. Shortly after, the yard boss came up to me; there were several other workmen near by.

"Look here, you," said the boss, "what in ——'s name

do you mean by coming to work one minute and a half late?"

"That's not so far behind the time," I answered, and then I went on to tell him the reason why I was a minute or two late, but he interrupted me, snarling out:

"Friends, hell, there are no friends in a case like this, and if it ever happens again, Mullen, you will be fired on the spot."

I flared up in a second, saying: "Oh, to hell with you and your blasted job. I want to get my time now; give it to me so I can go to the office and get my money."

I must be honest with him, though; he changed countenance and said:

"Well, there is no need for you to go to the office this time; you are a good man, but, mind you, I'd fire many another man for what you have done."

"No use," said I, interrupting him, "I couldn't work in this job now anyhow, I'd choke to death." I walked to the office, got my money, and left.

Unfortunately at that time I was pretty badly off and didn't know where in all America I could get another day's work.

I had a few slight mishaps during my stay in America, one of them being when I was kicked on the head and face by a vicious horse—the same horse had already killed a man but I suppose my skull must have been a bit thicker than his, because I am still alive! Another time I was cutting down a tree that had gipsy moth; these are pests in the form of a butterfly that lay their eggs on the leaf of a tree and usually on the topmost branch. Around the leaf they weave a strong web which they fasten to the branch so securely that the severest winter storms are unable to break it and blow the leaf away. In the spring or early summer when the trees are sprouting, these eggs hatch and a swarm of caterpillars crawl all over the tree, eating up all the young shoots and thereby killing the tree. In the winter time these webbed leaves can easily be seen, and men are often employed to cut them down and burn them. At the time of my mishap I had climbed a huge tree and had reached out with the cutting instrument to cut off a particular leaf. I couldn't reach it without going farther out on a somewhat shaky limb. I had forgotten about the exceptionally heavy frosts that we had been having for some time previously and which had made the tree limbs very brittle. The limb I was on cracked and I came flying to the ground, fully forty feet below. I managed to slide on my heels down a snowy slope when I struck the ground, otherwise I would have been killed, I think; but just the same it was a hell of a toss and it took me many months before I felt like doing much work again. However, little incidents happen in everyone's life, so there is no use in saying too much about them.

During these wandering years of mine I got into a share of labour troubles, but the world is so used to labour troubles and many other worse troubles that I will say nothing about them here.

I got married after many years of rambling, and kind of steadied down a bit and worked fairly hard till after the Great War was over. I should have been called in to prepare for the crossing to France, but there was some mistake made as to my age. I was quite satisfied, because I wasn't a bit interested in killing anybody or in getting killed myself, for that matter.

I may as well say here that in America I became an expert at making moonshine; as a matter of fact nearly everybody who cared at all about a drink turned their hands to the making of it during Prohibition.

In 1921 came news from home. Two brothers of mine, the two youngest, had died from flu—they had got out of bed and gone to work before they had fully recovered. The reason they got up too soon, I heard afterwards, was because of my father's impatience at anybody being idle and not working out on the shore. However, this may not have been the truth. But anyway one of them had died, and the other seemed to be careless as to whether he lived or died; so my father wrote me a letter asking me to return home. He had heard that I had done well and also that my wife was a very good woman. I talked the matter over with her and we came to the conclusion that we couldn't easily go back to Aran as we weren't very well fixed for travelling. I went to my brothers and asked them to make up their minds as to which of them should go back, but neither one of them would consent to go.

"We were there before," said they, "and we were glad to get away from it!"

I soon had another letter from my father saying that if I didn't come quickly he would sell out the old home and the little holding of land that we had all helped so hard to make and keep. That stirred my blood and after a final consultation with my brothers I made up my mind to cross the sea again and come back to Aran.

At this time my brother Joe and I had a very strange experience. I was running a turn of whisky one night in the cellar. Joe sat on a box while I read to him a book called *Napoleon and His Marshals*. Every once in a while we took a nip of the whisky as it ran out into the jug. About two o'clock in the morning I had tired of reading, so we talked of my proposed trip. Suddenly as I glanced sideways to where there was a trap door that admitted entrance from the back yard I saw two human forms coming without noise down through the trap door. I jumped up, believing they were Revenue Officers. I do admit that Joe and I had taken enough drink, but even so the two men, one tall, one short, stepped towards me. I had lowered down the light when I stopped reading. I fancied that the taller one spoke. His lips moved, but I heard no sound. They were not dressed in American fashion. One had on a grey shirt and the other a fisherman's jersey. I was so amazed that I blurted out with:

"Well, if you have no further business here you had better be going." They both stepped over to a dark corner of the cellar from which there was no outlet. I followed them and found the place empty. They had vanished. Joe stood up.

"Did you see them?" said I.

"Yes," he answered.

"Who could they be?" I asked.

"Didn't you know them?" he said, and went up the stairs.

I shut off the fire under the still. "Who were they?" I asked Joe again.

"Mike and Bart," he answered.

They were our two brothers. Bart had been dead some time, but we found out later that the time they appeared to us was exactly the time when Mike had died.

Soon after this a cable came from my father asking me to hurry home.

I booked a passage for myself and P.J., my boy. My two little girls and my wife I left behind, because there was some furniture and other things to be disposed of. They expected to follow us in the spring of '22. So P.J. and I bid adieu to America and sailed on our way to the bleak storm-swept rocks of Aran. Down past the North of Ireland our steamer sailed. The hills of Antrim was the first land we sighted. I have read many times of the thrill experienced by Irishmen, when returning home after a long absence, on getting their first glimpse of Erin. I experienced no such thrill. It was more with a feeling of curiosity I think that I looked at them. I had read a lot of Irish history, of course, but the glamour with which Ireland's story used to bind me in my youth had passed, and my thoughts were shaping along the lines laid down by Jim Connolly and, in his way of thinking, facts counted and not sentiment.

We landed at Liverpool, and there we met on the docks a woman who said she came from Dublin and that she ran a good house for returning Americans. Whoever she was or wherever she came from, I send her my curse, because she and her house alike were full of lies, dirt, and fleas. We were glad to be rid of them all when we took the boat for Dublin and then the train for Galway. I wired to my father. He came to town to meet us. He had aged considerably and had a lame step in him, but his eyes were bright and with the exception of the limp he was as sound as a bell. We had several drinks for which he paid, but while he appeared to be in good form, I caught him looking sideways at me several times. All Aran men who come back from America arrive well dressed and prosperous looking and most of them sport a watch-chain. I saw

44

one man who had two! I had neither watch nor chain. I had on old khaki trousers and an old coat, a fairly good pair of boots, and a battered rakish old hat completed my outfit. The first night in Mrs. Feeney's, he and I were to sleep in the same bed. The bed looked small to me, and when my father got into it, I pulled up a chair, and laying part of me on the bed I rested my feet with my boots still on, on the chair. My father was doing some thinking, I could see, and after a while he asked me if I always went to bed that way.

"That's the way I always go to bed," I answered, "I haven't taken off my boots at night for fifteen years." This wasn't the truth, but I wanted to take a rise out of him.

He said no more but turned his face to the wall, and on towards morning, when he thought I was asleep, he began talking to himself, saying:

"It's a queer son I've taken over. I'm afraid I made a mistake. Yes, I think I sent for the wrong man."

And I say now, yes, maybe he did.

P.J. was four years old. He slept in a little cot that was made up for him. Next morning we went down to breakfast and my father got talking to Mrs. Mitchell, Mrs. Feeney's daughter. I was washing my face in a little room next door and I heard Mrs. Mitchell say:

"The little boy is lovely and the beautiful curly hair he has!"

My father snorted in disgust, saying:

"He might be in your eyes, ma'am, but he isn't in mine. He didn't go with me. He is not a Mullen, and if he isn't, he won't amount to much."

We strolled about the town that day. My father put

45

himself out a bit to show me how well he was acquainted, but late in the evening when he introduced me to anybody there wasn't much pride in his voice. I believe I didn't have enough to say, anyway I was tired of it all and wanted to get back to Aran and go to work. Next morning we got aboard the *Dun Aengus*, and halfway across the Bay to Aran who should I see coming towards me, after having a short chat with my father, but the schoolmaster who hit me in the days long gone. He came to me with hand outstretched, a smile on his face, and he said:

"You're welcome back, Pat."

"Just a minute before I shake your hand," I said, "I want to tell you something."

He looked surprised, but he waited.

"I want to tell you," I said, "that there was a time I'd like to have seen you in hell. Do you remember that day long ago?" and I reminded him.

He backed away, and looked a bit startled. I looked him up and down for a second or two, then I added:

"But I forgive you, because you really knew no better. I will shake hands with you now, because it is all over."

We shook hands, and always after we were friends. He had changed for the better and was at this time as fine a man as one would want to meet. On the boat was a man in uniform, who had been a captain in the British Army, had married a beautiful Irishwoman and intended setting up in business on Aran, which he did shortly after.

CHAPTER III

*Aran once more—Changes at Home—Family
Friction—Death—Friends—Better Fortune*

★

We arrived at Kilronan pier and the only person
there whom I was interested in seeing was my
uncle, Coley Costelloe, my mother's brother. I
knew my mother would not be on the pier. Coley was
the best friend I had on Aran before I went away, and he
proved to be the best friend I had on Aran after I came
back, with the exception of course of my mother. I saw
him waiting there, a good bit away from the crowd,
some of whom had come to see me, and others who make
it their business to meet the boat whenever she comes; for
steamer day is always a big day on Aran. My uncle was a
man who never gave way to any emotion. Nor did I,
for that matter, and except for the difference in our ages
we looked very much alike. I stepped over to him. He
seemed to be very interested in the scenery because he
kept looking everywhere except at me.

"How are you, Coley?" I said.

He turned round, gave me a quick searching glance,
stuck out his hand and said: "Welcome." That was all.

We turned and walked up the pier together. He looked
at P.J.

"Is this your son?"

"Yes," said I.

"Huh," was all he answered.

"You have grown smaller, Coley, since I saw you last," said I.

"The world has a habit of doing that to a man. It will do the same thing to you by and by," he answered.

"How is my mother?" was my next question.

"No need of me telling ye. You will see her yourself in a few minutes." With that and after a few more similar remarks we came to the crossroads. He turned towards his house and, I taking P.J. by the hand, we headed for home.

My father had been delayed on the way. He was talking to some neighbours about fairs and markets.

P.J. and I walked into the house. My mother had heard us coming but instead of running towards us with glad tearful cries of welcome, as most people seem to imagine mothers usually do when this kind of reunion takes place, she had picked up the broom and pretended to be sweeping the floor. I took a couple of steps and placed my hand on her shoulder. She turned round to me. She gave me one look, and oh, such a look I shall never see again. Full up it was of joy and pride and love. Then she cast down her eyes as if she were ashamed. She had aged terribly. Her once strong frame had grown gaunt and thin. Her scant grey locks were tied in a small knot at the back of her head, and now I felt much ashamed, for it came home to me with a shock that during most of my wild years in America I had forgotten her. I felt very small and cheap.

"Mother," I said, as I lifted up her dear old lined face and kissed her.

"You shouldn't do that, Mac [son]," she murmured.

"Why?" I asked her.

"Because I am not nice to kiss with all my teeth gone and everything. Sit down in the corner there," she added, "and I'll have the tea ready in a minute for yourself and your little boy. He's a grand little fellow," and she stroked his curly head.

We drank tea together, then she showed us our room. Clean and tidy it was, and in a corner was a little stand with a towel and a big jug full of water, and a wash basin.

"You must be getting up in the world," said I, "to have these newfangled things stuck in the room."

"Well," said she, "sure I knew you were used to them in America, and I thought that the way we always wash in the kitchen mightn't be good enough for ye."

"Never mind," I answered, "let them stay here for to-day, but after to-day where you wash your face so do we wash ours, and where you eat, well, there we eat too."

My father had bought a horse when he knew for sure that I was coming home. Next day we went to look at it. I liked the horse and soon we hitched him into the old common cart and trained him to work, but there wasn't much to do, and that worried me. By work I mean labour whereby a man could earn a certain amount of money each week. I had been used to such a way of living for so long that I couldn't change my ways immediately. My mother saw this, and she told me not to worry.

"You will get work enough to do by and by," said she, "but whether you do or not, don't worry, because I have enough to keep yourself and your little boy until times get better."

My father was changing. He began to order me about, much, as I was told, as he had ordered the two other boys who had died. It struck me at the time that he couldn't see that I had grown up, and that he didn't realize how long I was away; he just went on as if I had never left home. Another thought—maybe it was wrong—but which nevertheless always persisted in coming to my mind, was that had I come home dressed up and with a few hundred pounds in my pocket, passing over a hundred of it to him, things might have shaped themselves differently. He grew very bitter, and cursed me as he gave orders. One day I turned on him and said calmly:

"Who the hell do you think you are talking to, a pup-dog or something? Now listen here to me. I never took kindly to being ordered about by any man, especially when ordered in the tone of voice that you use. Wake up, open your eyes and understand that you aren't talking to one of the boys."

He walked away after calling me his scoundrel of a son; next he began to talk about his property and how nobody could stay in his house waiting till he died to get hold of it. And what a property it was that he raved about—seven acres of land—the greater part of which we all had made ourselves by hauling sand and seaweed on to the bare rock until it formed a thin layer of soil! It was sufficient to grow a little crop of potatoes on, if the month of July came in showery! Also it could feed a cow and calf! Otherwise, so far as making a living out of it was concerned, it would starve the crows to death. He went so far one time as to say to a neighbour in confidence:

"How do I know whether that big devil is a son of mine or not. He might be some bloody ruffian that has come to get hold of all I have." And now came a worse change. I found that my mother didn't want him to send for me or any of us in America, she knowing only too well how difficult it was to get on with him. But now that I had come, she stood by me against him, with the result that he suddenly developed a terrible hatred towards her.

Strange it is how human beings can become so twisted, for I had known him as a great provider for his house and family, a tyrant over us for work, and a great worker himself. And now this, after all those hard years in the past. Had he asked me in a friendly way to go back to America, I would have gone willingly, but when he tried to force me to go, well, then all the devils in hell couldn't have driven me out of Aran.

I dug the poor potato crop, and between times I hunted rabbits with a dog the boys had. Speed was his name. Hunting rabbits didn't help me much, although my father said that I was good for nothing else! I had come home in September, and a few days before Christmas my uncle gave me a chance to earn my first pound since coming back. The job was hauling fish barrels from Kilronan to Kilmurvy where canoes were fishing mackerel. He paid me the pound on Christmas Eve. A bitter smile crossed my lips as I looked at it, for I remembered the many pounds that had flown from my hands in those other days that had gone. However, I walked straight up to the house and offered it to my mother.

"Thanks, Mac," said she, "for offering it to me, but I won't take it. 'Tis little enough for yourself of a Christmas Eve."

"What will I do with it?" I asked.

"Go out and buy yourself a cap with part of it, and then if there is anyone you have a wish for this blessed night, take them and give them a treat. But anyway," she added, "buy the cap first, because to tell you the truth I never liked that battered ould divil of a hat you have on you."

I bought the cap and have never worn the hat since.

On Christmas day there was a row in our house. My uncle, who had called in for a visit, tried to make peace. It was all about the pound. My mother told my father what had happened to it, but it was no use, my father kept on saying that we would stick to one another and that no one could tell what was happening between us.

The British Army officer had set up in business, and I began to do a little work for him. P.J. had begun to go to school, but he had a hard time because my mother didn't dare to be nice to him or treat him properly as a child ought to be treated. It would have only caused more and more trouble. Many a time she put a slice of bread and butter under her apron and made pretence of going to the village pump for water by taking a bucket with her. She really went to meet P.J. there at noontime to give him the bread and butter, then let him run off to school again. This secret kindness of hers to P.J. had to be stopped, because there are no eyes sharper than those of jealousy and hatred, and my father soon found out about her love for the child; then he raised such hell that my mother had to give up going to the pump.

I spoke to my uncle about it, and he told me to send P.J. to his house at noontime and evening, when he could have some cocoa and bread. At home things didn't improve, and my mother was failing rapidly. There are certain things that happen in families, at least there were

things now happening in ours, that stab too deeply to be written about. I must pass over those incidents and only say that because of them my mother had not long to live. One day I said something which made her call me aside and she said:

"Pat, I want you to make me a promise."

"Yes," said I, "anything you want me to promise, that I will do."

"Well," said she, "you must promise me that you will never raise a hand to your father."

I hesitated for half a minute, because I had many times thought that I should interfere and prevent his cruelty to her, but as it was for her sake, I finally promised.

"Now," she added, "I'm happy."

I think men should be very respectful towards all women, because I'm sure there was no woman ever born that didn't have a lot of good in her.

On Good Friday I had a long talk with my mother, and in the course of our conversation she said:

"I won't be here for very long now to look after you and your little boy, but whatever happens you must keep the horse. Your father will try to take him away from you. If you let him have his own way with the horse you are done, and you will have to go back again to America. Keep the horse," she said, making her words more impressive by laying her hand on my shoulder, "keep him and you will always have a chance to earn a shilling. And", she added, "try to get your wife over here as quick as you can."

I told her I would, but my wife never came because some neighbour wrote out a gossipy letter to America, and my wife heard how we were all quarrelling at home.

On Easter morning another of those incidents which can't be told happened, and my mother lost the use of her voice for part of the day. That night however she appeared to be in good form enough because she read a chapter from a novel to me. She smiled as she read, and winked one eye, knowing that my father who had gone to bed was listening—it was a habit of his to belittle the way anyone else had of reading, believing that nobody was as good as himself. And indeed, I must say, he was a very good hand at it. On Easter Monday morning I, as usual, brought my mother up a cup of tea which she drank in bed. I went to have my own breakfast when suddenly I heard a sound. I ran to her room and found her on the floor. I carried her out into the street into the open air, but it was no use. She just gasped, then with a sigh she died. I carried her in and laid her on the bed.

And now my father began to bemoan his fate. The neighbours gathered in and began to talk about the awfulness of sudden death, but I got into trouble immediately when my father said:

"Well, she is now before the Judgment Seat."

"Judgment Seat," I said, "what God would sit in judgment on a woman like her, a woman who worked hard and slaved to bring up a large family." I said some more, but stopped in disgust when the neighbours held up their hands in horror, saying:

"Pat Mullen, don't be flying in the face of God. That's the way with all of ye when ye lose your religion in America."

I walked out and went down to the army officer's pub, got a bottle of whisky and asked him to join me and as we drank we talked about other things than death.

Two days after the burial I drove down the road with the horse and cart. I stopped at the army officer's and went in to ask him if he would on his next trip to Galway Town buy me a second-hand sidecar (jaunting car). He was just giving his consent when we heard my father's voice outside, saying: "Get up, boy!" I rushed out in a furious rage, for he was taking the horse away from me. He had climbed on to the cart and was driving away. It was the last straw, and I had promised my mother to keep the horse. I shouted. He looked back, and whatever it was he saw in my face as I caught the horse by the reins and swung him across the road, I don't know, but he soon hopped down and hurried away leaving me in charge of the horse, and strange to say, that about finished our quarrels. Shortly after came a gradual softening of the strain between us. There were flares now and again, of course, but taking the whole situation broadly we began to get more and more friendly as time went on.

I got my second-hand sidecar and began to earn a shilling with it by picking up odd jobs, such as driving tourists from the steamer to see the ancient duns and churches, and so on. On one of these trips as I was driving down a hill on my way to Dun Aengus, I had three men and a woman on the car, when suddenly one of the shafts fell out of it. My passengers got a bit excited and began to blame me for taking them on such a trip in such a rotten old car. I needed a few shillings very badly, so, taking in the situation quietly, I said:

"Well, sure any fool could drive you on a car with two shafts, but it takes a man to drive you on a car with one."

This put them in good humour again; I managed to do it, and got them safely to the dun and back.

In spite of making a little money here and there I still felt dissatisfied. I was somehow a stranger in a strange land. My thoughts and ideas were different. Whether it was that knocking about had broadened my outlook or whether it was that Aran men had changed, I don't really know, but in any case things were certainly different. Later, after many years, I began to understand them better, and times became more agreeable to me. I began to make kelp again, but it was harder on me now than it was in my young days, because now I had to cook my own meals and dry and patch my old clothes. My uncle's company and advice was a great help to me at this time.

*   *   *

In '23 I met my first great friend, a lady who had come to Aran for a few days' holiday. My father had sold the horse and bought another. He named him Cannon Ball, a beautiful dappled grey. Next he went to town and bought a brand-new sidecar and harness with which to decorate him. Horse, sidecar and harness cost over fifty pounds, and he said to me:

"Now, son, go ahead and make a living."

I was admiring Cannon Ball one day in front of the house when this lady was passing by. I saw her look at the horse, then I spoke to her and asked her what she thought of him. She praised him highly. Next day I drove her to the duns and then she went away. But from that day on my star of luck began to rise, and though there were many setbacks, it has never set since. After this I conceived the idea of building a little cabin by the sea, so I could rest and have a cup of tea when worn out by kelp making.

In '24 I met my next great friend, an American lady, no

finer soul or truer friend ever drew the breath of life. And now the circle began to broaden and soon I had friends in Ireland, England, Wales and America. They began to send me good books to read, and I had some moments also for leisure and thought, and then it began to dawn on me gradually that what I had been looking for all my life I had found at last. Peace, home, happiness and true friends.

My eyes and my mind began to awaken to the beauty of my Island, the gorgeous sunrises and sunsets, the wild flowers, the lark's song at dawn with the soon following notes of the blackbird and thrush; the storms, the wild winter seas raging mountain high and covering our Isle with a mist of spray; the old duns that seem to gather in their walls closer round one when night pushes day away, and where the dead voices of the past come whispering again on the night wind and commune with one's spirit. Yes, at last Aran had laid its spell upon me and I could part with her no more.

While this transformation was going on within me, many incidents were taking place which would be discouraging to many a man. Cannon Ball was killed. I had lent him to a neighbour, foolishly enough perhaps, to haul kelp. The horse was spirited, and when my neighbour struck him a blow with a searod he went mad and tore with the cart of kelp down through the beach, where he fell and was so badly injured that he died shortly after. I had to slave again to earn the price of another horse, but in two months by working night and day, I made eighteen pounds worth of kelp and bought another great powerful animal, snow-white and wild as a hawk. I bought a canoe and prepared to learn how to handle her, my object being to be able to row my friends to the other two islands. In order to learn, I went herring fishing for one winter, and here I got the first great setback to my strength; having nobody to rinse the salt water out of my clothes or to dry them, I wore wet clothes all the winter, and rheumatism got its chance to take a fall out of me.

In order to reach true happiness I think a man's mind must rise to such serene heights that life and death are taken as a matter of course. Then, the when and where and how don't matter, and neither great adversity nor great joy can disturb it very much. I haven't reached those great heights by any means, but it is a goal I always try to keep in view. Perhaps, some time?

CHAPTER IV

I meet Mr. Robert Flaherty—Talk of a Film—The Flahertys' Return—Preparations for the Film—I become Contact Man—Mikeleen Dillane—Religion for Food—Selecting a Cast—Patch's Whiskers— Storm Scenes

*

O ne day, late in the year '31, I drove to the pier and met a man named Mr. Jaques, an Englishman. I drove him around. He was staying a week. He was very fond of fishing, so I got two other chaps with myself to row him out into the bay. He fixed up his own lines and killed, during the few days, a good share of mackerel and pollock. At night we used to adjourn to Daly's pub, have a few drinks, and talk over the sport of the day. I liked Jaques very much. He went away with a promise of coming again soon. He came back in a few weeks. It was about the end of November. He was on the bridge of the *Dun Aengus* as she came alongside the pier, and I waved my hand to him. When the steamer was moored, I jumped on board and we shook hands.

"Where is your bag?" I asked him.

"In a minute, Pat," he says. "First I want you to meet this gentleman, Mr. Flaherty," and he introduced us.

59

I shook hands with Mr. Flaherty who was a great giant-bodied man, white-haired and blue-eyed. He in turn introduced me to his wife and three very beautiful daughters.

"Drive us all up to Ganly's," said Mr. Jaques.

I did, and when we got there Mr. Flaherty said he'd be staying over until the next boat day, and asked me if in the meantime I'd drive his family and him around the Island and show them all the interesting places that were to be seen.

"I shall be glad to," said I, "because driving tourists around and showing them all the places of interest is part of my way of living."

That night they invited me to have supper with them in Ganly's. Mr. Flaherty talked, and talked well. Most of the time he kept asking me questions about the Island and the people, enquiring as to how they lived on it, asking if the sea ever washed away any of the little gardens we had made by the shore. We all, including Mr. Jaques, passed a very enjoyable evening.

Next day I drove the Flahertys around to see the duns, the cloughans, and the churches. They were interested in what I pointed out to them, but not nearly as much, so I thought, as other tourists that I had taken to these places before. But as I drove along the road Mr. Flaherty kept stopping me while Mrs. Flaherty took shots, as they called them, with a camera which she held up to her eye and clicked. However, I passed a very enjoyable day, for I like meeting interesting people, and the Flahertys were all of that. The girls Barbara, Frances and Monica were very jolly and friendly. Next day the three of them insisted on paying me a visit at my house. I refused at first, because a house like mine that had been for years without the touch of a woman's hand was no house to bring anyone into, especially when I had to be out of it night and day myself trying to earn a living. I had made several efforts to straighten it out, but it seems that to some people, as old age comes on, old memories freshen; and what I used to throw out of the house as useless, my father would, with tears in his eyes, bring back again, saying that this thing belonged to one of his boys or that to his wife, Mary. Anyhow, the girls won me over, and with a promise of helping me to clean the house they got in. They did help, and with a piece of cloth that I got for each of them they sent the dirt and cobwebs flying, and we all together puffed and spat till we made a fairly good job of it. Then we sat down for a while and had a chat, they talked about school and fishing, about Samoa in the South Seas where they had learned to swim, and they talked of New Mexico through which they had travelled and where they had spent some little time. They expressed a wish to go out fishing in a curragh, and though there was no sign of any fish in the bay, still, to please them, I got a couple of herring nets, put them into the canoe, and out we went. When we got out to where there used to be a good berth for catching herrings, we shot the nets, tying a buoy on the end, and then we came back home. Next morning I took two of the girls in a punt or small boat. The two chaps who were with me when we took Mr. Jaques fishing went in the canoe, and Mr. Jaques and Monica went with them. We rowed out to where the nets were moored and there wasn't a fish to be seen as far as we could see down through the water, but as they began to haul the nets into the canoe we saw that the bottoms of the nets were full of herrings. We had a grand catch, about eighteen hundred in all. We staged a kind of race coming in, but it wasn't a fair one. We were ahead in the small boat and we kept blocking the canoe every time she tried to pass us. I sold the herrings to a shopkeeper—I took Monica with me and tipped her off to help me with the sale, because in Aran as elsewhere you will find that the shopkeepers buy cheap and sell dear. This particular shopkeeper tried to bargain with me in Irish. It was one shilling and sixpence a hundred; but I would have none of his Irish; I kept answering him in English so that Monica could understand. I also kept asking her her opinion and she got excited.

"Why," she says, "Mr. Dolan, you don't mean a word of it. One and six for such beautiful fish. I never heard of such a thing. The least you can give the poor man is three shillings a hundred!"

We kept on at him—she did, anyway—and finally we got our three shillings.

Next day they prepared to leave Aran. Mr. Flaherty called me aside and said:

"Pat, I'm sending in a report on the conditions here, and don't be surprised a bit if you see me back here again making a film."

"I hope you do come back," I said, and with that we all shook hands and they sailed away.

That same evening I asked Mr. Jaques what he thought of Mr. Flaherty.

"He seems to me to be a very fine man. Indeed I think they are a very fine family," he replied.

"The family are all right," said I, impatiently, "anybody can see that, but there is something in Mr. Flaherty that I can't fathom."

"Do you think so, Pat?" said Mr. Jaques, "I didn't notice anything."

"There is something," I said, "I can see it by the look and the colour of his eye, but for the life of me I can't make out what it is. I can't lay my finger on it. Mr. Flaherty has a heart as big as a house," I added, "but yet——." And I may as well say here that later events proved that I was right. Mr. Flaherty came back, and what I didn't know at first I was soon to find out. It was this: that Mr. Flaherty was a man who was bound to be leader in any game where he played a hand, and I felt that, should we ever meet in any deal, there were bound to be some clashes, because I never had much use for leaders of men who believed that every man was as good as another; besides my nature always rebelled at taking orders from anybody. As things turned out we did have clashes. I have often since thought that there were times when he was right; but to be honest, there have been times when I felt sure he wasn't.

The time came for Mr. Jaques's departure. He sailed away with a promise to return on his lips, but he never came to Aran again. He had grown tired, that I knew, but I hadn't realized how tired. I would have prevented his going away from Aran had I known, and I know that he would have stayed had I asked him. Shortly afterwards came the news that he had deliberately crossed the Big Divide, and I was saddened because he was a true friend.

A few days before the New Year Mr. Flaherty sent me word that he was coming back, and now I knew that I would have to leave my kelpmaking and other work behind and start on an entirely new line of endeavour.

I had heard and read a little about film making, but in actual fact I knew almost nothing.

I had been able to make ends meet more easily of late years. I had become fairly expert at patching my clothes, and I had become a middling good cook when I had time enough to do it. Baking bread was hard to learn, and I pretty nearly gave it up after my first try. I kneaded the stuff together and put it into a big oven, and put a nice fire underneath it and a lot of red coals on the lid. After a while I fancied I smelt something burning. It was my bread. The fire was too big and the bread was burned black on top and had stuck to the bottom of the oven. I had to cut it into pieces with a knife in order to get it out. The bottom had also been burned black, but the middle of it was as soft and as sticky as ever; I threw the whole thing out in the garden, and sat down to think things over. Speed, my dog, came along and gobbled the whole mess up. It nearly killed him. It must have made a lump in his stomach, for he went around for the rest of the day with a sorry look on his face, and every once in a while he rolled himself on the ground trying to soften it!

My father, who was on his own hook at this time, made one try, and one only, at making bread. I came in one day and when I saw what he was up to I nearly died laughing. He had taken a large bowl, filled it with flour and water, and was mixing it up. It was too soft, and when I came in he had his two hands held out and was looking at them. The dough was dripping from his hands on to the floor. He was weeping at his sad fate and mourning all his relations that had died as far back as his memory went! I got a handful of flour and managed to get the dough off. He never tried again.

Mr. and Mrs. Flaherty arrived back, and with them a fine looking boy who would soon be a grown man. I was thinking about the film and forgot that Mr. Flaherty had no son, and I absent-mindedly called this young man Flaherty. His name was, however, John Taylor. He had come to assist Mr. Flaherty with camera work and also to develop the film in the laboratory. I drove them to Mrs. Ganly's again, and soon they began to talk about a cast for the film, also about the making of land and storm scenes, evictions and shipwrecks. They were indeed very keen about their work. After a week they decided to settle in Mrs. Sharman's house at Kilmurvy. It was near the sea and was in a central position on the Island. They began to get ready for making the *Man of Aran* film, as it was to be called. I was hired, and I was to be what is known as a contact man between Mr. Flaherty and my own people. Carpenters were put to work turning a fishing shed into a laboratory—part of the work was the putting in of developing and drying rooms. I knew nothing about this kind of work, and I never cared much about learning it. The fact is I never had the time, and even if I had, I believe I wouldn't have had the inclination.

An Irish cottage had to be built for the inside scenes, and Mr. Flaherty left this job to me. This was work I liked, and I took great interest in it. I searched the three most westerly villages of the Island for a gang of picked men, men who I knew were good at handling stone; then I searched through the different villages for a tumbled-down old house that had in it an arch over the fireplace suitable for our cottage. A friend of mine in Gortnagapple village owned one, and like the fine man he is, he tore down the walls of the old house, took out all the stones

that formed the arch, put them on his own cart, brought
them to where we were building the cottage, and made
us a present of them. While this work was bustling along,
I spent some days driving Mr. and Mrs. Flaherty around.
We met and spoke to many people here and there along
the road. Mr. Flaherty looked these people over very
carefully with an eye to finding suitable people for his
cast. We also visited people in their homes and chatted
with them partly to become on sociable terms with them
and partly with the idea to find out if they would be
suitable for the film. Both reasons were important. One
night there was a little bit of a dance in Killeany village.
The Flahertys expressed a desire to go, so that they could
get a chance to look the young people over. They did go,
and there they saw little Michael Dillane. His appearance
struck them so favourably that Mr. Flaherty was eager
to get some shots of him. A few days later he did, but he
had to take shots of Mikeleen's brother as well. The
shots of Mikeleen came out very well, and though
he took shots of many other boys, Mr. Flaherty never
took any that he felt sure would fit as well as Mike's;
so Mr. and Mrs. Flaherty then and there decided that
Mike was the boy they wanted for the film. So they
asked me to go to Killeany and speak to his parents about
letting him come to Kilmurvy to go to work on the film.
His father was away fishing, but a few days later when he
came home I asked him about it, and I painted Mikeleen's
future in glowing colours.

"Well now, Pat," said he, "you know yourself that it is
the woman who gets the most trouble from the children,
so whatever she says herself I will be satisfied with it."

I went to see Mrs. Dillane, and I went many times.

What questions she asked, questions which to me were absolutely senseless and time-worn, but which to her as to the majority of the people of the Island were questions of more than life and death, because they involved the hereafter and eternity.

*　　*　　*

The Great Famine and its aftermath had left the Irish people frightfully poor and broken-spirited, and it was unfortunate that at this time some Protestant proselytizers attempted to change the faith of the poorest of them by setting up soup kitchens. In these places they endeavoured to make the Irish people alter their faith in exchange for soup and a smattering of education! I'm not a bit interested myself whether a man professes any form of religion or not, because I believe God is so good that there is hope for us all. The incident I quote above was unfortunate because to this day amongst backward communities the fear of having their faith taken away from them by strangers, under the form of one line of endeavour or another, is a real fear. I can well believe of course that those proselytizers were sincere in their belief that they were rescuing the poor Irish from hell's fire, but that does not help the matter at all.

I do wish all such people would let us Irish go to hell or to Heaven in our own way, just as we feel inclined. Hell, yes, I'd rather go there just for devilment than to be pushed up to Heaven in spite of me. However, this idea has been handed down to us, and a few of the old people still remember those evil days.

*　　*　　*

Aran people were looking sideways at Mr. Flaherty

and his talk of making a film; some of them believing at the back of their minds that his talk of a film was only a blind, and that once he had got a foothold and a grip on things the same old story would begin again but in a new way. Mrs. Dillane asked:

"What does Mr. Flaherty do, Pat, when no one is looking at him? Do you think he says his prayers? Some people say that he is a queer kind of a man. Do you think if I send Mikeleen over to him my son will lose his religion? Will they try to take it away from him?"

"Musha, don't you know, ma'am," said I, "that there is no fear of that happening. Those days are gone forever. These days everyone has enough to do to make a living and they haven't time to care or think about what religion anybody else has. Besides," I added, "Mikeleen is a relation of mine through the Dillanes, and sure you know well enough I wouldn't be where anything like that would be tried on him."

She smiled faintly and said: "I believe that indeed, but if you want to know it, lots of people say that the divil a much you have of it yourself any more than Flaherty."

I laughed and kept on with my coaxing, and finally, after many attempts, she consented to come with me to the Sergeant of the Civic Guards in Kilronan village. Mikeleen was only twelve years old and she would have to give her consent before the sergeant in order to allow Mike to go to work on the film. It had to do with the school regulations. All signs pointed towards a favourable ending at last to the objections of Mikeleen's mother. We appeared before the sergeant, and he asked her if she were willing to allow her boy to go to Kilmurvy for film work. The question was, I thought, put to her a bit abruptly.

Anyhow, she suddenly got excited and frightened looking and said:

"Isn't it all right to send him there? What will they do
to him? Do you think they will try to take his religion
away from him?"

"My dear woman," said the sergeant, "that has nothing
to do with me. Are you willing, or are you not, to let your
son go to work for Mr. Flaherty?"

She got still more excited and rushed out waving her
arms, crying: "No! No! I will never give them my little
boy without knowing what they are going to do with
him."

And away she went home, and left me feeling very
crestfallen after all my wasted efforts.

Rumours were rife that Mr. Flaherty was a Socialist.
Not many on Aran know what Socialism means. To the
great majority it means an organization backed by the
devil. Other rumours said that the cottage we had now
nearly built was to be used as a "Birds' Nest". "Birds'
Nests" were buildings or homes that were put up in Ireland during the famine years, and there destitute Catholic
children were clothed and fed and brought up in the
Protestant religion. So after all it was rather hard perhaps
to place much blame on Mikeleen's mother. However,
after some months we managed to get her consent. Mikeleen came to Kilmurvy, but for many weeks he did nothing but fool around the place, doing whatever he liked,
except when once in a while I placed a little check upon
him. The rest of the cast had to be found before Mikeleen
could be used.

Amongst the men who had built the cottage was Patch
Ruadh, a fine honest old man with red whiskers. Mr.

Flaherty had noticed him and said to me: "Who is he, Pat?" I said he was known as Patch Ruadh or Red Pat, but that his right name was Patch Mullen.

"I must get some tests of him," said Mr. Flaherty, "he looks very dramatic."

I couldn't see where there was anything very dramatic about Patch, but I was no great judge, and I didn't voice my private opinion to Mr. Flaherty. I said instead:

"Test him any time you like. He is a friend of mine and anything I say to him goes."

Patch was tested and sure enough he came through with flying colours. Now I knew of course that he must be dramatic, even though I couldn't see where it was in him. I spoke to him in Irish, for he knows very little English, unless you put the words in his mouth and pull them out again, but having a quick mind he can do it that way. I asked him how he'd like to work on the film.

"Indeed, brother," he said, "if there is no harm in it, I will, and I'm glad to get the work. But I don't see the reason why I'm wanted when there are lots of finer men around."

"Well," I said, "Mr. Flaherty says your face is dramatic, and it seems that kind of thing suits the picture."

"What kind of a thing is it?" says Patch.

"Don't ask me, because I know nothing about it," said I, "but you have it a plenty whatever it is, and you are surely a lucky man. But if I was to give you my honest opinion," I added, "I'd say 'tis in your whiskers you have it!"

"Well, then, a thousand thanks to God that I have it in my whiskers or some place else. But anyhow, I may as well look after them now you say that 'tis in them it is," said Patch.

He knew from then on that his work would last until the film was finished. Days passed by and we were still trying to find the rest of the cast. Patch was doing jobs around the house, milking the cow that Mr. Flaherty had rented, and doing any other little things that turned up.

One never knew when a call would come for one of us, but there were times when Patch was called for and there was no sign of him. I soon noticed that always between nine and ten o'clock in the morning he disappeared for half an hour or so; so without saying anything, I set myself to find out where he went, though by the looks of things I had a pretty good idea. I watched out next morning and saw Patch, after giving a look around, disappear behind a huge boulder down near the shore. I slipped down the beach and peered around the corner of the boulder, and there was Patch, with a piece of a comb and a broken cracked piece of a looking glass, lovingly combing his whiskers. I made my way back silently. I explained to Mr. Flaherty about Patch's absence, and it was agreed between us that nothing should be said about it. Patch all through the making of the film kept his whiskers in order, and now that he believes they are so valuable, I think he will keep up the good work as long as he lives.

I don't know who discovered old Brigid, but she came to the house and tests were taken of her. At this time we needed, for *Man of Aran*, an old couple, a man and a woman, as well as a young married couple and a boy. But a change was made in the story, because the sunfish, or great basking shark, appeared off the coast, and we decided that the hunting of this monster of the deep was to be one of the great features of the film.

While driving around one day we saw Maggie Dirrane standing in her doorway with a baby on her arm. Maggie had been a beautiful woman at one time, but long before this, and though still young, she had been losing her good looks. Her husband hadn't been well for years. He had run himself out by making land, carrying baskets of wet dripping sand up from the sea, digging handfuls of clay out of the crevices in the rocks, hauling seaweed from the shore, and mixing the three of them together to make soil; also clearing the ground of boulders by smashing them to pieces with a heavy sledge-hammer and building these into fences. At one time he had been a hardy man, but the best of his days were now over because years of this work had sapped his strength and health and left him shaking and ailing and, though he tried to keep on working, his best wasn't much. Maggie had her four children to worry about, and I'm sure she was worried about her husband as well. So it was no wonder that a share of her beauty had faded. Her face was pinched and worn looking, yet full of resignation. Mr. Flaherty said he would like to take some tests of her. I spoke to her and explained about what was wanted. She consented readily. The tests were taken, but they didn't come out very well, and I was very sorry.

Later, when I was talking to Mrs. Flaherty, I told her all about Maggie's poverty. Mrs. Flaherty suggested that she should be taken over to the house and given something to do, such as making up beds, fixing up the rooms, and other odd jobs. I spoke to Maggie about her coming. She was glad to get the chance, and was very thankful to accept, because she needed a pound or two very badly.

The tests of old Brigid came out wonderfully well.

"Wonderfully dramatic," said Mr. Flaherty. Now I had

known Brigid for years, and I never saw anything wrong with her, not even, when in the year before this time, I had been partly the cause of breaking three score of eggs that she was carrying into Kilronan.

There was a wedding coming off, and the young man came to me and asked me if I would venture to run in a keg of poteen for him, for the Civic Guards might be on the look-out for *him*. The keg was in the far west of the Island. I got ready the horse and cart and away I went. I borrowed a big tub, put the keg under it, sat on the tub and headed for Kilronan. I saw Brigid ahead of me, and as I passed her she said:

"Take me up, Pat, I'm killed carrying this basket of eggs."

"Perhaps the eggs might get broken," said I.

"There is no danger of it," said Brigid. So I helped her up and she plopped down on the cart with her basket.

"Hu, hu," says Brigid, sniffing, "there's a smell of something."

Of course I knew it was the poteen she smelled.

"Hu. I smell something," said she again.

"It might be your eggs getting broken," says I.

"No fear of them," says Brigid.

So we rattled along, merrily bumping over the stones that were scattered here and there along the road. Two Civic Guards came along and I drove to the lee side of them and bid them the hour of the day. They passed on.

"Your keg is leaking," said Brigid, " 'tis a shame to have it going astray."

There was undoubtedly a seepage, but it wasn't from the keg. It came from the basket and formed a small pool between it and the tub.

"Perhaps it is your eggs," says I again.

" 'Tis not, don't I smell it. 'Tis a shame." And with that Brigid put the tip of her finger in the pool and tasted it.

"Oh, blood-an'-oun's, 'tis my eggs. I'm robbed! I'm poverised for ever!" she said sorrowfully.

Three score of eggs were broken, as I have said before.

So I knew Brigid of old and I had never seen anything wrong with her, but now she too had become dramatic! However, I said to myself, even though I don't understand it, Brigid is a first cousin of Patch's and maybe it runs in the family.

Mr. Flaherty took shots of many people, and the great majority of them, as did Brigid, believed that these were sent away by him immediately to be shown in America and everywhere, and that by this method Mr. Flaherty was going to continue indefinitely making money and making pictures. They were still very watchful and always kept an eye open for any signs of being approached in any way about their religion. I was sent to Brigid and I asked her how she'd like to work on the film.

"Hu. Why wouldn't I, if Mr. Flaherty thinks my picture will be able to help him? Everyone is beginning to think that he is all right, and anyhow what can he do to an ould woman like me? Sure, my mind is as strong as his. I'll stick to my religion forever." But she added wistfully: "I'm afraid that I'm no beauty and maybe soon he'll get a better woman for his pictures, a woman that people would like to look at better."

"She is not in Aran, anyhow," said I, "because he says your face is full up entirely of drama, and that is the kind of thing he wants."

"Oh, God, give me peace forever," said she, "do I look very bad?"

"No, you look all right to me. There is nothing wrong with you, is there?"

"Well, no—in a way—I don't feel too bad, but right enough for a spell now I haven't been feeling as well as I'd like to. It must be that it was this thing that Flaherty has been looking for that was coming out in me. Is there any cure for it?"

"I don't know much about drama myself," said I, "but I'd say that a dropeen of whisky oughtn't to be any harm at all for it." And she agreed with me!

She started to work, knitting stockings and spinning wool to keep her contented till the time came for her film work. Every once in a while additional shots were taken of her and she began to feel more independent. The men who worked around the place used to meet and ask her laughingly how she was getting on.

"Pat," she'd say, "'tis them that's proud. They let on they are earning their money, but if it hadn't been for my pictures that's earning the money that pays them, where would they be, I'd like to know?"

After some time we got three other women with Brigid for a scene. It was a rather foggy day and the scene was to be more of a test than anything else. They had to climb over a low fence on their way to the shore, as if they were hurrying down to meet the canoes coming in after fishing. Brigid isn't active. She is well over sixty years of age, and one of the new women, Noreen Shawn, told her to be careful and not to get hurt. They had to climb over a low fence. Noreen had been working off and on around the house doing odd jobs in the kitchen and so forth.

"Hu, me get hurt!" says Brigid in Irish, as she stumbled over the wall. " 'Tis time that I had knowledge of my work, I've been long enough at it and 'tis too much for anyone who started only the other day, to be trying to tell me anything about it."

Noreen gave me a look and a wink. We understood one another and allowed for Brigid's hurt feelings. Afterwards Brigid said to me in a hurt whisper:

"Well, Pat, did you ever hear the likes of that—Noreen Shawn thinking that she knows as much about film work as I do. How proud she is sure enough this hour of her life. But all the same," she added, "I'll say she knows a little about it. I noticed for the past week that she was walking very heavy in herself. Yes, I'd say she has a touch of that drama thing."

I agreed with her and then we had a long talk about the pictures, the Flahertys and about the kind of face drama was in and the kind where there wasn't any. I know all the old women in the three Islands. They are all my friends and I am very proud of the fact that they are, and Brigid is one of the nicest of them all.

Mr. Flaherty kept on taking tests of men and women. The women were all good looking, yet they didn't suit his idea of the woman for the principal star in the cast. One of the housemaids came out very nicely, but before a thought could be given as to whether she would be suitable or not, her mother swept her away, being afraid that the red flannel dress of the Island women, in which she appeared, would not be fine enough to be seen on the screen by her friends and relations in America, if the picture was to be shown there. Some years ago the Aran Island women wore red entirely, the same as the Middle

Island women do to-day. These women when dressed in
their Sunday best are strikingly attractive looking. Anyhow there was no great harm done, even though the girl's
mother was about the only woman in the Island who felt
that way about our native women's costume, because
later we got the woman who was really the only person
fitted for the part. The tests of the men didn't come out
any better and Mr. Flaherty began to get worried, fearing
he might have to look elsewhere outside the Islands for a
man and a woman to complete the cast. A good looking
young man came out fairly well, and he was kept working
around the place until some more tests could be taken of
him.

About this time we tried for a storm scene, with a four-
man canoe leaving Kilmurvy shore in a heavy sea. Big
Patcheen Conneely, Patcheen Faherty, Patch Ruadh, and
the young man who was on trial for the chief part in the
film, these four made up the crew. Big Patcheen was in the
bow, where the best man must always be. As a daring
oarsman in a canoe he is without a peer. He and I had
always been good friends and as one might say we had
been through the ropes together, such as having high old
times at weddings and a periodical now-and-again in
Daly's pub, whenever Patcheen came to Kilronan.

It was splendid to see the canoe take the breakers. A
huge sea broke down over Big Patcheen's head and the
big canoe almost stood straight up on her stern as she
leaped over to fight another sea. Big Patcheen shook the
water from his eyes, and as he bent to the oars for a powerful stroke he threw a quick glance toward the shore. I
was laughing with sheer joy and pride of how well the
canoe was being handled and of how I had picked the

right man for the bows. He saw me laughing and, strange as it may seem, as he drove the canoe up the next great sea, and in spite of the great risk he was taking, he laughed back at me. Later he told me that he had said in his own mind: "Ha, damn you, Mullen, you are the cause of my being here."

After going out some distance they turned back and were swept in on a gigantic wave. The stern man's legs were driven up under the thwart on which he sat, by the force of the sea, and he was hurt pretty badly, but otherwise they landed safely, though as the canoe struck the beach they were all knocked off the thwarts. But small things like that didn't matter very much.

CHAPTER V

*The Canoe and her Crew—"With a wave of his hat"
—In search of a Star—Maggie—Empty Handed—
Two Friends—News Gathering—The Great Bask-
ing Shark—With Harpoons to Galway—First Shark
Hunt—A Score of Flashing Fins—The Ancient
Mariner—We Sail for Home*

★

Now the fishermen of the different villages go to
sea from their own village shores, and they have
therefore an intimate knowledge of any sunken
rocks or reefs lying in or near the entrance, and they know
also about the currents and the twists and turns of the
sea, against which they are always battling, often for their
lives. Getting out from, and back to, these different
shores, each has its own particular difficulties, and it is
only fishermen who always use them who are really able
to overcome these difficulties, especially in stormy weather. For instance, a Bungowla village man will tell you
that a Gortnagapple crew are better men going to sea
from Gortnagapple than a Bungowla crew would be, and
a Gortnagapple man will say that a Bungowla man is the
best man leaving Bungowla shore when the sea is running
high; of course, all this is very true and obvious.

One Sunday we drove on the lower road to Manister shore. When we arrived there a great sea was running and Mr. Flaherty seemed to fancy the location.

"A great place for a storm scene, Pat," he said, "do you think you could get a canoe to go out in such a sea?"

After I had spent some time studying the breakers, the current and the passage, I said that I believed a canoe could live in such a sea.

"Very well," he said, "I will leave it to you to arrange everything. If to-morrow is like to-day we are coming here, so get busy and look up your men."

I went up to Manister village to get a crew for a four-man canoe. I first spoke to Tommy Fitz. We had been in the same class at school in the old days.

"Tommy," I said, "if to-morrow isn't any worse than to-day, could you get three more men and go out in a curragh for the picture?"

"Any worse than to-day," said Tommy, "man alive, you are mad! Sure, no canoe could live out there now, let alone being any worse."

"I am after telling Mr. Flaherty that I believed a curragh could live through that passage and gain the open sea, and," I added, "he will think I am a damn liar if I don't get a curragh to do it."

"A curragh might go out in it," said Fitz, "but I wouldn't want to be one of the men that would be in her."

"Well, anyway, Tommy," said I, "I'll depend on you to try and get a crew and be here to-morrow morning. Then if it is in any way fit to go out I know you will go for me."

"All right," said Tommy, "I will be ready; maybe be-

tween now and to-morrow the sea may have come down a little bit. Then we would stand a good chance of doing it."

Next morning we came to Manister shore—Mr. Flaherty, John Taylor, Tommy O'Rourke and myself. John was to help with the cameras and Tommy to help carry them around. I did the driving. P.J. who was hunting rabbits around the crags of Manister soon joined us. The sea was as rough as ever. Perhaps if anything it had risen still higher during the night. Tommy Fitz was waiting, but he had no crew. I caught sight of a man hurrying away. It struck me that he had put on extra speed in case he'd be asked to go out.

"Where are your men, Tommy?" I asked.

"You can't expect every man in Manister to be as foolish as you and me," said Fitz. "I couldn't get any man to go with me, and they are right. It isn't fit to go out, and besides that they say that Flaherty won't be satisfied until the curragh is put into the breakers. And what's more," he went on, "no man living in Manister has ever seen a canoe put out in such a sea."

So there we were, and Mr. Flaherty getting his camera ready! I turned to O'Rourke and said:

"What do you say, will you come with me, and we will both go with Fitz?"

"You know that I will go with you anywhere," said O'Rourke, and he would, though I don't know exactly why. Now, as there were only three of us, we had to go out in a three-man canoe.

Our work that day turned out satisfactorily, so always after this till the end of the film a three-man canoe was used.

Before our canoe left the beach Mr. Flaherty said to me:

"Now, Pat, I may not get what I want this first time, so if I want you to go out a second time I shall wave my hat. I shall very likely get it the second time, but if by any chance I don't, I shall wave my hat a third and a fourth time if necessary."

I didn't like the idea at all, and had I known that such a thing would happen, I might have backed out of it. Now I didn't dare tell the others. There was a frightful sea running, but I said to myself: Pat Mullen, you are going into a storm scene. I hope you will come out of it, but you may as well be in a storm scene on the sea, no matter how dangerous it is, as in a storm "scene" with Mr. Flaherty if you fail to go! I had caught a glimpse of Mr. Flaherty's face when Tommy Fitz said that he couldn't get a crew to venture out with him, and it looked as stormy as rounding Cape Horn. Of course, there was a far bigger reason than that driving me out that day. The months were flying past and Mr. Flaherty had only eleven months in which to finish his film. It was to be of my Island and of my people, and seeing that I had a little to say in the making of it, well, as far as I could help I would. And I made up my mind to show my people in their true light.

Anyway, we got under our curragh and carried her down to the sea. We let her slide off our shoulders on to the beach. Then we walked out to above our knees in the water with her. Fitz jumped into the bow, Tommy O'Rourke in the middle, while I held the canoe by the stern with her bows to the sea, steadying her till Fitz gave me the word to shove off and jump in over the transom to my seat. After about ten minutes Fitz shouted:

"Now, out with her and jump in! Hurry and grab your oars!"

I did and away we went. These great seas usually come in threes, rolling in one after the other, then there is a bit of a lull while smaller seas come rolling in. Then suddenly as if it had only been waiting to gather strength, comes the first of three great seas, and so on. Fishermen watch for the lull and take advantage of it when leaving or coming back to a shore where these seas rise in bad weather. On the other hand one can never be sure of the sea, and oftentimes when one expects the lull it never comes, instead a great mountainous wave may rise up unexpectedly and come rushing in as if bent on destruction. Many a canoe has been lost in this way while waiting and watching for a chance for the run home—they have been caught and overwhelmed. We got clear from the shore and brought the curragh's bows to the wind in a spot inside the passage where there was deep water, and here Fitz gave his final orders.

"Do you see those breakers to the eastward?" he shouted, "well, while you keep the height of the grave-yard in line with Mickel Shawn's little house you are clear of them, but one curragh's length to the eastward of that line and we are lost. When we go through the passage the closer you keep to the western breakers without going into them the better. But we must bring out Straw Island light before we face her to the westward. Then we go to the west until we get Shawn Mor's house in line with Oghil Lighthouse. We can't go far then, unless we go away out on the deep. These marks", he went on, "would bring us safe on any other day, but to-day the seas are broken everywhere."

"We don't want to go so far west as that," I said, because I knew we would be too far away for Mr. Flaherty's camera if we did.

"Now," said Tommy, "in the name of God let ye do your best!"

The three great breakers came rushing past, and then we swung our curragh out, and stretching manfully at the oars we cleared through the passage and headed to the west. Soon we saw the signal to return—Mr. Flaherty waving us in. Coming through the passage we managed to dodge the breakers and came through without much risk. We were now inside, feeling a bit excited but steady, and Tommy Fitz said:

"Well, now Flaherty has got what he has been after and I'm damn glad he has."

"So am I," I replied, hoping it was true, but out of the corner of my eye I watched the hat, and sure enough Mr. Flaherty took it off and began waving us out.

"What is that?" I said. "He is waving his hat. He must want us to go out again."

"Ah," said Fitz, "what the devil does he think we are, him and his ould hat. Why didn't he take the picture when he had it. Come on in and let us put up our curragh."

I explained that maybe the camera got jammed and for the matter of one more trip we oughtn't to let him down.

"Down or up," says Fitz, "it isn't fit to be out in such a sea."

And right enough it wasn't. A breaker might at any time roar down on top of the curragh, and if it did we'd be done for. However, out we went again and sure enough a mighty sea broke a curragh's length from our stern. Manister men who were watching us from the hills around said later that if one more sea like it had followed immediately after, we would have been drowned. Anyhow, two powerful strokes had brought us clear, and we rowed westward. Silent we were now and tense, watching every sea, ready to bring her bows by a few strong pulls clear of any sea before it broke, or dodge it and run a couple of curragh's lengths here or there. Again we were signalled in, and after some minutes waiting for our chance we made a run for the passage, rowed for all we were worth through it and got inside.

"Now," said Fitz, "he has something he never had before, and we are lucky men to be safe out of it."

When up goes the hat again and Mr. Flaherty waved us out.

"What the blazes does he think we are," said both Tommys, "him and his pictures; he must want to drown us, then perhaps he will be satisfied."

"It begins to look that way," I agreed, "but just the same he is a good man, and if he had got what he is after he wouldn't be wanting us to go out again. Let us not give it to say that once we are here we failed."

So after some more grumbling we tried again, won through, and headed west. On our return a great sea came rushing along after us. We swung the canoe around in a second, faced the sea, and with a few furious strokes we climbed up and cleared it with a jump, and let it rush toward the shore where it crashed with a roar that made us grip our oars tighter, set our teeth, and prepare for the rush through the passage. After riding several great seas in the mouth of the passage, where they broke in wild fury with great white manes flying, we headed our curragh in and we were lucky enough to get clear inside.

"Good boys," said Fitz, "for two men who know nothing about this shore ye have done well. Now, thank God, 'tis over."

As a matter of fact we had all had a bellyful of it by now and were glad to be finished with such risks. But I was still shaky about the hat, and sure enough up it went and waved us out again as calmly as if we were about to go out on a pleasure trip on a millpond. We sat on our seats and held our curragh's bows to the wind. We argued, we cursed and swore on Mr. Flaherty, Fitz saying: "To hell with him and his bloody pictures!"

"Once more," I pleaded, "just one more run out and after that he can go to blazes," and though I don't know why they agreed, out we faced once again.

P. J. on our last trip had stood on a high boulder; I knew he was getting anxious and as we rowed out this thought I well remember came to me: Well, my boy, you are rather young to face the world alone if I go under, but after all you may be as well off if I do go, because my example to you, I'm afraid, has sometimes not been of the best.

We had to make two attempts this time before we cleared the passage. We rowed farther westward than on any of our other trips. We turned back at the signal and made our final attempt to run the passage between the reefs, but when halfway through we saw great towering seas coming after us. I shouted to Fitz asking him if we should turn and try to ride them or keep running for the deep spot inside the passage.

"Row! Row!" yelled Fitz, "we have a chance to run it."

And we rowed as we never did before, for death was coming behind us, and we only just won through. Those huge seas came breaking in and had they caught us—oh, well, they hadn't, and that's all. Nothing could have driven us out again and, although the hat went up once more and waved us out, we rowed ashore. A crowd was there to meet us, wanting to see how we looked after taking such desperate chances. Mr. Flaherty soon joined them. He was in fine form, for this was the first real piece of work he had done. The Cape Horn look had gone from his face. Forty feet more of film was all he had left, he said, and he wanted to use it up, that being the reason he waved us out for the fifth time! He was sure he had got a good storm scene. When I saw it on the screen, though it passed all right, it didn't look half as thrilling to me as it was when I was in the curragh doing the work. Still it had that dramatic quality, so Mr. Flaherty said, that is needed in the making of a film. The sun had shone brightly on that day with the wind from the north-west. West or north-west wind makes the sunlight softer and more suitable for film making. On Aran it does, anyway, for Mr. Flaherty could never do much good work with a south-east or east wind.

Tommy Fitz is a descendant of the old Fitzpatrick family who owned these Islands some centuries ago. He has a medal from the Royal Life Saving Institute for bravery in saving life at sea. He said after our storm scene that Tommy O'Rourke did very well by doing what he asked him to do, but as far as Pat Mullen was concerned he either didn't see the danger, or didn't care a damn what happened. However, 'twas all over and done. I saw the danger, of course, but Mr. Flaherty had planned that a storm scene was to be one of the most important parts of the film, and I had begun by this time to put all my energy into the work so far as I was able. I was very anxious that the film when finished would be a really great piece of work.

During April and May Mr. and Mrs. Flaherty and many other people made frequent remarks about Maggie, such as "Isn't she looking well?" "Did you ever see anybody improving like her?" "She looks brighter and so much happier," and so on. It was true. Maggie was earning a bit of money. She was now able to buy flour, tea and sugar with which to feed her family, and now and then a dress for her little girls. The wrinkles were disappearing from her face, and a soft, happy light shone in her eyes and her laughter could be heard again.

So far we hadn't found the woman we wanted for the film. There was seemingly none in Aran suitable, and I proposed to Mr. Flaherty that we should go over to the Middle Island, telling him that there were some fine girls there. I mentioned that one of them especially was very beautiful. To tell the truth I was a bit discouraged on account of my own Island having failed to produce a woman fine enough to fill the cast. Mr. Flaherty agreed to go, and in a few days' time we sailed for Middle Island in a motor fishing boat, one of the only two now left in Aran, the last remnants of a once fine fleet. When we arrived, there were some curraghs out to meet us and take us ashore. We walked up the hill to the first village, and there we received a great but rather inquisitive welcome, something like this: "A hundred thousand welcomes to you all." "What brought ye over here?" "Will ye be staying long?" "What is Flaherty going to do?" "Will he be taking pictures?" "They say he is rotten with money." And so on.

Mr. Flaherty inquired about a public house, and we all went in to Peadar Mor's, where we had several drinks. We intended to use a white horse in the film, so I inquired if there were many white horses on the Island. This of course was only a roundabout way of doing things in order to get better acquainted with the people. We wanted a horse, but not at this time, but it would have been the height of folly to speak immediately about the real object of our visit. If the name of the girl had been mentioned first thing in the village, gossip would be flying from lip to lip long before we could explain why she was wanted or what benefits might come her way if she could be used in the film. Some other construction would be put on our visit and very likely we could never set eyes on her. It turned out that way at the finish, anyway, in spite of all our endeavours. However the horses were brought out on the road outside Peadar's, most of them old hard-worked creatures, and the few that had spirit had their tails badly clipped. None of them was suitable for our purpose, for we wanted to get a white horse with a flowing mane and tail. After a couple of hours I began asking in a careless sort of way about the girls. It didn't sound strange coming from me after all the horse talk, also I knew all the women young and old in the Island. I praised one young girl as the finest looking, but most of the men disagreed with me, saying that such and such a one was the finest. I knew quite well that such and such a one was the finest. It was she we had come to see, and as a matter of fact she and I were fairly good friends. Towards evening Mr. Flaherty and I rambled along the road towards the house of the young girl we wanted to see. On reaching it we went inside, and after the usual Cead-Mile-Failte we sat down. Two old women were there, one in each corner by the fire. One of them was thin and sharp-featured, the other stout and heavy, very old and good-natured. The beautiful young girl and her sister stood looking at us smilingly. The two old women had lost their husbands, whether by drowning or not I cannot say, so the young girls had to do all the outside work, pull seaweed for manure, plant the potato crop and all the other little jobs that go with living on these islands. The girl whose picture we wanted to take was tall, black-haired and blue-eyed, friendly and altogether a very fine girl. Her sister was plump and pleasant. We got talking about trifling matters. Mr. Flaherty didn't understand a word of what we were saying, of course. Soon the thin old woman wanted to sell us crisses or girdles which are hand-made of woollen threads of many beautiful colours.

"This is Flaherty," I said (there is no Mr. before any man's name in Irish).

"Isn't he making a film?" she asked.

"Yes," I answered.

"They say he has plenty of money," she said, "and 'tis little he will feel to throw some of it away, so do you get him to give a good price for those crisses."

"Well," I said, "to be honest with you he has a share of money, but when he spends it he wants something for it in return, and what brought us to this Island was to take pictures and spend a share of money. But I will get him to buy your crisses just the same; he won't feel the price of them and I will add on a couple of shillings extra."

"Indeed, I knew you'd do it for me," said she.

"Now that we have made a good beginning," I continued, "and while we are here I'll ask Mr. Flaherty to come in the morning and take the two young girls' pictures. We will be taking pictures of lots of other girls of course, but I'd rather your girls had the first chance, and besides that, if any of them come out all right no one knows what money she will make out of it."

I couldn't tell the old women that we wanted a star for the cast, because Mr. Flaherty was always against raising anybody's hopes too high when taking tests, in case they didn't turn out well enough, and then the people might feel terribly hurt and disappointed. We chatted and talked and we were all in good humour. As we were about to leave they agreed that it would be all right for us to come with the camera the following morning and take pictures of the young girls. My dark-haired friend was pleasantly excited and Mr. Flaherty thought her very beautiful. It doesn't matter now what happened after we left the house, but I know that at the time they were all sincere and were quite satisfied that Mr. Flaherty should take their pictures. Next morning we took the camera to the house. Mr. Flaherty set it up in the yard and I went in to get the girls. There was nobody there except the two old women. I asked them where the girls were, and I was told that they were in the garden at work some distance away. I suggested sending a messenger after them.

"No," they said, "the girls wouldn't come and wouldn't get their pictures taken for anything."

I went outside and told Mr. Flaherty, his face became like a thundercloud, and this was one of the times I didn't blame him for being angry. However, he spoke calmly enough when he said:

"For God's sake what's the matter with those people; don't they know what's good for them?"

I told him I didn't know what was the matter. A Middle Island man who was helping us carry the camera lens cases around whispered in my ear:

"Pat, I don't think they are in the garden. I believe they are in that room."

Mr. Flaherty spoke again:

"Heavens above, here we come to this Island specially to get this picture. Is it possible that we shall have to go back without it? Is it money they want, or what?"

I knew it wasn't money they wanted, because I had been doing some quick thinking in the meantime, but in order to make sure I asked the old woman if the tall young girl would let us take her picture for five pounds.

"No, no, you won't take her picture for five pounds."

"Ten pounds, then," said I.

"No use in your talking," said she, "she won't have her picture taken at all."

"Well," said I, "this will be my last offer. Will you let us take her picture for twenty pounds?"

"No, not for all the money in the world would she have anything to do with you in any way," the old women replied.

Then of course I knew it could be only one of two reasons, their refusing. Middle Island people are, in one respect at least, like most people everywhere else. They don't turn their backs on money, and twenty pounds, I well knew, represented a small fortune to this poor family. It was as I say one of two things, fear of the evil eye—that is if too many people saw her picture and spoke a great deal about it—or a fear of her losing her religion in case she came to Aran and associated with the Flaherty Socialist family. They must have talked it over at night with some of their neighbours and made up their minds that our dark-haired girl friend would be lost if she had anything to do with us.

So we bid good-bye to Middle Island after first asking some of the men if they would go out in a curragh scene on the south side of the Island. The sea was rough and they said it would be daring too much to try it. We returned to Kilmurvy by motor boat and had no more dealings with Middle Island except when we came to take shots of cattle being hauled through the sea and hoisted on board the *Dun Aengus*, whence she sailed with them to Galway Fair. On the beach, when we took these shots, was the dark young girl holding a rope in her hand and running to and fro with many other women. Boys and girls kept the cattle from running away across the strand while the men were busy wrestling with them and tying ropes around their horns and driving them into the sea, where they were rowed out to the steamer by men in canoes. I spoke to the young girl and asked her what had happened on the day when we wanted to take her picture. She laughed, looked a bit shy and confused and refused to tell me.

Anyhow it was just as well that things turned out as they did, because soon after this Maggie was tested again, and she came out wonderfully well. It was a good thing, because not many other women in Ireland could do what Maggie has done in the filming of *Man of Aran*. Her joy at being able to make both ends meet again was beyond the telling, and she showed her gratitude in every possible way. Absolutely without fear, she would have risked her life (as indeed she did) if told it was needed for the making of the picture.

I had to give up kelpmaking entirely, because of the film work, but there was another line of endeavour that I didn't want to give up entirely, and that was the driving of my friends whenever they visited Aran. I spoke to Mr. Flaherty about it, and he said:

"Why, certainly you must drive your friends, that is of course unless we are doing some special bit of work on the film. Then the film must come first."

I realized that, and I thanked him for his kindness.

*   *   *

On our arrival back from Middle Island word was waiting for me that my great friend from America was coming, but instead of staying over from one boat-day till the next, her trip this time was to be a hurried one and it would give her only about one hour and three quarters in Aran. I have always been in the habit, when driving along the roads, of giving the people of the Island a lift on my sidecar, especially the women, but as I drove down to the boat to meet my friend whom I had not met for three years, I swore to myself that come what might and no matter whom I met I wouldn't take anybody up on my car. I met my friend and we drove up to Ganly's where she had dinner. She didn't take very long over it and soon hurried out and got on the car. We headed up the road toward the west of the Island. We were looking forward to having a talk about old times and about our friends, but as we jogged along the road who should I see ahead of me but a woman from Onaght village. I didn't notice her getting off the steamer, but I knew she had

been to a hospital in Galway with wind on her stomach.

It is a common complaint amongst old women of Aran to have lumps of wind rolling around in their stomachs. I really believe it may be indigestion, this complaint, but I never heard it called by any other name than lumps of wind rolling around in the stomach.

This woman had been kind to me the year before. She had given me half a dozen fine dried pollock as a Christmas present, but even so this was the one time I intended to leave her to carry her own weight, because I knew that if she ever got on the car—well, good-bye to my talk with my friend for another couple of years. The old women of Aran never travel very far away from home, though most of them have sons and daughters in America. They all nevertheless love to hear about the outside world and especially about the land of the Starry Banner. When a woman from the West of the Island goes to Galway Town, she considers it her duty to observe everything, so that when she returns home the old women of the village can hear all the strange news of the outside world. Kilronan villagers, on the other hand, going more often to town and being a bit more sophisticated, do not nowadays trouble to bring back any news.

Anyway I knew that this old friend of mine would be able to tell us what her doctor was like, whether the nurses were pleasant or whether one of them had been especially charming, how many beds were in the room and how many windows let in the light, who the other patients were, where they came from and what they all suffered from, in fact everything and anything that amounted to news both inside and outside the hospital.

This old idea of gathering the outside-world news is

dying fast, but in my father's young days when the black hookers did all the sailing to and from the Islands and when they were often three or four weeks weatherbound in Galway or in Clare in the winter time, the arrival of the boat in Aran was always awaited with the greatest interest. Men and women who were especially qualified for the dispensing of such news were able to keep their audience hanging on their words for fully two weeks. One of these old-world news carriers lost his reputation for some years because of what was considered to be the greatest lie ever told by man. He said that he had heard that it was a fact that the news of the world would soon be running on the top of a stick (meaning the telegraph)!

However, I drove past the old woman and pretended not to see her. But I had only gone about twenty yards when my conscience began to bother me and I looked back at her. She had been keeping an eye on me and immediately began to lengthen her step and hurry.

"I'm afraid I won't be able to take you up," said I. "I'm going to the Seven Churches, and I must be back again before the steamer sails."

"Oh, sure, you can do that easy, because I'm not very heavy after the hospital, and indeed," she added, "you won't feel me at ye or from ye."

I stopped the horse, jumped down and helped her up alongside my American friend, who had been looking on smilingly. I explained to her how weak the poor woman was after being in the hospital. My friend turned to her and said: "I'm sorry you are not very well."

The old woman puffed for a minute or two, and with little moans in between began to settle herself so as to get the last ounce of comfort out of her seat. She opened out her shawl a bit to get more air and mopped her face with a large handkerchief.

She then turned to me and said in Irish: "Pat, is this woman from America?"

I had known what was coming of course, and I realized that I wouldn't be able to have a talk with my friend on this trip.

"Yes," I said, "she is." The old woman didn't know much English but that didn't seem to matter. She was in quest of news and this trip with the lady would put a fitting finish to her journey when she arrived in state in her own village.

"You are from America, ma'am?" was the first question. "Yes, 'tis a great country they tell me."

"Yes, it is."

"Do you live in Boston?"

"Not exactly, I live some miles away from Boston; but I have often been there."

"H'm. I have two girls in Boston, God bless them, Mary and Una. They live in the Back Bay. Maybe you've seen them. Conneely is the name, Mary and Una Conneely."

"I'm sorry," said my friend, "but I haven't met them. However, if you give me the address where they live, I will call to see them when I go across."

"Yes, do, and tell them I've been in hospital, but that I'm middling now. I will give you the address when I get as far as the house."

The conversation continued all the way to Onaght village, six miles. As we entered the village the old woman made herself more comfortable and independent looking.

"Pat," said she in Irish, "I'll bet you anything that a lot

of the women are looking out through their windows at us, but they won't let on that they ever saw me because I'm coming too grand to the village, especially when I have this lady beside me."

I agreed with her. However, when we arrived at her house, three or four of the neighbours came out to welcome her.

"A hundred welcomes back home, how are you after the hospital, and what's the strange news?"

"Faith, I'm middling after the hospital, but as for the news I'll never be able to tell the half of it, for this lady has told me all about America as well."

"Well, well," said the neighbours. "Isn't that a wonderful thing?" They looked at one another and bobbed their heads together in agreement.

I helped her down off the car. "Come in," said she, "and I will have a cup of tea ready in a minute for ye."

We went in, the other women following. The tea was soon ready. We drank it and then to put the right touch to arriving home, the old woman stood up and after looking around at her audience (several more women had come in by now), she said: "And now, ma'am, I'll give you the address of my girls. Be sure to call and see them."

The other women bobbed their heads again and said: "Isn't this American a fine woman."

My friend promised to go and see the girls, and as a matter of fact she did. We hurried out to the car and trotted fast for Kilronan and the steamer.

My friend turned to me with a smile, saying: "Pat, our talk will have to be postponed."

"Yes," said I, "but as you have seen, it could not be helped."

She knew that, so she sailed away till the next time.

The following day I had occasion to pass through Onaght village. I met three of the women who had been in the house the day before.

"How is Maureen?" I asked.

"Oh, musha, she is all right," said one.

"Arrah, sure, half of them old women do be only letting on. They don't be half as bad as they say they are," said another. "But," she added, "she has the world entirely of news, wherever she got it. I don't know myself whether she's putting anything to it or not, but we must go in again this evening, because she hasn't come to America yet, and we all want to hear about that, more than anything else."

* * *

We had been trying to do some work on the land sequence when the days were fine and the sun shone, but it was difficult to get what was wanted for the film. Clouds bothered us a good deal and for weeks at a time nothing much could be done. Whenever the sea ran high Mr. Flaherty continued taking seascapes.

At night we had long talks about the sunfish or great basking shark, known in Irish as the Levawn Mor. I set about collecting all the information I could from the old men of the Island about this fish. In the old days these monsters were hunted by fishermen off the west coast of Ireland for their oil. Black hookers, boats of from about ten to twelve tons, were used, with five men to each crew. It was the one big moneymaking industry on the west coast of Ireland about a hundred years ago. My grandfather hunted them, and down in the old house tied on to a rafter over the fireplace I found two rusty harpoons. In Killeany village I found two more tied up in the same way. The flanges were encased in leather sheaths. In those old days the liver of the basking shark was worth as much as thirty-five to fifty pounds, it yielding up nearly two hundred gallons of very fine oil, and was used principally for lighting purposes, in lighthouses as well as dwelling houses. The harpoons, including the flange, were from four to four and a half feet in length, the flange being about a foot long. Old tales of sunfish hunting have been told around our firesides for generations. One tale tells of how Bartly Shawn and his crew harpooned a large sunfish which towed the boat westward for two days and a night, and finally they had to cut the line and let the fish go because of an easterly gale that had sprung up, and after terrible weather they barely reached home. Another true tale is one about the *Pine Boat*, a new hooker built specially for sunfish hunting. She was planked with pitch-pine. She sailed out of Killeany Bay one fine morning, and outside Gregory's Sound they sighted a sunfish. Other boats were running on it too, but the *Pine Boat* was first. They harpooned the sunfish, and when the boat was last seen it was being towed towards the setting sun into the western ocean. The boat and crew were never seen again. It was believed that the sunfish must have smashed the boat's side in with a blow of its tail.

For years and years, for some unknown reason, these monsters practically disappeared from our coast, but about six years ago they came back in great numbers, and Mr. Flaherty decided that if the reports and the stories that he had about them were true, he would throw back the film into the Aran days of long ago and take scenes of the hunting of the sunfish.

One day I was driving along the road, and as I drove I let my eyes rove over the North Sound, and there sure enough I saw the great black fin of a sunfish flashing in the sun. I turned back and reported what I had seen to Mr. Flaherty, who went to have a look at it, but the fish had disappeared. Next day we sighted two of these monsters close inshore. They swam around in wide circles, for this is the way they feed: they surround whatever it is they live on, and with their great mouths wide open swim around in ever narrowing circles, until, I suppose, they swallow the feed all up. These giant sharks have horrible looking mouths. Indeed the fish itself is an awful looking creature. Its mouth could easily take in the stern of a four-man canoe. Mr. Flaherty took quite a lot of shots of them from a platform fixed up between two canoes. We laid planks across two curraghs and with ropes that went from these planks around the bottom of the canoes we bound them firmly, keeping the canoes about four feet apart to give the whole thing steadiness. A platform was erected on the planks between the two curraghs, and on this Mr. Flaherty stood working his camera. Two oars on the outside of each curragh were used for driving them ahead and on fine days they were pretty steady.

Mr. Flaherty made up his mind to go hunting the great basking shark. We sailed for Galway in Pat Fitz's motor boat, Mr. Flaherty having engaged her to take him to the Islands and elsewhere. On arriving in Galway we took the old harpoons up to Flanagan the blacksmith and gave them to him for the time being, so that he could use them for models.

We ordered half a dozen new ones, and asked him to hurry.

I went rambling through Claddagh village seeking information about the sunfish. I learned from the Claddagh men that in the old days their forefathers too had sailed in hookers to the westward of the Aran Islands in quest of these fish. Those men had been great harpooners and they shared with the Aran Islanders the honour of being the best men at this very tricky work. I spent a good part of the afternoon and night without getting much information. It seemed that all knowledge of how to harpoon the fish had died out amongst the younger generation in Claddagh. Finally I went into a small thatched cabin, where an old man sat by the fire. He was in his stockinged feet, had snow-white hair and a ruddy complexion. He wore a blue serge suit and an orange-and-white scarf was around his neck in a half turn with both ends hanging down in front to his waist. He looked a picturesque figure. He welcomed me and we got talking. He said hunting sunfish was before his time, but when he was a little fellow he believed the Claddagh men did hunt and kill them.

"You will get no knowledge about the sunfish here, sir," he said, "unless you can get any from Martin Quinn. He ought to know something about them because he is up and down to a hundred years of age. But even if he does see you," he added, "I'm afraid he won't be able to give you much information, for I hear he is very slack. They say he is dying."

Though I hated to go into any man's house, bothering him, and he in such a weak condition, yet I badly wanted to find out how the great sunfish was harpooned, so I made up my mind to take a chance on going to Martin's house and maybe having a few words with him. I found the house and went in. An old woman was fixing jugs on a dresser. She was Mrs. Quinn, and after "May God save all here" and a few other remarks, I asked for Martin.

"You can't see him, sir. He is very sick. I am afraid he won't last long," said Mrs. Quinn.

I told her that I was sorry to trouble her, but I had come in for information about the sunfish, or as he would best know them, Levawn Mor, having been told that he was the only man now living in the Claddagh who could give me any information about them. If he could manage to speak at all, and if it didn't hurt him to do it, I would very much like to hear what he had to say about them. I also told Mrs. Quinn that I had known her daughter Mary in America and that she had often visited my house there, all of which was of course true. We talked about her daughter for a while and then Mrs. Quinn took me into a clean little room, and in a nice clean bed I saw an old man covered up with the bedclothes, nothing of him to be seen but the top of his head which was covered with wisps of snow-white hair.

"Martin," says Mrs. Quinn, "this man has called to find out if you would be able to tell him anything about the sunfish, the Levawn Mor he tells me they used to be called. He is from Aran and he knew Mary well in America. He is married to so-and-so."

"Did he know Mary?" asked the old man as he feebly pushed the bedclothes away from his head. "How is she? And what do you want to know?"

"When I saw her last, the day I left America," said I, "she was very well; of course you know that she's married to Tom Brown. They are very happy and have a lovely home. But," I added, "I want to know how you used to harpoon the great Levawn. We are going to hunt them again."

"Ha, the Levawn Mor," said Martin, " 'tis well I know them and 'tis them that's hard to kill," and his faded blue eyes shone brightly and took on a faraway look. Then he spoke again:

"You must have two hundred fathoms of line, with ten fathoms of it sarved near the harpoon end, so that when the Levawn rolls around on the bottom of the sea trying to get the harpoon out, the cable won't be cut on its skin. It is very rough and full of little sharp points and many a good boatman lost a Levawn that way long ago, for want of the cable being sarved properly."

"Where will I harpoon it?" I asked.

"On the grey streak under the big fin, but you are never sure of your Levawn till you drive home your second harpoon."

Then old Martin turned over on his other side with his face away from us, and as he pulled the bedclothes up around his head he again murmured: "The Levawn Mor."

That was all, and bidding good-bye to Mrs. Quinn I left the house and went on my way. The old man died the following week. God give his soul rest, that is if rest is good for it. Perhaps Martin, when his spirit grows young again in Tir Na nOgue may like to roam the seas in his black hooker in quest of the Levawn Mor.

When the harpoons were ready we bought two hundred fathoms of strong manilla rope and took them on board Fitz's boat. We sailed for Aran, and the first thing

Mr. Flaherty did after we arrived was to place sentinels on all the high points of the Island on the look-out for the sunfish. It was done the same way in the old days. Each boat's crew had a man stationed on some high point from where could be had a good view of the sea. Then on sighting the sunfish he rushed down to the harbour with the news. The boat put to sea immediately and if a sunfish was captured the sentinel came in for a share of the money. Mr. Flaherty bought a Connemara pookawn, a strongly built boat able to carry about two and a half tons, to be used in the film for the sunfish hunt; for the crew he picked the young man who was on trial to represent the Man of Aran, also Patcheen Faherty, Patch Ruadh, Tommy O'Rourke and myself. Patch Ruadh was to be the steersman.

A sentinel sighted a sunfish out to the south-west, off Dun Aengus. We put to sea and our boat was towed by Fitzpatrick's motor boat from Kilmurvy to the north, then to the west part of Rock Island and then south. Fitzpatrick's motor boat was now to be used for camera work, until we reached—as near as we could figure it—the place where the great fish was sighted. Shortly after, we saw the sun flashing on a big black fin as the Levawn cut through the water. As we sailed up to the fish Mr. Flaherty came to me and said:

"Pat, I think we ought to try and harpoon this one from the big boat. After all, we don't know very much about them, and the art of killing them is lost. They look very powerful monsters to me, and not for the world would I have any accident happen to any of you men, which might be the case if you tried harpooning it from the small boat. Let us try our hand out of this boat first, and then as we gain experience we can later on try harpooning them from the small one if we think that it can be done."

All this was very true and fair, and now as we came close up we tried our hands at harpooning for the first time. Mr. Flaherty said: "Pat, you will be the harpooner, and the young man can help, if you think you will need him."

Naturally we were very excited over our first encounter with the great basking shark. In our hurry we struck too soon and missed. When we again approached it, it sank slowly and I could only just reach its back with the harpoon. We learned afterwards that the haft of the harpoon, when being used from a large boat such as Fitz's, should be from fourteen to sixteen feet long instead of the ten-foot haft we were now using. We failed again and again to drive the harpoon home, but on the fourth attempt I struck the shark on the grey streak under the big fin. The shark lashed the sea into foam with its tail and sent showers of water flying over the boat. The line went out with terrific speed as the great monster went down in a slanting dive. The line went out so fast that it smoked on the combing of the hatch while running from the hold where it was coiled. We were told that when the fish dives after being struck and fails to get rid of the harpoon by rolling on the bottom, it heads for the open sea. However, this didn't happen in this instance, for the shark headed towards the cliffs at Dun Aengus, about a mile distant. Our line which was two hundred fathoms long was fast going over the side, so we knotted the end to a line belonging to Fitz, which was also about two hundred fathoms in length.

When the shark, which was now towing the boat

through the water, neared the cliff, it headed down and brought our boat much too near the rocks. While we were considering seriously whether we should cut the line or try and pass it into the smaller and shallower-drafted boat, which could be more easily handled near the rocks, the line suddenly stopped running out. We began to haul, but we were only pulling the boat nearer to the rocks, so we had to pass the end of the line into the pookawn. We rowed in all directions trying to get the line clear, for we now knew that it had fouled the rocks at the bottom. When the shark was circling down by the cliff, the line must have got entangled around the rocks. The harpoon was torn out and the shark gone. We finally got the line aboard. Parts of it were very frayed where it had been drawn around the sharp rocks, and several fathoms of it near the harpoon were covered with a thick greasy slime from the shark's skin.

The wind had been coming in heavy puffs as we re-covered the last of our line, and soon it began to blow from the north-east. We rowed hurriedly to Fitz's boat, got on board, and with the pookawn in tow headed for Brannagh Island Sound. By the time we had passed through it into the North Sound it was blowing a whole gale. After much buffeting by the heavy seas we finally reached the mouth of Kilmurvy Bay; but it wasn't safe to land there, so Fitz kept his boat battling away, with the pookawn still in tow until we reached Kilronan and landed at the pier.

Next day another sentinel came with news that a great number of sharks were off Brannagh Island Sound to the south-west of the Island. The day being fine and Fitz having sailed back to Kilmurvy, we decided to go out after them, and as we sailed out through Brannagh Sound we saw about a score of flashing fins. As we came closer we slowed down and swung around to head off one of the sharks. We came closer still, and when I saw a chance I made a drive for the grey streak with my harpoon, but I failed to strike it properly because the haft of the harpoon wasn't long enough. When the fish was three or four feet below the surface of the water Mr. Flaherty and I talked things over and we decided that we would lead the line from the big boat to the pookawn, harpoon the shark from the pookawn, and then let Fitz's boat, which had the other end of the line attached to it, hang on. Mr. Flaherty was to come with us and work his camera from our boat, while John Taylor was to try and get some shots from Fitz's boat. We hauled our pookawn alongside and got into her. One of Fitz's crew, an old man whom we called the Ancient Mariner, looked down at us as we were about to cast off and gave us a little friendly advice.

"If ye take my advice ye will be very careful how ye go about harpooning them whale-sharks. We know Aran men used to do it long ago, but they knew how and their boats were at least three or four times as big as that little pookawn, and if one of them sharks gives her a clout with its tail she will be smashed to pieces. If anything like that should happen we mightn't be able to save the half of ye, so I'd advise ye to be very careful when ye go in amongst them. Why, by the looks of them every one of the devils is able to swallow your boat, and now after what I have said," he added, "ye can do as ye like."

I thought it was a very fair and square talk, but I knew that Mr. Flaherty didn't like it. He didn't want us to feel too nervous, at least that is what I thought at the time.

I respected the Ancient Mariner's advice, for I knew that in his day no tougher or braver man of his weight and inches had ever put a foot onto a boat or curragh. He had gone to America early in life and had spent the best years of his life fishing on the Grand Banks and had fought his way up and down the waterfront of Boston and never backed down from any man. The waterfront along old T Wharf in Boston in those days was a pretty tough place, where strong men gathered and drink ran free; there were fights often, and the Ancient Mariner was considered one of the best men sailing to the fishing grounds. Fond of drink, yes, but he had a great big honest heart. I remember I was seventeen years of age when Martin Dillane's four-man canoe, laden with herrings, went down in a gale about half a mile out from Kilronan pier. The Ancient Mariner, not ancient in those days, ran down the road to the pier. He had seen the canoe go down. I had run to the pier myself too, with no definite object in view, for in those days I knew hardly anything about canoe work. The Ancient Mariner ran up to me. His blazing eyes thrilled me.

"Pat," he said, "there is a curragh at the quay, will you come with me if I can get another man, to try and save those men out there?"

"Let's hurry, I will go with you," said I, though I had an idea at the time that I should be more of a hindrance than a help.

We jumped into the curragh shouting to a man who stood at the end of the pier to hurry and come with us, but he refused. I heard afterwards something about the fairies having moved the man's curragh the night before.

He believed that it was a sign warning him not to put to sea that day. The Ancient Mariner and I could not put out because without the aid of a third man we couldn't have made any headway against the gale that was blowing. Instead we should have been driven to leeward and lost on the bar.

It was on this day that Tommy Fitz had won his medal. He with his crew saved two of the four men who manned Dillane's canoe. The other two were drowned.

However, on this day when the Ancient Mariner spoke to us about the whale-shark, he was an old man, dying on his feet, but trying to earn a shilling in order to keep things going for the short time left him. Living or dying, fear could never touch him.

Just as we were pushing away from Fitz's boat, the young man who was on trial for the chief part in the film had a sudden idea. He jumped aboard her from the pookawn, took out his pipe, lit it and sat down on the butt of the bowsprit to smoke. He looked quite calm and had an expression on his face that said: "Well, so far so good. I think I'm safer here."

"What's the matter now?" asked Mr. Flaherty.

"Nothing at all," I answered. "Let's shove off and row out to those fish. It's time we had a shot at harpooning one of them."

We didn't have much trouble in getting near to them as they swam around feeding close to the surface of the water. Underneath them at a depth of about a couple of fathoms could be seen great shoals of mackerel flashing past. The rays of the sun shining down through the water made it so clear that we could see to a great depth. A huge shark swam past our boat. I struck at it with all my might. It was a good stroke but it entered about two feet behind the right spot under the big fin. The fish with a mighty splashing dived to the bottom. We immediately threw everything clear. The shark with great speed worked around the stern of Fitz's boat. Fitz's boat was going slowly ahead and the shark was rushing astern so that, when the strain came, the harpoon was at once torn out. We hauled the line in and found the harpoon twisted out of shape. The sharks seemed to get a bit shy after this and swam deeper in the water, though they still moved around in circles feeding. They had also moved closer inshore.

We made several attempts to get near them in our boat, but it bothered us having the end of our line in Fitz's boat. However, it was not wasted time, because we were getting more used to our work and were gradually growing bolder, though I must confess that I always felt a thrill of fierce excitement as we rowed up in our small pookawn to harpoon one of these monster sharks. Clouds came up that evening, so we sailed for home. I don't know why the sharks' feed only comes to the surface of the water when the sun shines, or why the sharks should go under when clouds come over the sky.

Two old men from Kilmurvy village met us at the pier as we landed.

"Where are your Levawns, Mullen?" one of them shouted in derision.

"Oh, we are only making fun with them yet," I answered. "We aren't in any great hurry to kill them."

"Yes, and it's fun ye will be making with them *forever*," he jeered.

"Ye don't know how to kill them, and furthermore ye aren't *able* to kill them."

Then, as old men will, they went on to talk about the great days of their youth and of what they had heard of the feats of some of the old harpooners. But what they said about the great Coolawn was the yarn that pleased me most and stirred my blood.

Maurteen Mor Coolawn's name will go down forever, in Aran Island history, as being just about the most powerful giant who ever lived. We had all heard tales of his great strength, but what these old men told me seemed to me almost beyond belief.

Coolawn had hunted the basking shark and being of such prodigious strength he was made harpooner on his very first trip. Once, as the boat approached the shark, so these old men said, he became terribly eager and excited and disregarding the advice of the older men he struck with his harpoon just as soon as the first chance offered. The Levawn was swimming past the boat's bow and Coolawn struck at its head with such terrific power of stroke that the harpoon pierced the shark's skull, the flange actually going right through its head to the other side. The Levawn didn't even thrash with its tail, for it met instant death. I have sneaking doubts sometimes about the truth of this story, but they disappear always when I remember that Coolawn was reputed to have had the strength of ten full-grown men put together.

CHAPTER VI

Coley King—After the Sharks again—Bad Light—
Good Dog, Speed—Inishboffin—In Search of Shark
—We drink ourselves into Trouble—The Visitor
and the Harpoon—Keening—The Evil Eye

*

The young man having failed us, I again tried to
get Big Myles Joyce to come and have his picture taken. I had asked Myles many times before
but he had refused, saying:

"What business would Flaherty be having of a man
like me?"

He seemed to be very bashful and was always in good
humour when refusing. I had always entertained the idea
that he would be the right man for the film, because of
his iron constitution and the never-say-die spirit which
he had so well displayed five years before. He with two
other men in a canoe were caught out in a snowstorm,
and after forty-eight hours of battling with it, trying all
the time to keep the curragh's bows to the gale, he was
driven ashore on the mainland and was able to haul his
curragh some feet up on to the beach and reach a house
nearby. The other two men had died on their oars and
had slid into the bottom of the canoe. Myles stands six
feet three in height. He is a great blond good-humoured

giant. After many friendly talks and a few pints of porter
in Daly's, Myles at last said with a laugh:

"Well, that will do. I will go to Kilmurvy. Sure, nobody can hold me there if I don't want to stay."

Next day Myles came; Mr. Flaherty and I both thought
that he was the right type for the film, but it was a disappointment for us to find that he did not photograph
well. So we had to keep our eyes open for someone else
to take the part of the Man of Aran. Maggie, Mike and
Patch were all right for the film, but it began to look as
if we would never be able to find the right man for the
star part. Frances Flaherty, Mr. Flaherty's daughter, was
on Kilmurvy pier one day when she saw a man sitting
there, and she was much impressed by his appearance.
Knowing that we still wanted a man for the cast, she
brought him to her father's notice. This man's name was
Coley King. Mr. Flaherty sent for me and asked me about
him. I said he was a fine looking man and a brother of the
young man we had asked to come for a test some time
before, but who had never put in an appearance.

"Oh, yes," said Mr. Flaherty, "I remember now. They
are the people that have so much to say about our being
Socialists. Better not get him, Pat, because even if he
comes here and the tests turn out well, his work is sure
to be unsatisfactory, because anybody who entertains
those ideas about us won't be interested in our work.
We will get a man somewhere," he added.

I agreed with Mr. Flaherty, but as the days passed by
I made up my mind that I'd try to get King to come along
and have his picture taken. I met him on the road one
day and spoke to him about it. He said he couldn't see
how he stood to benefit much even if he were found to

be suitable. I explained about the steady employment and the good money that I believed a man would get who fitted the cast. Next day we talked the matter over again and finally he agreed to come. That night we called on Mr. Flaherty, who was much surprised, but he asked King nevertheless to call the next morning. He came, and his picture was taken. It came out so well that we at once decided that he was the man for the part.

King is a fine looking man, six feet in height, supple as a deer and as light on his feet as a cat. In a day or two he was ready to start working. He and I stretched a new coil of rope, taking the kinks out of it so that it wouldn't foul when running out after we had harpooned a shark.

It was May, and the weather was cloudy and windy, with showers. We put to sea and sailed around the Islands, but sighted no sharks; after a couple of weeks we received word that some had been seen off South Island. It was too far to row or tow the pookawn because the weather was too rough, but as we were anxious to get a shark by hook or by crook we sailed for South Island in Fitz's boat. When we came near the strand there, we saw three huge fins close together about a quarter of a mile away. We steered straight for them, and King now being the principal man in the cast was to be the harpooner, but as we wanted to improve our chances of catching a shark we all agreed that I should assist him in driving the harpoon home when the chance came. As we approached nearer the sharks they gradually went down, and although we now had an eighteen-foot haft in our harpoon we failed in our first try, the fish being too deep in the water. The weather became worse, and we believed afterwards that it was the cause of their being so hard to approach, because any change in the weather makes them restless. King was all over the boat in his endeavour to get a chance to use the harpoon. At last we came shoulder on to a huge shark. It was about thirty feet in length, but as we approached it began to go slowly down. However, King and I reached its back with the harpoon, and exerting all our strength we tried to drive it through the tough skin. The harpoon bent like a willow and we hauled it on board all twisted out of shape. King knocked it off the haft and fitted a new one on. We came up to another shark that was just showing the top of its fin. We made a fierce drive at it; the harpoon struck hard on its back. It splashed the sea all over the boat and then with a mighty swish of its tail dived for the bottom, leaving the harpoon behind. Once again we hauled our harpoon aboard, to find it was bent as badly as the other. All three sharks had now disappeared and we didn't see them any more. We now understood why the old harpooners struck at the grey streak under the fin. It is the most vital spot in which to strike them. The rough scalylike hide on the backs of these sharks will easily turn and twist any harpoon out of shape; this we had to find out for ourselves. We learned some time later that there is a small spot just behind the big fin where a harpoon will enter fairly easily, but as it is so small it is almost useless to try for it.

We headed about and had started sailing back for Kilmurvy Bay, when suddenly there appeared a lone shark. King at once got ready his harpoon and as we got close up he made a mighty drive, striking the fish on the grey streak exactly under the fin. The harpoon went through to the rope which was fastened to the upper end.

After a terrific thrashing of the water the shark went down—but soon after reappeared on the surface some distance away, swimming at a great speed.

The rope was smoking as it went out, so great was the friction.

Mr. Flaherty worked hard with his camera, trying to get something worth while, but he shook his head hopelessly.

"It won't be any good," he said, "the day is too dark. There's hardly any sun."

The shark towed the boat for four or five miles, then it seemed to weaken and we took a turn of the rope around the capstan, and by degrees we brought the shark up to the bow of the boat and then drove in our second harpoon. At nightfall we put in our third harpoon and lashed the huge fish to the side of Fitz's boat and towed it in to Kilmurvy and there tied it with chains and ropes to the pier. But our labour went for nothing. The weather continued cloudy and was getting worse, so after a week we towed the shark out on the deep and sunk it by tying heavy stones to it. Unfortunately Mr. Flaherty didn't manage to get anything worth while for the film as the light had been so bad. In film making there are lots of ups and downs, I understand. This great shark measured twenty-nine feet eight inches in length, and from the upper tip of its tail to the lower tip it measured six feet six inches, and I'd say it weighed about seven tons.

The sharks entirely disappeared from the waters around these Islands after this, so Mr. Flaherty got into touch with the mainland and prepared to send word all round the west and north-west coast of Ireland in order to get tidings of them. He meant to follow them up, because he intended having the film finished by the end of November if it were at all possible. I told him that I had heard the waters around Inishboffin Island, about twenty miles to the north of Slyne Head, were considered in the old days to be one of the best places around the coast in which to hunt the sharks. Word was immediately sent there.

In the meantime we searched the Island for a suitable location for the land sequence, or in other words a place suitable for making a garden.

*   *   *

One morning I was told to be at Kilmurvy very early. I got up at dawn and hurried to the field where I had placed the horse the night before. I broke down the fence and went in through a little potato garden to get the horse. Speed, our old dog, had followed on my scent. We found him in the house when P.J. and I returned from America. He was getting very old and for some months now he had been blind. Of Airedale breed, and though not a big dog, he had been a terrific fighter. He was a wise dog, and I hadn't been long back on Aran before we became friends and he soon followed the side-car everywhere. Oftentimes when going along the road, three or four dogs would suddenly appear ahead. Speed would stop immediately and trot back to the car, at the same time looking up at me with a look full of understanding. All I had to say was: "Good dog, Speed, it's all right," then he faced ahead and gamely went into the fight. The first dog to attack him was the only dog he was allowed to fight, for with a long whip I always drove the others away. Then it was a case of let the best dog win.

People talk about separating dogs and not letting them
fight. I think it is useless if one has to pass the same places
every day, for they will continue to fight until some dog
becomes the master, and even then the losers will try to
gather a pack to pull the best dog down. It isn't very
surprising, because in my ramblings around I have seen
human beings do the same sort of thing to one another.
Anyway, I took the horse out of the field and built the
wall up again, not knowing that Speed had followed me
in the darkness of the early dawn. He had come in
through the gap in the fence while I was putting the halter
on the horse, and had strayed off into the ditches of the
potato garden, and it was not until two days later that I
heard about his being there. P.J. had missed him but
didn't know where he had gone. I talked things over with
P.J. and we decided that it was time to drown him, because he had become blind and weak and was now a
nuisance, so we went down and fetched him from the
garden. He wagged his tail when he got our scent on the
wind. He didn't hear us coming because age had made
him deaf as well as blind. I found a pitchfork inside the
fence, putting it under him I lifted him over the wall on
to the road. Then we went down to the shore with Speed
following us, staggering with hunger and sometimes falling. I myself had often staggered with hunger and I didn't
mind the dog doing it very much, but what began to
hurt P.J. and me was that Speed seemed quite certain that
he was all right when we were near him. He kept wagging
his tail and showing his pleasure in every way that he
could, and all the time we were helping him down the
rough shore to where there was deep water inside the bar.
He was pretty far gone anyway and though we kept on

saying to one another that it was a shame considering what a warrior he had been in his day, still we agreed as we approached the sea that it was better to drown him and be done with it rather than let him live on in such a wretched state. I took him on the brink of a rock, where the ledges underneath sloped down rapidly, so the water was quite deep about fifteen feet from the shore. I looked at Speed and decided that he was too far gone to bother about tying a stone around his neck, a thing that is always done on Aran when getting rid of a dog. I put the pitchfork under him, lifted him up and threw him far out into the water. I expected him to sink almost immediately, but the old dog was built of sterner stuff and he headed out toward the bar, swimming strongly; this surprised me considering his weak condition. At last he reached the bar, where the seas were breaking. One of them broke slap in his face, which threw him back and turned him in again. I looked at P.J. and I saw that he was thinking much the same as I was, but neither of us spoke. The dog swam in closer to the shore, but he was nearly done. He was tired out and was now beginning to swim round in circles. He began to whine a little as he felt the last of his strength ebbing away; at last his head went under. He came to the surface and floundered around in a circle which brought him a little nearer to the shore. I glanced quickly at P.J. He stood with his hands clenched and his eyes flashing. I spoke no word but jumped into the sea up to my shoulders, reached out with the pitchfork and as Speed was going slowly down I brought him back to land. It was a long time before he revived. We both sat by him with our minds too full for words, especially when the dog began to wag his tail again feebly on getting our scent again as much as to say: "Ha, I knew while ye were there that nothing could happen to me." I felt mean and cheap as I looked down at that old blind dog. We carried him up to my little cabin by the sea, there we laid him on a warm clean bed of straw and every day while he lived P.J. brought him half a loaf of bread and a good drink of water, and when we could get it, a drop of milk. He never got much more than that because there is no fancy food on Aran.

*   *   *

After a couple of weeks a message came back from Inishboffin saying that sharks had been seen around there a few days before.

Mr. Flaherty in the meantime had come to the conclusion that Pat Fitz's boat was not the right boat for camera work. It rolled too much in any kind of a seaway. She is a stout blocky boat, good in heavy weather even when she did roll, but it was very hard to do any good camera work on board. So Mr. Flaherty paid a visit to Galway and hired a splendid motor boat called *The Successful*. She also carried sail, and had been doing some trawling in the bay, but as fish were scarce her owner was quite satisfied that she should work for Mr. Flaherty. I believe her owner was anxious that the film should turn out well. As soon as she arrived at Kilmurvy we got our gear on board, and under motor power as well as all sails drawing full, we made for Inishboffin. We didn't bring the pookawn on this trip, fearing she would be towed under in the heavy seas we expected to meet when rounding Slyne Head. We intended getting a boat at 'Boffin that would look enough like her, so that nobody could tell the difference between them when seen on the screen. We rounded Slyne Head in great style and sailed into Inishboffin harbour late in the evening. The harbour is well sheltered and the island looked very green. We anchored, lowered our curragh and went ashore. We met some of the islanders. They said a shark had been seen outside Inishshark the day before.

Inishshark Island is separated from Inishboffin by a narrow channel. The name had been given to it because of the great numbers of basking sharks that appeared in the spring in the old hunting days. Claddagh men and Aran men, as well as men from as far north as Donegal often sailed their boats for 'Boffin Island to take part in the hunting there. Among other things, the 'Boffin men told us why they had stopped hunting the shark. It wasn't because paraffin oil came on to the market, but because of a monster seventy-five foot shark that had been harpooned and had attacked a boat, smashed it to pieces, and drowned its crew. Mr. Flaherty thought that this monster might have been a finback whale which has a great fin very much like a basking shark's and also has the same shaped tail.

While I'm on the subject, I will mention here that one day during the past season, while we were working on the land sequence, we saw from the top of the cliffs a number of sharks close in, and amongst them was a fin that didn't belong to a basking shark. It was about five feet out of the water, but much narrower towards its base than a basking shark's fin. We couldn't tell the length of this strange fish—the sea was rough and we couldn't see down beneath the surface.

The men of 'Boffin treated us very kindly. Among the people along the west coast, the Aran Islanders are well known for their hospitality to strangers from the mainland, and when any of the Island men trawl along the seaboard they are treated kindly by everyone.

Next morning I explored the island, which is of sandstone formation. A man showed me a part of the cliffs where an English company had taken some shiploads of rock away in order to get soap out of it or something. The business fell through and a good thing for the 'Boffin men that it did, otherwise in time there would be no 'Boffin Island left!

We on Aran Island have always been grumbling because we have no bogs where we can dig our turf; instead we have to get it from the mainland and pay a big price for it. Of course if our Island had been boggy, we would have burnt it from under our feet centuries ago!

I borrowed a sledge-hammer and broke off a lump of rock from a ledge. There was a lady in Aran who was a sculptor, and I had an idea that this kind of stone would be suitable for her to work on. I carried the stone to the pier. It weighed about half a hundredweight. After I got it aboard the boat, I rowed back again to the pier. I found half a dozen old men gathered round Mr. Flaherty, and when I joined them the oldest man was telling about a great shark that had been driven ashore long ago, when he was quite a small boy. This monster, he said, had been fully seventy-five feet long.

"Do you hear what this old gentleman says, Pat?" said Mr. Flaherty, "a shark seventy-five feet long. Good heavens, if we could only harpoon and capture a shark as large as that we would surely have a marvellous film."

Mr. Flaherty had for a long time past been searching for facts about these sharks, and it is very surprising how little has been written or handed down about them. We didn't know whether to believe that they did reach such a great length or not, for what we had seen of these sharks they certainly didn't appear to be any more than from twenty-five to forty feet in length.

One day in Kilmurvy Bay—it was a Sunday, and we didn't do any work on Sundays until late in the last hunting season, because if any accident happened on Sunday it would ruin the whole picture. The reason for this was that the people would have said that we were flying in the face of God by working on Sundays, and they would have stayed away from us altogether. By the second year of the film, however, we had nearly all the film finished when the season came to hunt the sharks so we were quite safe in working on Sundays, because all we wanted was the shark sequence. But on this day in Kilmurvy Bay we saw what we took to be a monster shark about sixty-five feet in length, circling around. It had two big fins instead of one. All day it circled about and swam around, huge and frightful looking, and in the evening it sank down and disappeared. We didn't learn until long after this, that what we saw must have been two sharks instead of one. We found that sometimes they feed that way, male and female swimming and feeding with the snout of one touching the tail of the other, never changing this position during the course of a whole day. But this Sunday in 'Boffin we didn't really know what to believe. I was afraid that maybe the old 'Boffin man was talking more with an eye for porter than anything else. But one couldn't be sure.

"Yes, sir, there are seventy-five foot sharks swimming

around the coast here, and if you get a chance of one you are bound to kill him."

This ended the conversation and we all went into the public house. Drinks were ordered, and we lifted our pints of porter brimming full and drank: "Here's hoping for the seventy-five foot shark and likewise a health to the *Man of Aran.*" And there were blissful looks in the wise old eyes of the 'Boffin men as they twirled their long moustaches. Sentinels had been posted on the high points of the Island, but no fish were sighted. We went on board our boat about twelve o'clock midday and cruised round about the Island, and then we sailed out ten miles to the westward and did some more cruising there, but we never had a glimpse of a basking shark; so next day we sailed away for Clifden, a little town on the mainland a short distance from Slyne Head where hookers came in with their cargo from Galway, our idea being that from these hookermen we might get some information about the sharks. We anchored in the shallow passage that leads up to Clifden and launched our curragh. Mr. Flaherty and John Taylor went to an hotel. King and I rambled around to see the town and to pick up news from the hookermen, but they had sighted no Levawn Mor and they didn't think we would either. It was getting late in the season, they said, it being now July, and the Levawns had probably left the coast as they always did early in the month. We know now that changes of weather make a difference of two or three weeks in their migrations.

Tommy, Patch Ruadh and Patcheen stayed together. We all met at a corner of the street and had a chat. Tommy said that he would get a haircut. He is a swell-looking young man and when in town he wants to look well and have a good time. I objected to his having his hair cut because Mr. Flaherty wanted us to look about the same always so that on the screen there would be no change in our appearance. But it was no use. Tommy had an idea, I think, that all the beautiful girls in Clifden would think him a savage if he didn't have his hair cut, and with this on his mind away he went. King and I strolled into a public house owned by a man named King. We had a few drinks and talked to the landlord about the film. I introduced the Aran Island King to the Clifden King, explaining that he was our star. I believe that Mr. King of Clifden and Coley King are distant relations, anyway they said they were, and after that we had a good time. Mr. King of Clifden is a thorough gentleman. He and his family treated us very hospitably. We left there that night with many a friendly handshake and a promise on our part to call in the following day. We then roamed around quite happily, looking for a place in which to put up for the night, and we arrived finally at Gerald Bartly's Hotel. Tommy and his two comrades had found their way there before us and had already gone to bed. The hotel was full up, but I said that all we wanted was a seat by the kitchen fire for the few short hours till daylight, which they very kindly gave us. When morning came, Coley and I went back to Mr. King's house to say good-bye to him and his family before going aboard the boat. However, instead of saying good-bye and hurrying down to the beach in order to be ready to row the other two men and Mr. Flaherty out to *The Successful*, we stayed at the public house, having one drink after another. Soon we were quite happy with that false happiness that goes hand in hand with drink. We forgot all about *The Successful* and Mr. Flaherty, and

though Mr. King strongly advised us to go and get ready to row to our boat, we said that there was time enough and that there was no need for us to hurry. Finally he had his car brought to the door and he said he'd drive us down himself. Just as we were getting ready to go Tommy came in and said that Mr. Flaherty had sent word that if we weren't on the beach by ten o'clock and ready to go on board he would sail away without us.

"And Pat," says Tommy, "he is raging mad because I got my hair cut and because you and Coley are drinking."

"Tell him we will be down right away," said I, and then we had a parting glass with Mr. King.

He then got ready to drive us down, but we didn't accept his offer. We started on foot towards the beach. We were about halfway down when we saw a car with John Taylor on the running board rounding a bend in the road at great speed. The car stopped when it reached us and John Taylor jumped off, saying:

"Oh, Pat, do hurry. The chief is raging."

"I'm sorry he isn't happy like we are," said I, "energy used in raging is badly wasted."

However, we got into the car and were driven to the beach. Our three steady men were already in the curragh and Mr. Flaherty told John Taylor to have them row us two hard cases out to *The Successful*. The curragh was then to return and pick up the others. King and I got into the curragh very meekly and everything would probably have gone on all right, had not the three steady men begun to abuse us for letting Flaherty down and keeping him and his business waiting.

The idea suddenly began to dawn on me that Mr. Flaherty was damn well able to take care of himself and

that his anger was sufficient for the time being for two
such meek-minded men like King and myself to endure
without having to take further abuse from these three
steady men, any one of whom would drink the cross off
an ass's back if he could only get a chance to do it. So
when we came alongside *The Successful* I told them
politely that King and I were the only two men that were
worth a damn anyhow and the only men who were fit to
go back in the curragh to row Mr. Flaherty and the
others on board. King backed me up, saying:

"You are right, Pat."

So I told the steady men to hop on board *The Successful*
or I'd sink the curragh by driving an oar through the
bottom. They did hop on board and they hopped lively.
King and I rowed back for the three men on the beach.
I never even glanced at them as they got into the curragh;
then King and I rowed our somewhat erratic course back
to *The Successful*.

Mr. Flaherty gave orders to start for home and he,
John Taylor and a visitor went into the cabin; but before
Mr. Flaherty disappeared down the ladder I had a look at
his face and it was frowning as sternly as the cliffs at Dun
Aengus. I got hold of a book and went down into the
forehatch to have a read. I pulled a sail around me but
instead of reading I fell sound asleep. I don't know how
long I had slept when I was awakened by one of the crew
gripping me by the shoulder and shaking me, saying at
the same time:

"Pat! Pat! For ——'s sake get up and try to stop ——
from killing the visitor in the cabin."

I jumped up and stuck my head out of the hatchway,
and sure enough there I saw one of our steady men stand-

ing over the entrance to the cabin. Later we heard he had taken a bottle of whisky on board with him. He had on neither shoes nor stockings, no coat and no cap. In his hands he held a razor-edged five-foot long harpoon, with a fourteen foot haft out of it. He had it raised on high, and as he glared down the cabin way, he shouted:

"Come up. I dare you to come up. We came on this trip to harpoon sunfish or basking sharks or whales, but as we can't find any of them a man will do just as well. Come up," he shouted, "you that passed the remarks about me."

This man with the harpoon had earlier in the day told me that he had heard the visitor say something unpleasant about him.

"Just one sight of ye till I drive this harpoon through your body!" he shouted.

The Successful was heeled well over. It was blowing strong, and as the spray flew over her our man gripped the deck with his feet and indeed in all my life I had never seen a wilder or more dangerous looking figure. The captain of the boat and the other two men of the crew were making every effort to appear interested in steering the boat and in coiling ropes! However, I sized the situation up pretty quickly, and I said to the man who had awakened me:

"Well, so far so good. I can't see how we are going to better matters by butting in. While he stands there he can't harpoon the man in the cabin. If he tries to get down into the cabin he can't take the harpoon with him, and the three men below should be able to master him. On the other hand, if the man below is foolish enough to show himself before things cool down, well he deserves to be harpooned!"

We left it at that, and after a time the man growing tired of hurling his challenge began to look around at the sea and got a bit unsteady on his feet. A heavy sea struck the boat, our man lost his balance and, taking a quick step to recover himself, struck his foot hard against my piece of soapstone. The harpoon was sent flying out of his hands as he stumbled, and then he crashed down on to his knees. He leaped to his feet. His toes were cut. He looked to see what had thrown him, and then with a yell he grabbed the rock in both hands and hurled it into the sea. We ducked back into our hatchway and listened for a while. As we heard no further outburst, we stuck up our heads and we saw our man sitting on a coil of rope filling his pipe with tobacco. He lit it and smoked away calmly. We got out on the deck and looked at the sea for a while, then we went up to him and passed some remarks about the weather. There the matter ended. We never mentioned it again except that he afterwards told me that he felt very sorry about the whole affair. Anyhow, this trip of ours was a wild and unprofitable one for all concerned.

We sailed into Kilmurvy Bay late in the evening, all discouraged and grouchy. I know that I felt awfully ashamed of myself. Mrs. Flaherty asked me what had happened.

"We didn't harpoon any fish," said I.

"I know it, but there's something more than that. You sailed away from here full of hope and in great form, but you have come back silent and dejected looking. You look as if you all thought the world was coming to an end right now."

"I cannot tell you, ma'am," I answered, "I think we all feel in fairly good health. I know that I do, anyway."

But whether she ever heard any more about it I don't know. I must say that at this time Mr. Flaherty showed great patience; I never heard him speak about that wild trip of ours again.

The Successful made one more trip to 'Boffin. We got word that another shark had been sighted, but in spite of sailing for miles we never sighted even one. Mr. Flaherty brought back with him a harpoon gun that a man in 'Boffin had used in the 'eighties when hunting the basking shark for sport. By now the season of the basking shark had passed and the sequence for the film had not been completed. So Mr. Flaherty made up his mind to stay on Aran until another hunting season came round.

★   ★   ★

Wakes and weddings still interested Mr. Flaherty, and one night after coming back from 'Boffin he asked me about an Irish wake. I told him all about it. How the women used to keen, crying their dead. Then thinking he didn't understand, I said I'd lay myself out and get old Brigid to cry me. Mrs. Flaherty said that she would lay herself out, but I explained to her that Brigid would feel a bit strange crying her, as Mrs. Flaherty was a stranger, and I didn't think Brigid would put her best into it. So I got a sheet and laid myself down on a couch. I put the sheet over me with only my face showing. Then I closed my eyes to make myself look natural and old Brigid got down on her knees and began to cry, and she cried me so well that after a while I thought I was dead. I suppose nobody ever hears anything good about themselves until they are dead, and so now it was with me! Brigid, in her crying, told about how never again would I drive along

the road and take up the poor old women and shorten
their way home, never again would I be seen holding the
reins as my big white horse dashed and tore along, and of
me and my people who were always decent and of my
mother who never let anybody out of her house without
a cup of tea. And so on for a full half hour she keened, and
at the end she said:

"And now your great big bones will soon be laid away
in the grave forever. I hope when your soul goes into
God's presence that there it will find salvation and peace."

I was very glad to jump up off that couch. I was feeling
rather queer and a bit saddened. Mr. Flaherty was impressed, but there was no opportunity of bringing into
the film any keening or wakes. This keening is as old as
our race and it is usually done when mourning the dead,
but in the old days of sailing ships, when Aran young men
and women were going to America, keening was much
indulged in, because most of those who went away never
came back.

They sailed in hookers to Galway, there to take the ship
to America, but long before the ship hove in sight the
women of the Island used to gather on the cliffs at the
Glassin Rocks near the mouth of Gregory's Sound. They
sat in the shelter of a little hill—it is about the only green
spot on those barren cliffs and has always since those days
been called the Glen of Tears—and when the ship appeared
beating up the Bay they speculated tearfully as to whether
she would sail out through Gregory's Sound or not. If she
did, they waved their shawls and their keening swelled
out on the wind until the ship grew small in the distance.

My mother's aunt was one of the few of these emigrants
who went away and returned. I remember a little about

her and how she spoke about her trip to America—of the ship she was on being eight weeks tossing about the Atlantic, and of how in one terrible storm when the ship had made a lot of water the rats ran screeching up the rigging to the tops of the masts. As time went on, of course, conditions became better, and when my own sister went to America a little steamer was sailing twice a week from Galway to Aran. Nowadays when young people sail for America they bid good-bye to everybody who lives in the two or three villages that are nearest to their own and they all go together to the pier. There is much crying of course and amid tears and the waving of hand-kerchiefs the young people sail away. However, they go usually with the conviction that they will be able to pay a visit back home sometime.

On wet days we gathered together in the Irish cottage and sat down on the stooleens round the turf fire, while Patch Ruadh made baskets from sallys, which are long willows grown specially for the purpose; we talked and told stories of great curraghmen, of the fairs and markets on the mainland, folklore stories, and also there were many told about the evil eye. I think of the latter that the one that happened in my own family was as strange as any. As I have said before, I remembered a little about my mother's aunt, but this, that I am going to tell you, happened when I was about two years old.

My aunt had relations living on the mainland in Connemara and once every year she packed up her green trunk with little presents for them of one kind or another. My father then took the trunk to the pier where it was put aboard a hooker; then the old lady sailed away with her trunk for five or six weeks. One of my elder brothers,

Martin, was sick, but not bad enough for her to postpone her annual trip. That same evening, as my father was coming home from milking the cow, he saw a hooker put into the pier and was much surprised when he saw a green trunk being hauled out of her. He hurried down and sure enough it was the old lady back again and she all excited. My father asked what had happened.

"I can't tell you here. Wait until we get to the house," she answered.

They hurried home and she then told my father what had made her decide to come back.

As she had journeyed along the road in Connemara, with a man carrying her trunk, she went into a house to see some people she knew, and sat by the fire and had a drink of milk and a rest. She hadn't been there long before a gipsy woman walked in to kindle her pipe; as she stooped to catch hold of a piece of lighted peat or turf she glanced at my mother's aunt, and said:

"You are from Aran."

The old woman said she was.

" 'Tis in Aran you should be now," said the gipsy, "because that little boy you left behind is very sick. The evil eye has been laid on him, so hurry back home if you would save him. You know the house in Killeany," continued the gipsy, "where he used to go for a drop of milk when your own cow was dry. Well, the old woman there has laid the evil eye on him. She told him one day to come down to the fire until she could see whether in his forehead he looked like a Mullen or a Costelloe. She looked at him and admired him a great deal, but she never put 'God Bless' on him. So hurry you now back," said the gipsy, "and sleep not a wink to-night until you see that woman. Bring with you there a piece of red flannel; sit by her side and get her to smoke a pipe and then, when she throws out a spit, you manage to get it on the red piece of flannel. Then hurry back home and rub the flannel three times on the boy's forehead in the name of the Father, Son and Holy Ghost. If you do that you have him saved, but you must hurry."

While my mother's aunt was telling this to my father the evening had almost turned to night, but she at once began to make preparations for her mile journey to Killeany. My mother said that the sick boy was no worse than he had been for a long time and that there was no fear of his dying at all, and she added:

"If you go all the way to Killeany now, the people will think it a very strange time for such an old woman as you to go visiting. So rest yourself well to-night and about ten o'clock to-morrow it will look natural enough for you to be seen going to have a chat with an old woman like yourself."

So next day my mother's aunt went on her journey, bringing a piece of red flannel with her; but as she turned down the boreen to go into the house, the man of the house ran out in a great hurry, and as he passed her he said he was running for the priest, for the old woman within. She was feeling very ill, and he was afraid that the priest wouldn't be able to catch her in time. My mother's aunt hurried in, but she was too late; the old woman was dead. So she came back home empty-handed. Three weeks later my brother was buried.

CHAPTER VII

Land Scenes—Shore Work—Wreckage—To Galway to buy a White Horse—Storm Scene on Kilmurvy Strand—Goose Dinner—Gortnagapple Shore —A narrow Shave—Sharing the Jobs

★

The land sequence of the film was very difficult, and we did a lot of work up around Dun Aengus. It is a famous old prehistoric fort, the finest I believe in Europe. Most of the tourists who come to Aran come specially to see it. The peace of the Islands and of these old duns makes a stranger feel that he is in another world.

From Dun Aengus Mr. Flaherty took several shots of Gortnagapple village where Liam O'Flaherty was born. It lies not far from the edge of the cliffs; it is very bleak-looking and for weeks, I might almost say months, in the winter time the foam and mist from the raging seas blow over it. We did some work near the village, smashing rocks and building them into high fences and making gardens, doing the work in the same way as the people of these Islands have been doing it for centuries.

Mr. Flaherty found this work very difficult to film, because through the limestone run particles of shining rock which throw back bright beams of light. Also it isn't

easy to show a small stretch of limestone on the screen and at the same time to get people to understand thoroughly what heartbreaking work it is making land on Aran. However, we kept on at the work while the sun shone, Mr. Flaherty trying all kinds of angles with his camera. This work had to be done if the life of the Aran Islanders was to be shown accurately to the people of the world.

There were a good many landless families on these Islands in the old days. The Great Famine of 1847 had driven many from the mainland away to the Islands where there was a plentiful supply of fish. These families were often hard pressed for food in the stormy winter months. Then the owners of the little holdings of rock-stretches engaged them to work on the land, giving them their food and a few pennies a day. After a time the landless people began to make land on contract, that is to take over a stretch of rock from the owner, clear it, build walls round it; and when the stretch of rock was levelled to their satisfaction they began to gather and haul sand from wherever they could get it. They were allowed very little seaweed from the shore because seaweed rights have always gone with the land. They scratched up baskets of clay out of the crevices between the rocks, and mixing seaweed, sand and clay together they made a fairly rich soil. This they spread out over the cleared space. Then in spring the potato seeds were planted and if the season was showery a fairly good crop was harvested. These contracts only lasted for two years; after that the made garden went back to the owner of the rock, who in the meantime had been clearing some ground himself—either that or kelpmaking—and the landless man after the two years would start making a small garden on another stretch of limestone, and so on.

Making land on Aran is killing work. A neighbour of ours would willingly take down all the mearing walls that ran between his land and his neighbour's, so that he could take the small amount of clay that had gathered underneath during the past years—he would then build the walls up again, higher and stronger.

Mr. Flaherty wanted some seaweed work done, and the best shore I knew of was the one where three generation of my own family had worked; and where my grandfather often cut seaweed, until the water went into his mouth when he stooped to catch the seaweed in one hand and to cut it with the other! We managed to get a white horse (not the beauty that we had in mind for the film) and a donkey, and with Patch Ruadh and Mikeleen cutting and loading seaweed on the smaller animal and Maggie and King on the horse we began our work. It was a lovely day and turned out to be a very successful one too. Unfortunately very little of it could be included in the film owing to lack of space, but what has been left in gives a very good idea of the work. The shores of the villages have different regulations about the cutting of seaweed. If the shore slopes gradually and offers no resistance to the sea driving the seaweed in, then in such a shore the seaweed is cut in partnership. The flood tide drives it up, and there it is divided after the tide has ebbed a little. In such a shore a man to be fully qualified must be able to change his knife into either hand and with each be able to cut equally well. I remember once I got a chance to go cutting on such a shore. I was to get my first man's-share as a cutter. I felt very nervous as a full score of men walked

down the path toward the shore, each man having made, long before, his choice of a sharpening stone—and on these they were carefully whetting their special knives to razor edge. I also had a special stone and I sharpened my knife on it and pretended to be very unconcerned. It was my father's job as every man there well knew. He was a first-class knife man, but he was now looking for some better work somewhere else and threw me in his place, he intending to earn a man's wage in one place and give a chance to me to get it in another. In some shores at low water men wade up to their waists in order to reach the best seaweed. They work (as they say in Irish) as if there was fire on their skins. On my first day I kept close to my Uncle Jim, thinking it would be safest to be under the arm of a relation; but I was mistaken because he soon began to give me hell, shouting out so that everyone could hear, that it was a shame that I should be looking for a man's share.

In other shores where a current may wash, or where ledges run, donkeys and horses are used, while in the wildest and roughest shores a man or woman must carry the stuff in baskets on their backs. Mr. Flaherty was very anxious to get Maggie to carry seaweed on such a shore, as he thought it would make an interesting scene in the film. I explained to Maggie in Irish what Mr. Flaherty wanted her to do, and she did it so well that after this Mr. Flaherty gave me the megaphone. I felt very shy of it at first, feeling that it was being put into the hands of the wrong man, but I got used to it, and very shortly after this I felt lost without it when working on location. We took months trying to get this land sequence together. A great deal of time was wasted owing to clouds and rain, which of course made filming impossible. However, with the work in the shore, the collecting of the soil and King's work with the sledge Mr. Flaherty decided finally that he probably had enough material to make a land sequence that would be easily understood by an average audience. He had only about fifteen minutes to show this work on the screen! However, up to the end of the film we worked at it, always trying to improve on it and make it better.

When making land on Aran all the large loose stones on top of the crags have to be cleared away; oftentimes a whole upper layer of rough rock has to be cleared. This must be smashed with a heavy sledge, or by raising a granite boulder over one's head, and then bringing it down heavily on the large rock to be broken; all this must be done in clearing the land and in making the rocks small enough to handle, so that they can be built into walls.

Families on the Islands differ in their ways of judging values. It seems to be born in some (it was born in me) to have an especial craze for seaweed, others for fishing and others for land-making, and practically all of them are crazy after driftwood, or in fact wreckage of any sort.

I remember once, a ship called the *Bandon* went ashore on Straw Island point; the crew had gone home, and she became a total wreck except for the possibility of removing her gear and cargo. The Coast Guards were left in charge of her. But the men of the three Islands tore her to pieces. The sea was black with curraghs, and while the Coast Guard boat chased a curragh laden with spoil, scores of others darted here and there around the ship, men climbing up everywhere and tearing away anything they could lay their hands on. My father with his crew and curragh had joined in, and one dark wet night they

made a raid on the ship. They took what spoil they could and were back home before daylight. They divided the haul, our share being several heavy glass salt-cellars or shakers, an enormous, heavy tackle block and a heavy pump which my father said could turn salt water into fresh. One of the salt-cellars is still in the house. I don't know what became of the block, but for years and years the heavy pump stayed hidden up in the loft. It could never be used except in a big ship and why he tore it out of the *Bandon* I don't know, but I do know that for years he spoke very pridefully about it to any stranger he trusted or to any neighbour he cared about, and many a time when friends came in my father would say with swelling chest:

"Pat and Peter, let ye go up and lower down that pump."

Then when it had been thoroughly examined and praised it was hoisted up again to be hidden away. My father's eyes would sparkle and he'd say:

"Arrah, what, man! That pump is worth a fortune!"

Usually while this conversation went on my mother sat on a stool knitting, and she'd once in a while give a look sideways at us hauling up the pump and draw a deep breath as if tired. All of which said plainly: "My children, Pat and Peter, we will be a long time waiting for that fortune."

★   ★   ★

In August some strangers drifted in. A few of them were looking for work. One of them came with the intention of picking up some easy money.

"For", said he, "Mr. Flaherty must get some man from

the outside to run these Aran men while he is working his camera."

I don't know if he ever asked Mr. Flaherty for a job, but he got none, anyway. We were able to do our own work and the cast always worked better when told how to do it in Irish. There wasn't any room for strangers.

Time was slipping by and the big September horse fair was soon to be held in Galway. Mr. Flaherty still had in his mind the idea of having a beautiful white horse in the film and spoke to me about it. We were pretty busy at the time, so I told him that my father was the right man to buy it, for he is never rightly in his glory until he is selling or buying cattle or horses. After every big fair he comes home tired and says:

"This last trip has me finished. I will buy no more, I am a little too old to be jumping around after cattle or horses."

But when the next big fair is coming on he gets terribly excited. He can't stay sitting down for a minute on end; he walks around the kitchen swinging his stick, talking to himself if there is nobody else to talk to, and picking out the little farmers of the Island who own good cattle, because he always buys the best.

"Patch Feadar owns a great spotted bullock. He ought to fetch so-and-so. Patcheen Maura, they say, has an out-and-out heifer. She's older than a two-year-old, she'll hold her weight at the Fair and stand the hardship of shipping better than a younger beast. I wonder myself what he'll be expecting for her. Divil have him, anyhow, 'twas always hard to buy from him."

And he talks on and on like this to himself. On fair morning in Aran we have a bit of a fair before the cattle are put aboard the steamer *Dun Aengus*. My father stands at the gate of our house and yells out to the owner of the first bullock or heifer that is driven down the road: "What price for that little article you are driving?" And then goes on a bargaining that is well worth while listening to, my father pretending that he is buying in order to help the owner, and the owner saying flatly that he intends going to the fair in Galway and has no intention whatever of selling in Aran.

However, my father was the right man for the job of buying the horse for the film. He is a youngster of eighty-five and during his life he has dealt with all manner of men and women, tinkers and gipsies included, and though sometimes he would be cheated in a deal he always managed to be some pounds up at the end of the year. I said to him:

"Go to the Fair. Mr. Flaherty wants a horse for the film. Buy a snow-white three-year-old with a flowing mane and tail."

"All right, I'm your man," said my father, "it seems that Mr. Flaherty wants a regular Arabian steed, the kind that Saladin used to ride long ago when he beat the Crusaders. Well, if there is such a horse for sale, I'll get it, in spite of all the buyers in Ireland or in England either."

As the *Dun Aengus* sailed from the pier for her trip to Galway I shouted up to my father: "Remember, a snow-white horse."

"All right, son, I understand," he shouted back.

Two days later a wire came from him, saying: "Horse, Erin's Hope, coming on *Dun Aengus*." I was very excited, but being busy I got Tommy Fitz to meet the boat and take charge of the horse. So impatient was I to see Erin's Hope that on the first chance that presented itself I hurried to Kilronan. All Aran Islanders have a great love of horses, and visions of a beautiful snow-white Arab steed floated through my mind as I drove rapidly along the road. I met Fitz.

"Where is the horse?" I shouted.

"He is in the field back of the schoolhouse," said Fitz, "and a finer horse I have never seen."

"Snow-white?" I asked eagerly.

"What!" said Fitz. "Snow-white? Not at all, the horse is a bay, a splendid animal. It's many a long day since the likes of him was seen in Aran."

I nearly fainted, but as I had come so far I had to go in and see him. He was a fine powerful animal but a bay, with some white hairs in his mane and tail. I went to see my father, but before I could say a word he said with his voice full of pride:

"Did you see the horse?"

"I did," I answered, "but why the devil didn't you buy a white horse, or if you weren't able to get a white one, well then, the nearest thing to it, a cream coloured?"

"There weren't any to buy," he snapped. "There wasn't a white or a cream-coloured three-year-old horse at the fair. Didn't you know very well that I wouldn't leave Mr. Flaherty without a horse if I had to go to Dublin to get one; and besides," he added, lowering his voice and speaking in great confidence, although nobody was listening, "do you think that I'd let any man on Aran say that Johnny Mullen went to Galway to buy a horse and had to come back without one. I'd rather see the whole damn lot of them in blazes first!"

Luckily it turned out that no white horse would be

needed after all. Ideas of using a horse with Tiger King handling him were dropped.

*　　*　　*

One stormy, cloudy day we went to Bungowla shore and looked the place over, the reefs and breakers and so on, and we came to the conclusion that it was far too dangerous for a curragh storm scene. The shore slopes away in ledges for a great distance out to sea and in rough weather I believe that there is no place in the world where the great breakers, line after line (caused very likely by the ledges underneath), rise to more terrific heights or wilder grandeur. One could watch, day after day, these mighty seas break and rush madly towards the shore. They make one stop thinking of the worries of life and time seems to stand still. Bungowla is Big Patcheen Conneely's shore.

We tried a curragh scene in the mouth of Gregory's Sound at Glassin Rock point. It didn't come out satisfactorily. Another scene was tried at a rugged point west of it. We had another try at Kilronan Bar; both these places are exceptionally dangerous for canoe work except in fine weather. None of these scenes turned out satisfactorily, some being a bit too far away from the camera and others being bad owing to clouds coming up. Mr. Flaherty wanted another curragh scene to tie up with the one in Manister, so as to have that sequence the right length to suit the film. The reason why Mr. Flaherty was so insistent in trying to get storm scenes in such dangerous places was that he wanted to show Aran men at their best in a storm scene, because he knew well from the tales that I had been telling him, that no matter how good the camera work, and no matter how good the curragh work, nothing could be shown on the screen more thrilling than what curraghmen are doing in the seas around the Islands.

One morning, it was before a break in the weather, we looked out to sea. The sea was getting up and a heavy swell was pounding on Kilmurvy Strand, which is Tiger King's shore—the place from where he always fished. Mr. Flaherty made up his mind to get King and his crew out and then try for a landing that was needed for the film. He asked me what I thought of the sea.

"It is a tricky sea," I told him, "it is a sea before a storm, see how it's getting up gradually, and look at that steady line of rollers coming in, but perhaps it's not too dangerous."

Suddenly, almost as soon as I'd said these words, seemingly from nowhere a huge sea reared itself up and struck the beach with a hollow roar. Then for a long time a steady line of rollers came sweeping in again, but as suddenly as before, as if pushed up from the bottom of the sea, one or two huge waves came rushing in. I spoke to King about going out.

"I've seen worse days," he said, "yes, we'll go."

So I told him to get Patch Ruadh and Tommy O'Rourke and to get their curragh out and ride in on a sea with it breaking from the fore thwart. Coming in that way would, by very good management, carry a curragh clean up high and dry on to the beach, and we believed that it would look good through the camera. The men launched the curragh and got out clear, then after rowing out some distance they turned the curragh back. The Tiger timed the sea to a second and they ran in with the wave tumbling white from the fore thwart and they made a

146

beautiful landing. Maggie and Mike were in this scene. They ran down the beach to meet the curragh. Again the Tiger went out and came in the same way on a rushing wave. He went out a third time, but as the seas weren't as big as the previous ones he hesitated about coming in. He followed one for a curragh's length then stopped and prepared to go out again, when suddenly a huge wave reared itself up outside. I yelled through the megaphone, but it was too late. The Tiger couldn't make the beach quick enough to get clear, nor could he get out far enough. So he steadied the canoe and prepared to take the wave squarely on the stern. The sea broke clean over the canoe. One moment we saw them on the oars, the next moment the canoe was swung sideways, had turned over, and the crew disappeared beneath the water. Maggie forgetting everything but her desire to help rushed headlong into the sea. But the water was too deep and she disappeared. Tommy was the first to come to the surface, clutching hold of an oar. Next came Patch. Then came Maggie, and after much struggling they found a footing and reached the shore. Patch was pretty frightened looking and he looked a sight with the sand and water falling out of his whiskers. I shouted through the megaphone:

"Patch get out and try to save your curragh."

"Oh, the devil take the curragh," spluttered Patch, but he turned out into the water and made the attempt.

The Tiger was underneath the canoe and it was quite a little while before he put his head up through the water. The curragh was thrown in a few moments later by the sea. The Tiger caught hold of her, and with the others helping they managed to drag her ashore. Tiger was all right except that he had taken in a lot of water. Maggie, being a very strong woman, just put on a change of clothes and was ready for the next scene. Mr. Flaherty's heart was in his camera and he continued to take the scene until the whole thing was over. The Tiger stated afterwards that when under the curragh the thought that was uppermost in his mind was how Patch and Tommy were getting on: he feared they had been drowned. Alas, the camera cannot take such thoughts. This scene was developed and shown on the screen but unfortunately it didn't come out very well. The seas in the background didn't look anywhere near as big as the Manister seas where Mr. Flaherty had taken his first storm scene. However, in case it might be made all right by the further addition of having a canoe come in from a distance farther out, and so make up the connecting link between the two, Mr. Flaherty asked me a few days later if we would get the canoe out and try it on Kilmurvy Strand.

I didn't want to. I hated the Kilmurvy Strand stuff, but I didn't hate it half as much as he did. Still, in case he might be missing anything, he wanted the men to make the try. I spoke to the Tiger; he got his two men and they put down their curragh and rowed out; on the signal they turned back and landed. Mrs. Flaherty had noticed my hesitation on this trip about getting the curragh out. I made some excuses but they didn't satisfy her. She looked me straight in the eye and said:

"Pat, what is it. There is something on your mind?"

"I don't like it," I said, "I'm afraid that Mr. Flaherty might not wait to give us the right chance to help him make the film, and I don't like to have anything shown on the screen about Aran men and women if it is not up to the mark."

Mrs. Flaherty laughed and said: "Pat, you don't know him yet as well as I do. It is only that he doesn't like to let anything pass without taking a shot at it. Don't worry. You will get plenty of chances yet. Though I must admit", she went on, "that at present what we want seems most elusive. We can't reach out and lay our hands on it."

"I'm sure", I answered, "that we'll get what we want as regards the curragh work, because the best man, Big Patcheen Conneely, is yet to be heard from. I have kept in touch with him and told him that sooner or later I felt sure his time would come."

"Yes, I understand that," said Mrs. Flaherty, "but I thought we had given up the idea of trying anything in Big Patcheen's shore. It is so frightfully dangerous and as you know we don't want people to lose their lives while making the film if we can help it."

"I know that," I answered, "but lives lost or not, the *Man of Aran* ought to be made the real thing or nothing. Besides we can also try Gortnagapple shore."

Mrs. Flaherty looked at me queerly, but never said a word.

The curragh work on Kilmurvy Strand also turned out to be unsuitable.

*   *   *

While waiting for the weather to break again and for the seas to rise we turned our hands to landmaking. Mr. Flaherty had fancied a craggy slope near the Glassin Rocks. It was strewn with granite boulders that had dropped from the ice, ages ago.

During one of our trips to this location a woman living in a cottage nearby invited us in for a drink of milk. She is a relation of mine and a very kindly woman. Mr. Flaherty was much pleased and spoke to me about it.

"Pat, it was very kind of your friend to give us that milk. Couldn't we do something for her in return?"

"I don't know of anything we could do," I answered, "except to thank her, and that we have done already!"

"Yes, I know, but . . . oh, I have it," said Mr. Flaherty. "We'll be coming here to-morrow, so why couldn't you get her to cook a good dinner for us. We can bring a basket of food as usual for the men carrying the cameras. The dinner will be more in the nature of a treat in return for her kindness. We can give her something that way." And he added: "I have seen a lot of geese along the road. If she owns any of them she might give us one for our dinner to-morrow. If she doesn't own one, then let her buy a fat one. I'm sure all these housewives know how to cook, don't they?"

I agreed with him that they did, so I turned back and went into the house and asked her about the dinner.

"Get a goose," said she, "why, you couldn't buy one of those geese for love or money. I haven't one myself and none of the people here ever sells a goose whether they are laying or not."

"A goose you must get," said I, "and a fat one at that, for the gentlemen's dinner." (Mrs. Flaherty hadn't come with us on this trip, but John Taylor had.)

"You can pay a good price for it, and Mr. Flaherty will settle up with you later," I added.

"Well, the only goose that I can get is an old one that Mickeleen Paudeen's wife has, but I wouldn't call her a goose because she is as old as myself and I know that no matter how she is cooked she will be as tough as a pampootie," and she added: "I wouldn't like to put a thing like that in front of a fine man like Mr. Flaherty."

"How old is the goose?" I asked.

"Oh musha, she must be well over twenty years if she is a day. Mickeleen's wife has had her since I can remember."

"Get her, anyhow," I said, "I will call in to-night and have a look at her. Maybe when you stuff her well she will turn out all right."

"Pat, you were in America and you must know all about grand dinners," she said. "You can tell me what to stuff her with because I have never done anything like this before."

"I know something about it all right," said I, "but you get the goose now and have her plucked by the time we pass in the evening. Then I can give you a lift into Kilronan on the sidecar where you can buy the things for the stuffing."

I called in that evening on our way home. The goose was plucked, but what an object it was to look at! It was so thin that the bones almost stuck out through its skin and its flesh was dark with age. I didn't know what to do or to say as I turned it over, for I realized that all the cooks or cooking in the world couldn't ever make a good meal out of it.

A sudden thought crossed my mind as I caught it by its long scrawny neck. I looked at it and I said to myself, well, here is a blasted old bird that's probably the last of an otherwise extinct breed of geese. We only want to do the woman a favour after all, and for some time now our work has been rather dull, without any excitement. Not many men on earth would dare to try and play a joke on

Mr. Flaherty, but here was a chance, if one only had the courage, and I said to myself, live or die, I'd venture it. In other words if we couldn't make anything better out of it than a bad good dinner, then it would be ten times better to make a good bad one! However, I took my relation, Mrs. Dillane, up on the sidecar, and on the way to Kilronan I told her what to stuff the goose with.

"Stuff her", says I, "with potatoes and bread, onions, milk and oatmeal, but above all things put a couple of boxes of pepper and a great deal of ginger into her. She's tough and nothing will ever soften her except plenty of pepper and ginger. And," I added, "don't tell the people at the shop what you want it all for."

She got down off the car and went into the shop and we went on our way to Kilmurvy.

Next morning when the girls in the kitchen were making up the basket of food, I told them to put something extra in for some other men who might be working on location. Of course I knew there wouldn't be any extra, but I wanted to play for safety, because with plenty of food to spare it wouldn't matter so much about the fancy dinner. Next day as dinner time drew near, Mr. Flaherty said:

"What do you say, John, are you ready for the big dinner?" and John, always polite, said:

"Yes, Mr. Flaherty."

"Come along Pat," said Mr. Flaherty. "The others can have lunch out of the basket while we are gone."

I started off with Mr. Flaherty and John, but when I got just beyond the first wall I ran back and told the men not to touch the basket until Mr. Flaherty came back. Then we headed for the house. It took about ten minutes to get there through the crags and boreens. We went inside, and as usual Mr. Flaherty took a great interest in looking round the kitchen, admiring the beautifully white-washed walls, the clean floor and the turf fire with the blue curling smoke going up the chimney. Hanging in the smoke from the pot hooks was a pot oven, and no man living could find fault with the smell that came out of it. The goose was sizzling within. Mr. Flaherty some-times when he wants work done has a fairly hard eye, but now as I watched him look at the pot his eye softened wonderfully. A fat goose is his favourite dish.

Mr. Flaherty looked at the poreens or square holes built into the chimney. One of these was for placing a partly knitted stocking in when the woman of the house had to get up to do some other work. The one in the other corner was used for holding the pipe of the man of the house, while still another was used, long ago, for the hens to lay their eggs in. Now it was being used as a bedroom for the cat! All Aran Island houses nowadays have beauti-fully clean whitewashed poultry houses, built some dis-tance away from the dwelling house. The white Wyan-dotte breed is I think the favourite one, but there are many others.

I often visited this relation of mine. She is a very kind-hearted lovable old woman. I have played many tricks on her, but of course I was always forgiven and I already knew that I'd be forgiven for the little one I was now playing on her. I used always to tell her about them after-wards and the scolding had always been: "Oh, musha, Pat, that you may be lucky. You are a queer man entirely, God bless you." As she sat by the fire I have watched the cat many a time jump from the floor to her knee, where it purred for a while, then jump from her knee to her shoulder where it purred and stroked her grey hairs with its whiskers. From her shoulder it jumped into the poreen where it purred away in a bed of straw finally to fall asleep while she calmly went on talking and knitting her stocking.

Mr. Flaherty admired the great big conger eels and ling hanging on pegs which were stuck in the wall over the arched fireplace. These fish were kept drying in the smoke and heat of the fire for winter use. The dresser was placed near the front door so that it could be seen from the street, its shelves being covered with big, beautifully coloured plates and dishes; but the grandest dish of all had been taken down for the goose. Hanging on nails driven into the two lower shelves were many mugs of various colours and on nails driven into the top shelves and on the shelves were a dozen or more most gorgeously gilded jugs; some of these jugs were centuries old and came from foreign countries when Aran men were smugglers and sailed to France and Spain and other countries in their hookers and dodged the British law. These beautiful old jugs are never used. The dresser with its delft is the most valuable possession of the old-time Aran Island housewife and is placed in front of the door as a sort of challenge to other housewives, or in case a strange lady passes by and admires it. This cottage was like scores of others. Of course it had the stooleens in the corners by the fire, also clean scrubbed forms by the walls, and near the front little window a table. In the loft was piled up the winter's supply of turf, and from a rafter was draped a cowhide skin which would be made into pampooties for the family. From another rafter hung a couple of pieces of rope a few feet long. These were to be used later in hanging up the spilliards or long lines when not being used during the great winter storms. Seeing all these things of course took only a few seconds, and while Mr. Flaherty, who sees everything, was admiring the kitchen and its furnishings, Mrs. Dillane had been talking to me as she took the stuffed goose out of the oven, laid it on the grand dish and hung the kettle over the fire.

"Pat," says she, "I'm ashamed of my life. This old goose is as black as the hobs of hell and twice as tough. What will I do with it at all at all. I think I ought to throw it out of the window and give them some fresh boiled eggs with bread and butter and tea instead."

"You are a very foolish woman if you do," says I, "there is a fine smell out of her and I'm sure the pepper and ginger has made the flesh on her, what little there is of it, as soft and as tender as a gosling's."

"Well, all right so, and now in the name of God I better leave it up to them."

And so she did. Dinner was in the big room, which contained a small table, already laid with knives and forks and plates and so on, and the big dish with the goose on it was laid gravely in the centre of the table. A couple of chairs were close to the table. Blessed pictures were on the walls and on a little mantelpiece over a small fireplace were standing some photographs of relations in America, and in the far side of the room was a bed. A gorgeous coloured, hand-made patchwork quilt covered it, and a snow-white valance draped along its side almost down to the floor. I brought up the potatoes which had been kept warm in an oven; Mr. Flaherty and John Taylor sat down. The scene was lit by the light from one middling-sized window.

"Come and join us Pat," said Mr. Flaherty heartily, "there is enough for all three."

"I know that well," say I, "and there will be lots left over too. But thank you just the same; the ways of the gentry are not my ways, and I would rather have a cup of tea with my friend here, Mrs. Dillane."

We then left the room, she shutting the door behind her out of a sense of decency, so that the strangers should have the privacy of the room entirely to themselves. Mrs. Dillane and I talked about the dinner as the kettle boiled; she then poured the water on to the tea and placed the teapot on a little separate red coal of turf a bit away from the main fire, so that the tea could get strong without boiling. While doing this she had her ear turned, listening in case she might be wanted in the next room. She poured out our tea and we were drinking it peacefully enough when she suddenly became very nervous; she said she couldn't believe that the dinner could be any good if all the women in Ireland had taken a hand in the cooking of it. I too didn't feel very well, because I knew that soon this cottage where a good many big men had been reared would be much too small for one certain man!

"Hist!" says she. "You would think he is cursing or something."

"I wouldn't say that," says I, "Mr. Flaherty says a lot of prayers. He must be at one of them now."

And he was, because I fancied I heard a gurgle of laughter from John Taylor. Soon, much too soon, they came down out of the room, and I never saw Mr. Flaherty with a rosier complexion, and it wasn't because he had fared well inside him!

"Ask him how he liked the goose," says Mrs. Dillane,

adding an aside to me, "sure we know very well how he liked her, but I did my best with the stuff I had." (Of course she spoke in Irish.)

"She wants to know how you liked the goose, Mr. Flaherty?" I asked.

"Goose!" says he in disgust, "where was it? If you mean the thing that was on the dish there in the next room, that was no goose. That was the raven that Noah let go out of the Ark and never came back. But how the blazes it ever came to Aran to live till your friend could lay hold of it to put before me for a goose dinner is a very great mystery."

"The stuffing ought to be middling," says I.

"Stuffing! It would have burned a hole in the side of a battleship!"

And with that he went out and down the boreen with John Taylor following. I turned to my friend and said: "The divil a bit of us can help him."

"Indeed we can't," she answered. "Sure, we knew ourselves how it would be, but anyway sure we were only wanting to oblige him."

I followed Mr. Flaherty to the location, and when he saw the men sitting around the untouched basket of food he asked them why they hadn't had their lunch.

"Pat told us not to touch it till you came back."

Mr. Flaherty looked around at me and suddenly he smiled broadly and said: "Well, I'll be damned."

"She did her best," said I, "that raven was very old."

"You bet it was," he answered, "and Pat," he added, "see that you give her five shillings extra."

★   ★   ★

Mr. Flaherty's brother, David Flaherty, and an English-man named John Goldman arrived in Aran about this time. Goldman was sent to speed up the cutting of the film and David to keep accounts and help with camera work. They are two very fine young men, and I hope as the years pass by that they will always remain true friends of mine as they have always proved themselves to be.

Early one morning we were awakened by the noise of the sea breaking on the rocks and after breakfast Mr. Flaherty asked me what I thought about Gortnagapple shore for pulling off a landing, taking into consideration the sea that was now running. I said it was worth a trial. Gortnagapple shore is on the south and wildest side of the Island. We had looked it over many times previous to this but, like Bungowla, it was very dangerous with any kind of a big sea running. It is a shore where, if a curragh were upset, the current would drag curragh and men around the point and batter them to pieces against the high cliffs that are on either side of the entrance. Big boul-ders strew the shore of the little harbour. A curragh when ready to come in must take it on the run and men must be waiting inside on the shore ready to snatch it out of the sea; that is, of course, unless the weather is very fine. Cameras were got ready in a hurry, because the morning which had been dark now showed signs of clearing with the sun likely to come out at any moment. We drove away on our sidecars. When we arrived at Gortnagapple I found that Dan Flaherty (Liam's cousin) had gone to Kilronan, so I went to the next best curraghman, Anthony Flaherty, and asked him what he thought of the day and the sea for getting out in a curragh.

"An hour ago it could have been done," said Anthony,

"but the sea is getting higher every minute and soon we will have the turn of the tide. After that no man can tell how it will be."

However, he agreed to get his crew, and if it were at all possible he would make the attempt, so we hurried out through the village carrying cameras and tripods; but we found we had forgotten the caps. Somebody had moved them from where they had usually been placed, and in the rush we thought they had been taken. These caps were used in the film. They are woollen and hand-knitted and were much used formerly—the broad felt hat is and has been worn, but the broad brim throws too much shadow, consequently they could not be used in the film. I hurried back to Gortnagapple village and jumped on the sidecar. I drove as fast as my horse could gallop to Kilmurvy, got the caps, and tore back again at full speed—too much speed, for when I rounded a corner with the car on one wheel it upset and I was thrown out against a wall and then on to the road. I had lost the reins and away went the horse dragging the car after it upside down. Up the hill he ran. The caps and cushions were scattered all over the place. At the top of the hill a man ran across a field, jumped over a fence on to the road and, the horse being winded, stopped as the man caught the reins. I gathered up the caps and didn't bother about the cushions, being in too much of a hurry. We righted the sidecar and away I went once more. My ribs on one side, where they came against the wall, were hurt a bit, but I wanted to see the curragh go out, so I didn't care much about my ribs. I arrived at Gortnagapple and ran through it to the shore. I fancied that everything looked hopeful in spite of a big sea running but, as I came near, Mr. Flaherty said that the curragh crew had just told him that it wasn't fit to leave the shore. I was terribly disappointed. I had hoped that we might have taken enough storm work to tie up with the Manister scene. I spoke to Anthony and explained to him what the going out of the curragh meant to us. His crew said it wasn't fit, so I offered to go with him myself, though I knew that the men he had with him were better men than I on this shore.

Anthony answered me by saying that he wouldn't ever have it said that any other man would leave that shore when a Gortnagapple man had refused, and with a wild yell he shouted to his men. They caught up the curragh and rushed down to drop it over a ledge into the sea. When this is done a man springs into it, grasps his oars and keeps the canoe's stern about a yard away from the ledge while the other two men each in turn jump in. Just as they were about to drop the curragh down on the water a terrific sea came rushing in. With another wild yell he ordered his men to hurry and carry her up again, and it was well they did so, because the onrushing sea covered the ledge to a depth of six feet with foaming, treacherous water. The tide had turned. Anthony looked at me with a wild light in his eyes and shouted:

"Now, you devil, is it fit to go out?"

And indeed it wasn't. Anyhow, the film had to be made, and I still had an idea that by watching their chance carefully they could try to get out in a rush as the biggest breakers spent themselves on the rocks; then when out on the deep, and watching the different points till the right time came, they could run her in so that a landing scene might be pulled off which would finish the storm part of the film. It was just a chance at best, yet I am al-

most sure that if Dan Flaherty had been with Anthony they would have ventured out. Anthony is famous as a curraghman, but Dan is by all accounts considered the best man in Gortnagapple. I don't know how Mr. Flaherty felt, but I was thoroughly discouraged. We had tried the other Islands and couldn't get anything done that was worth while—that is anything with this elusive dramatic quality which seems so necessary for the making of a good film. There was just one more place left before we should be compelled to face the dreaded Bungowla shore.

One day I took Patcheen Faherty with me, and we went out in a curragh and we rowed around west from Kilmurvy where there is a dangerous reef separated from the shore by a fairly deep narrow passage. It was a rainy day with a light east wind, and a fairly big sea was running. We rowed and drifted around the reef studying it and figuring if the passage could be run in a storm. Patcheen who knew the reef better than I, said:

"Now take my advice and don't go in any farther. We are as far in now as it is safe to go."

"It doesn't look too bad," said I, "and if we keep on we will very likely be in past the corner of the reef before the big seas come."

So we talked and drifted and grew a bit careless, when suddenly Patcheen shouted: "Look! Look! We are done!"

I glanced over my shoulder, and it looked as if we were about to be finished. A great sea had risen up and came rushing towards us. We were caught in the breakers. At such times I don't think anybody thinks much of the hereafter. Just one swift fleeting thought, then hope or whatever it is springs up. There is a fighting chance and one's thoughts are centred on the fight. Muscles become taut and a man prepares to battle it out to the finish. I shouted to Patcheen to keep a grip on his oars whatever happened, because if a man loses an oar at such a time he is lost. We faced the sea, and with a mighty pull we tried to drive the curragh over it. She went part way up but not over. I was in the bow and the sea broke down over my head; it lifted our oars off the thole pins and then rushed past with a roar, leaving the curragh half filled with water. She was now heavy under us and felt like some live thing that had been almost broken with a blow, but we had held our oars.

"One half length," I shouted, "one half curragh's length on to the deep and we will make it yet."

We tried to turn her head out swiftly, but she came round slowly. If only we could get the half curragh's length before the next breaker caught us we would be safe. The next great wave came and we barely had her bows to it; Patcheen cursed me bitterly, but my delay in helping to bring her head to the sea was caused by my efforts to bring her a little farther on to deep water. The wave broke, but it wasn't so strong as the first. It filled the curragh to the thwarts and we were nearly under. We worked hard to bring her head away and at last we were clear. Then we staggered into the pier. We had not brought an old can or anything with us to bale her out, in case of a leak. Patcheen blamed me, of course, as by right he should.

The damn film was beginning to get on my nerves. These storm scenes were becoming a nightmare. Next day we laid our canoes on the water, two crews of us intending to try and get a storm scene in the passage by the reef

—the Tiger with his two men in one; Patcheen Faherty, another man and myself in another. A heavy sea was running, and after some five or six attempts to run the passage we gave it up. A curragh couldn't run it and live, because the sea that was running so high continually broke across the reef and across the passage to the shore and also to the west of the passage. It was an almost endless line of breakers. This day's work was developed and we had a look at it on the screen. It looked very good but there was some doubt about its being used, as Mr. Flaherty said it lacked the finishing touch, the touch that goes between a good piece of work and the work of a master. That evening he called me into the big room. I went in and sat down. He was drinking his black coffee as usual. He looked at me with an unspoken question in his eyes.

"Yes," I said, "it has to be Bungowla shore and Big Patcheen Conneely."

"I dread the thought of it," said he. "I don't want any lives lost."

"Never mind," I answered, "Big Patcheen is the master curraghman of the west. He is a powerful and fearless man and I'm sure he is fit to bring his curragh home through almost any kind of a sea. We will get those storm scenes yet."

"I hope so," he answered. "We have good stuff already in Manister, but we want some more, and I do wish we could get it finished."

We were much bothered by the shortage of water, which kept the developing of the film back, oftentimes for weeks. This caused Mr. Flaherty much anxiety, because he couldn't ever be exactly sure of his work till he saw it projected on the screen, so during the weeks of waiting he had to work more or less in the dark.

We were now starting to build another cottage for a projecting room, as by this time Mr. Flaherty and his family had, as one might say, become Aran Islanders. There was no more fear of what might be in the back of the Islanders' minds with regards to religion. So that while we had a hard time to get anybody to come near us at all in the first place, now the trouble was to find excuses to keep them away! I had no easy time, because all this fell on my shoulders, and even though I divided up the work so that every family in turn was earning a pound by working on the film, still some wanted a little more than others. A man came to me one day, his eyes flashing angrily as he approached, saying:

"What the hell kind of work is this you are doing, giving work to everybody and not giving me any?"

"Well," said I, "you earned five or six pounds before, that isn't bad, is it, and besides," I added, "I'd say that you are a good deal better off in land and sheep than lots of other men who are looking for a shilling to earn here."

"You might think so," he said, his eyes still flashing, "but you ought to know that you couldn't get a penny for a sheep or a cow now."

"Kill them and eat them," I suggested.

"Yes," he said, "and leave myself and my family without anything by and by when the times maybe might pick up, and when a few sheep and a cow will be a great help to a man. Come, come," he said impatiently, "put me to work."

"I cannot see my way of doing it," I said, "I'm sorry."

He blazed up in anger, saying: "Look at the family I

have behind me. Ten of them and more to come. What am I going to do with them?" he shouted, looking at me accusingly in anger.

"Man alive," says I, "sure it isn't my fault if you have ten in family and if there are more to come. What has it got to do with me anyway? Sure I haven't had anything to do with it!"

"Oh, I know that well enough," he answered, somewhat pacified, "we all know, Pat, that big families are due entirely to the will of God."

But as he said it with all appearance of sincerity I could nevertheless have sworn I saw a flicker in his eye, and I knew that somewhere in him was a sense of humour which appealed to me, so I said:

"Well let us put our heads together and see what is the best way to get you a job, because without some kind of a plan the other men working on the cottage will know that I gave in to you; and if they ever thought they could force me to do anything I'd have to leave Mr. Flaherty, because half the men in the Island would be clamouring around here and trying to frighten me into giving them jobs."

So we plotted, he and I, as to how he could earn three pounds more on the film. Finally we both agreed that the most diplomatic way was to get his wife to come and see Mr. and Mrs. Flaherty and tell them of her big family and of her poverty, then when Mr. Flaherty sent for me, which I knew he was sure to do to talk the matter over, I could easily manage to put the man to work, even though I had to lay another man off to do it. I could give as my excuse for laying him off that I was under orders from Mr. Flaherty to do so, because of Mrs. —— coming to see him and pleading her poverty. There would be a few curses of course on Mrs. —— but that would be all. Next day Mrs. —— came to see me; she was very bashful about going to see either Mrs. Flaherty or the Chief. I had a hard time coaxing her into the kitchen and through it into the hall. We had much whispering outside the door of the dining-room, she refusing and I encouraging her to go in; at last with a few reassuring taps on the back and telling her to keep up her courage, I pushed her gently through the door and I hurriedly tiptoed out through the kitchen.

Mr. Flaherty soon sent for me. I came in.

"Pat," he says, "can we do anything for this poor woman, couldn't you give her husband something to do, put him building the house or hauling seaweed? She has a large delicate family and they are desperately poor."

"We are full-handed as we are," I said, "but if the case is as bad as that, I can lay a man off and put her husband to work."

This being agreed on I went to the man that I intended to lay off and told him I was sorry to do so but that Mrs. —— had come herself specially to Mr. and Mrs. Flaherty, and she had been crying bitter tears when she was telling them her story of her weak family and of how badly she needed a few shillings. The man stood up and looked at me; he spat out a stream of tobacco juice, looked very solemn for a minute, and then he said:

"Mullen, I don't blame you at all for letting me go, but damn her soul," he added, "wouldn't you think she'd be ashamed to go in crying like that before any lady or gentleman, and all for the sake of a couple of pounds; and besides, she and her husband are better off than a lot of us."

166

The woman hadn't cried, of course, but it was just as well to say so.

A relation of mine came to me one day. He is not a relation by blood, but it was near enough for him. He is a tall, middling old man with wild red whiskers, and he carried a blackthorn stick in his right hand.

"Pat," says he, "what the divil kind of a man are you? Every place I ever heard of where a man would have a bit of a say in the spending of money, he always gave his own relations most of it. But here now you are doing the other thing. Everybody is getting just as much chance to earn a pound as me and my family, right enough, and I have no complaint to make in that way. I have earned as much as anyone, but", he continued, "relationship ought to count for something, or if it doesn't, what's the good of it."

"Well," I answered, "I was just reading the life of a great man the other day. He was at one time the President of the United States of America. His name was Abraham Lincoln. 'Tis said of him that he was one of the greatest men that ever lived, and he never put any relation of his first; when jobs were going and when easy money was to be had, they always came last. He was killed. . . ."

"Ha! Of course he was killed!" shouted my relation, interrupting me, "and his own relations killed him. They had a right to kill him," he added, hitting a large empty tea box a clout with his stick. "The damn scoundrel," he went on, "but sure anyone would know that he was bound to be killed; sure we never heard of any man that didn't give his own relations the first chance when a shilling was to be earned!"

He glared at me fiercely and I saw that I was on the

wrong tack and nearing dangerous reefs, so I put myself about, trimmed my sails and steered a course for deeper and safer water.

"Well, right enough," said I, "there is a lot of truth in what you say, and though I couldn't tell everybody, there is no harm in telling you; I am doing my best to favour my own relations on this job. But this is how things stand: every shilling that any relation of mine makes above any other man, Mr. Flaherty is told about it. He wants me to let the money go around as evenly as possible. Now if I favour my own people too much he will pretty soon be told all about it, and the next thing I shall lose my own job."

"Well! well! Can you beat that?" he said. " 'Tis the devil for a poor man to look out for himself on account of them," and by "them" he meant those busybodies of talebearers I had told him about. He continued: "Keep your job, you, because if you lost it the sorra bit at all we will get. Isn't it a terrible world when people want to cut one another's throats that way?"

He went away fairly well satisfied. However, there were many others, and one of these was a very hard case. A stocky man, named Cook, with a beautiful pointed beard, came into the Irish cottage one night, and after a sit down and a smoke in the corner, he carefully knocked the ashes out of his pipe and stood up. He stuck out his chest, raised his arms above his head, and stretched himself.

"Mullen, I'm coming to work in the morning," he said.

"Are you?" says I.

"I am, and it's pretty near time I did," he answered.

"I've let things go on long enough as it is, and I'm sorry now I didn't come to work long ago."

"I don't think there is any man wanted now," said I, "but maybe you are coming to work for the good of your health, and that you don't want any money at all, and besides that," I added, "don't forget your son earned a few pounds the other day."

"What he earned was no good to me. The blackguard drank it or something, and I got very little of it," he answered. "However," he concluded, "I will stroll over here in the morning and I will start fiddling with something. 'Tisn't work you will want me to do, because I hear all ye do here is put the time past ye."

With that he walked out, saying: "God give ye all a good night."

Sure enough next morning he appeared on the job.

"What kind of fiddling are you going to put me at, Mullen?" he asked, as he looked me over calmly, but his look had a little superior touch in it.

"Faith! I couldn't tell you," says I. "We have too many men here as it is and I don't know what to start you at."

"Why, Mullen! You haven't half enough men here; a place like this where everyone says money is more plentiful than the grains of sand on Kilmurvy Strand! 'Tis only lately that I have been thinking this way myself, and now I'm sorry that I didn't come in for my share of it long ago. I am not extra well in health, anyway," he added, "so I'd better put a spade on my shoulder and start walking around with it, because I get dizzy when I bend down."

I think that he must have hypnotized me—because he went to work. Dinner time came round and the men from Kilmurvy village began to hurry home for their meal.

Cook, my stocky friend, though living in Kilmurvy, didn't bother himself to go with the others.

"Aren't you going home to dinner, or do you work better when your stomach is empty all day?" I asked him.

He roared with laughter and as he wiped the tears from his eyes with the sleeve of his bauneen (long white woollen coat), he said:

"Well, Mullen, you are the devil for making fun. Go home to dinner when there is more thrown away out of this house, they say, than would give food to half the villages in the Island? Where there are quarters of beef and quarters of mutton and millions of tins of everything that come from every land on which the sun shines! Me go home to dinner! Well, well, Mullen!"

I was very patient with him, so I said: "Those other men who come from your village have all gone home to dinner. Why can't you do likewise?"

"Oh, them damn fools! Sure 'tis only by chance that God threw the soul into them. Come, come," he added, "hurry up and get half a dozen of those cans out of the house. We will break them open and see what's in them. Anyhow 'tis near time, after my life of rough food, that I began to eat some of those dainty things."

I looked at him again and turned towards the house. I got together four or five tins of food—one of salmon, one of rabbit, one of beef, some pineapple, and I also brought some bread. We sat down on a slab of limestone. I opened first the tin of salmon.

"What's that?" he asked.

"Salmon from North America," I replied.

"Wait till I taste it," says he.

He stuck his knife into it and put a little bit of it in his mouth.

"Oh, darn it! Throw it away," he said, as he spat it out. "Sure, it tastes as bad as any other fish; we are sick and tired of eating fish all our lives and I can't understand at all why people buy fish when they can afford to buy better stuff, unless it be that when they get too fat eating meat they eat the fish to cut it down again. What have you there?" he said, as I opened the next can.

"Beef," says I.

"Ah, that's the stuff that's able to put the strength in a man," and he started eating it with great gusto. "What's in that next can?" he asked between mouthfuls.

"Rabbit," I told him. "Shall I open it?"

"No, don't, there is no strength in rabbits. Beef is the right and only food for a man in order to keep him in full strength."

I pecked away at the salmon while I watched him eat. He wasn't surprised at my eating fish, because he believed that I too was lined up with too much fat on account of being so long on the job. Finally he heaved a sigh of fullness. (Aran men aren't big eaters anyway.)

"I have another can here," I said.

"What's in it?" he asked.

"It grew in a very warm country," says I. "It must be great stuff entirely, because my brother Peter told me that once when he was going through the Panama Canal, he was fined five pounds for going into a garden and taking one of them."

He got all excited.

"Fined five pounds! Open it, open it quick, so that we can see what's in it."

I did. He looked at it, then tasted it.

"Why," he said, "isn't it queer the notions people have? That thing tastes like some kind of a root, and I'd say it's raw along with that. I wouldn't give you a halfpenny for a shipload of them, and Peter got fined five pounds! Well, well, Mullen!"

He soon got tired of fiddling around with the spade on his shoulder. So I put him to work sitting down to break some stones with a small stone hammer. I placed him opposite the cottage window for reasons of my own. Hoping to startle him into doing some work, I came around next day. He was spending a lot of time with his pipe and heartily bidding the hour of the day to everybody who passed. He praised the loveliness of the day and the glassy smoothness of the sea, as he lifted up his small hammer and then took it down again carefully, hardly ever hitting a real blow with it.

I came up to him and said: "Well, for God's sake why the devil don't you do something? Here you are opposite the window, and every time Mr. and Mrs. Flaherty look out they can see you sunning yourself. I'm going to lose my job over you, if I'm fool enough to keep you any longer. I saw them both looking out at you a minute ago, and they were out of their minds with anger."

He looked at me pityingly, saying: "Mullen, there is a lot of your head empty, if you can't see that it's only letting on they are. They must pretend like that sometimes. The real truth is that Flaherty is getting about a thousand pounds a week to spend, and if he spends more than that he will get two thousand a week, and so on. Of course," he added, "he doesn't want to tell us that straight out for fear the people he works for might hear of it, but I'm telling you the Gospel truth."

"How do you know?" says I.

"Why shouldn't I know?" he answered. "Didn't I hear it was in the papers?"

When I told him to go, I had to lay off two other men with him, otherwise he would never have left the job.

CHAPTER VIII

Mikeleen goes Fishing—"Of doubtful fragrance"—
Maggie on Bungowla—In the Nick of Time—A
strange Tale—The day before Christmas—To the
dreaded Shore—By the Hair of her Head—Making
a Garden—With Sticks and Stones

★

Little Mikeleen had been working on his part—that is
doing what most of the young boys used to do—fishing from the cliffs for rock fish, bream and pollock.
Fishing from a cliff three hundred feet high requires a
steady head and hand and also a great deal of experience;
but Mikeleen, before he joined us, had fished off the
Glassin rocks. His people have, as far as we know, always
been landless, and have had to earn a living by fishing, so
that at the age of thirteen Mikeleen was already an old
hand. He is as surefooted as a goat, and is as much at home
sitting on the edge of a three hundred foot cliff as if he
were in bed.

Mr. Flaherty had asked me if we should try to put a
rope around Mikeleen and lead it back to a cleft in the
rocks where it would be unseen by the camera's eye.
Mikeleen would be safer that way. I didn't like the idea.
Besides, Mikeleen had often told me that he wouldn't be

able to work right unless he were free to hop around just as he always did. I also believed that had we put a rope around him it might have instilled in him a sense of fear, while being free would help to form his character—that is of course providing he didn't fall over! There was always the chance of his doing that.

On one of these fishing days, Mikeleen got ready his line, and we all went up towards Dun Aengus. Mr. Flaherty picked out with his camera the spot where Mikeleen was to fish from, and I must say that this same damn camera seemed to be possessed of the evil eye. It had the faculty of picking out the hardest and most dangerous places to get at. Mikeleen took up his position, and Mr. Flaherty shouting, "All ready!" Mikeleen swung his line around his head, letting it out in ever growing circles in order to get the proper drive to it. Then he let it go. It sailed far out because of the stone attached to the end; this is also used as a sinker for the line, and is attached to the line by a slender cord so that if the stone gets caught among the rocks, the cord can then be broken by a sharp pull and the line saved. This sinker helps to place the line and bait in the chosen position, which is usually at the edge of or between sunken boulders, under which the fish hide.

Mikeleen jumped to the other end of his line, and lifted it high, letting it run out over his right arm to prevent it from being cut on the edge of the cliff, and also from burning his hands. When the line reached the bottom, he darted out to the edge of the cliff and sat down, his legs dangling over. He began to fish, feeling for a bite and balancing his line on the side of his pampootie to prevent it from being cut by the rocks underneath.

The place where he sat was split wide about four feet

back from the edge, the crack being about three feet wide and six or eight feet deep. The sea is forever gnawing underneath these cliffs, and in places they overhang fully a hundred feet, and are continually falling away into the depths below. Mikeleen was sitting on a large slab of rock that appeared to be about evenly balanced. One never knew when the cracked and broken cliff beneath would give way, but it had been like that for years, so we weren't much worried about it, and besides it seemed to be the very spot that suited the camera.

Mikeleen fished away, and after a time, believing his bait to be gone off the hook, he began to haul in his line. I shouted to him to hurry, because clouds were coming up and we wanted him if possible to catch a fish while the light of the sun was good.

When Mr. Flaherty had stopped using his camera, I jumped out on to the slab of rock to help Mikeleen haul in his line quickly. He looked up calmly from his perch and said:

"Pat, when you jump like that again, jump easy. The rock is stirring and it might fall out."

I was so shocked that I caught him by the collar of his jersey and dragged him and his line back to safety. I tested the ledge after that, and sure enough it was very shaky.

Mr. Flaherty sang out through a megaphone, enquiring what was the matter. I told him.

"My God!" he said. "If anything had happened to that boy I'd never again touch a camera."

So, owing to the shaky rock we had to look for another location. We found one inside Dun Aengus, and on these high cliffs Mike has done most of his fishing. Not long after this, after a night's heavy rain, the broken rock, where he had been sitting when it stirred, fell away, several tons of it.

We had to spend many days and months on the Dun Aengus location in order to get this part of the film as good as Mr. Flaherty expected the rest of it to be. It was tricky work because Mikeleen had to have a live fish so that it could be seen on the screen. He caught many, but most of them were either killed against the rocks on the way up the face of the cliff, or died "naturally". For rock fish as a rule do not live long when taken out of the water. However, one day he hooked a real big fellow, and after great efforts and seemingly endless hauling, he landed it on top of the cliff. The day was fine, and luckily this fish, being very strong, stayed alive long enough for the camera to get a good picture of it. This completed Mikeleen's fishing scene, and needless to say we were all very glad when it was over.

It was only a few days before this that Mikeleen called me aside and said: "Pat, I nearly fell over a while ago."

"I know that," said I, "but I didn't say anything when I saw that you weren't frightened, and," I added, "you remember I told you to be very careful to-day because the wind is blowing strong from the north and against your back. I told you to brace yourself back against it in case it might blow you over."

"Oh, I know that myself," said Mikeleen, "but what I didn't think of was my pampooties, and that the weather had been very dry for the past couple of days. The grass had dried and the rocks had too, and my pampooties were dry, hard and slippery, and I nearly fell out when I slipped."

On the other hand, our work had its amusing side.

Mr. Flaherty had an idea of having Mikeleen come home to his mother riding on a donkey, with his day's catch of fish tied to a string and thrown over his shoulder. When one least expected it, Mr. Flaherty would say:

"Pat, I have been thinking over Mikeleen's part. We will try some more shots of him to-day on his donkey going through such and such a village."

These shots depended a great deal on the situation in which the cottages were built, whether they were close to the road or not, and whether the gables faced the road, and also of how the sun shone on them at a certain hour of the day. At the same time Mr. Flaherty always had his eye ready to catch any stray bit of drama that he might see in any of the women who owned the cottages—whether it was in her nose, in her eyes, or her mouth, in her hair or in her old pampooties, he never missed it. I have spent many heartaching hours trying to catch a glimpse of this will-o'-the-wisp vision—the something which Mr. Flaherty would call dramatic but which I could never manage to corner rightly.

Anyway, Mikeleen always had to have a string of fish over his shoulder when riding his donkey, and as sometimes one couldn't have fresh fish because of stormy weather, I bought a hundred horse mackerel and gurnets from a Kilmurvy man and threw them into a barrel so that we could always have a supply on hand. I threw a shake of salt on top of them, but it didn't do much good. We couldn't gut the fish because they had to look natural, as if they had been freshly killed; and the salt couldn't do its work properly because Mikeleen used to have a score of these fish knocking about the villages on his donkey. The result was of course that a most abominable stink began

to come out of them. At first the women used to put their heads out of their doorways when they got wind of it, wondering what foreign element of doubtful fragrance had spread through the atmosphere, but after a time they just said, as they sniffed the air: "Huh! Theirselves are coming."

One day when the wind blew from the south-west, which meant blowing from the fish and our starting point in the morning, towards the house where Mr. Flaherty and his family lived, I saw Mrs. Flaherty come to the door all ready to come with us, then as if growing a little faint she put her handkerchief to her face and disappeared into the house again, and Mr. Flaherty, growing impatient of waiting, went in to see what was the matter. Later, after we had started out, he'd say:

"Pat, Mrs. Flaherty is not very well to-day. She is not coming with us." He never let on that it was because of the fish.

On these days he fairly bubbled over with energy, as if he were afraid that if he gave a thought to the fish the drama would run like the devil out of the scene.

Once when he spoke to me about Mrs. Flaherty not being very well, I said jokingly: "Yes, people should look out for themselves this weather, because there is lots of flu and other queer things drifting around in the wind." None of this work appears in the film, and perhaps it is just as well!

*　　*　　*

One day I went with Mr. Flaherty to Bungowla, and showed him parts of the shore where amongst the rocks at low tide, landless men and women had to come and cut seaweed for manure. He decided that at the next spring tide he would take some shots of Maggie cutting and carrying a basket of seaweed.

Now it is one thing to go to a shore, cut seaweed and carry it to a garden, and another thing entirely to do the same kind of work for a film. In the first case a man can be ready about three-quarters of an hour before low water. He can go to work immediately, cut and carry as much seaweed as he can in the short time that he has to do it in —which is about one hour and a half. He then leaves the shore when the flood tide puts him out of it, and his work is finished. For a film there are clouds that bring delay, there are dark backgrounds which prevent a person from being seen clearly with the camera, and in order to be in the best position for film work, one may have to be outlined against the sea and may have to go in a dangerous place for that purpose. During all this waiting, picking and choosing, the flood tide may have crept in, and at any moment a sea may come and break over that particular location, submerging it entirely—especially at the south side of the Island, where there is no shelter from the Atlantic.

The spring tides set in. This doesn't mean, of course, that these tides come only in the spring. There are neap or low tides and spring or high tides, following one another all the year round, though it is a fact that the tide ebbs farther and flows higher in the spring of the year than at any other time.

Anyway we got ready. We drove our sidecars to Bungowla, and got Big Patcheen to come along and carry the camera cases. Mr. Flaherty set up his camera on the edge of a high cliff almost overlooking a great hog-backed ridge of rock that ran out to and beyond low-water mark. The ridge ran south-east with deep water on both sides of it, the inside, under the towering cliff on which the camera had been set up, being dotted here and there with great hundred-ton boulders, between which the sea ran swiftly. To one looking down from the high cliff above, the ridge appeared to be fairly smooth, but when Maggie, Big Patcheen and I scrambled down the perilous slanting pathway where she was later to carry up her basket of seaweed, we found it terribly rough—fit only for a curlew to perch on.

The great seas for ages had been doing their work and the ridge was scarred and cut so that now it stuck up in jagged spikes from a foot to three feet long. Here and there, between these sharp points of rock, were deep green pools of water, at the bottom of which were swarms of spiked blue-black Coontha Morras. These spikes are so sharp and strong that they can go through a bad pampootie.

I remember in my youth that when some of them had pierced my foot and broken off, my mother wouldn't touch them until the ebb tide had set in, because these live spikes or needles tend to go in with the flood and out with the ebb tide.

Yet men and women had cut and carried seaweed here for centuries and the pampootie is the only shoe that I know of that can pick out a foothold in such places.

The signal flag went up—a sign that Mr. Flaherty was ready to begin. Maggie went to work cutting seaweed. She filled her basket with it, lifted it on her back, and picked her way slowly up the long ridge of rock. This day she seemed very lifeless in her work. I asked her what was wrong.

"Nothing," she said.

It didn't look very good from the camera, for a runner came and told me to place Maggie farther out on the point, and that she should carry her basket of seaweed along the outer edge of the ridge, so that the camera could pick her up outlined against the sea. I knew this should not be done, for a quarter of an hour before this the tide had turned and now at any moment a sea might come rushing in and breaking over the ridge sweep her in amongst the boulders, from where a strong current ran out to the deep. I hated to place Maggie so far down, and then have her walk along the edge where points of the ridge stuck up as sharp as needles. At the same time I didn't want to take her up to Mr. Flaherty and tell him that it couldn't be done. He wouldn't have understood, because from the great height from which he looked it appeared to be quite an easy thing to do. I asked Big Patcheen what he thought of it. He said that it was an awfully bad place, without any footing, and now getting dangerous because of the flowing tide, but he added:

"You know best. No man can judge it any better than yourself."

I made up my mind. I looked far out to sea before we went down, then we hurried as best we could. We filled Maggie's basket with seaweed. I told her that when I yelled through the megaphone she was to rise up under her basket and hurry along the edge of the ridge as she had never hurried before.

I didn't know till long afterwards that Maggie had spent many sleepless nights nursing her youngest child who was very ill. She never told anybody about her home affairs. Had I known that she was spent from loss of sleep

and worry, I would never have placed her where she now was.

I told Patcheen to run up the ridge and get out of sight; and I took one final swift glance out over the waters. Yes, the sea was coming. I could see it breaking high on the shore to the west as it swept along towards us. But it was still far enough away for Maggie to have her work done if everything went right. I raced up the ridge to get out of sight of the camera, waving my megaphone to Mr. Flaherty as a signal that everything was ready. I dodged out of sight, but I was in a position where I could keep my eye on Maggie. I yelled to her to get going, but to my horror she seemed in no hurry to do it. Slowly she put her arm through the rope that is fixed to the basket so that it can be carried on the back. Slower still she made a half-hearted attempt to rise up under it. I shouted, cursed and implored her for God's sake to hurry. It seemed an eternity before she began to move. She looked around as if in a daze, then she began to pick her way slowly over the sharp-pointed spears of rock. But by now I felt it was already too late. I had judged the sea well. Maggie should have been by now well on her way and clear of danger, yet she had only just started.

Still hoping against hope that Mr. Flaherty might get something worth while, I waited. The film had to be made and one never knew what unexpected twist of fortune would help in the making. Also I now realized that I couldn't reach her in time in case anything was about to happen, so I hoped that I might have been mistaken in the sea, but I wasn't—it came roaring in. It crashed against the ridge and rolled, boiling and white over Maggie and her basket, dashing in amongst the boulders on the other

183

side. In an instant she and her basket were tossed in the foam, and as I rushed down to help her she had disappeared. As the sea poured down on the inside, the ridge began to show itself and I saw Maggie; the basket had been swept away and as she was being tumbled across the ridge, her long red petticoat had caught in the tall spikes of rock; this had prevented her from being dragged over the ridge and into the main current.

Big Patcheen was now running down. He had been further away than I. I helped Maggie to her feet and shouted to her to grip the sharp rocks and crouch low when the next sea came. I did the same thing with one hand, while I gripped Maggie with the other. The next sea almost covered us, but it wasn't nearly so bad as the first one. Before the third sea came, with Big Patcheen helping me, we managed to get her safely back.

We sat down to rest. The flag was still flying, showing that Mr. Flaherty was ready to go on with the work. But there was now no way of working, as the basket was gone. Besides, the place had become frightfully dangerous, and Maggie was much scratched and cut about her knees. She looked at me with a world of reproach in her eyes, and said:

"What did you try to do to me? Is it true what the people are beginning to say about you?"

I asked her what they were saying.

"They say that all you care about is the film and that it wouldn't worry you a bit whether people working on it lost their lives or not, provided it suited the picture."

After a while we climbed up to the higher cliff, where Mr. Flaherty was. He asked me what was the matter. I told him. He had seen the sea break over the ridge and sweep Maggie off her feet, but from the great height from which he looked it didn't seem to him to be so very serious. Mrs. Flaherty dressed the cuts on Maggie's knees, which fortunately were not very bad.

When Mr. Flaherty understood the situation thoroughly, he got angry and told me never again to do anything like that when I knew there was such serious risk. However, Big Patcheen knew as well as I that had Maggie been her old self this accident would not have happened.

This was the first and last time that I broke in on the camera's work. There were many occasions after this when I felt like doing so, but thoughts of what might be got for the film always held me back.

*　　　*　　　*

Winter was coming. It would soon be in on top of us, and while waiting anxiously for the storms that must now soon come, Mr. Flaherty used up the time by taking "tie-up" shots of Mikeleen and Maggie in curragh scenes, and also shots of groups of people looking out to sea, watching for curraghs to come in.

Many a time in the old days when big fish, ling, cod and eels were plentiful, old men and women watched for the coming in of the curraghs. The fish were caught in the winter or early spring, and consequently in the roughest weather. Fish, as I say, being plentiful, the canoes were out in all weathers.

I can barely remember what is said to be the most anxious day in the memory of any Islander. This is what happened.

The canoes of the three Islands had shot their lines at night out at the south'ard end of the Islands, at different distances from the land: some a mile, some four miles, and the farthest about eight or ten miles to sea. They, as always, left the shore hours before day, in order to be over their lines at the first streak of dawn, taking with them as food a piece of dry bread and a can of water. Some who had no bread had to take with them boiled potatoes, which of course were stone cold when eaten.

It began to blow a whole gale from the north-east when the men were hauling their lines. It was a head wind, and a fearful row back to the Islands. The people stood on the high points of the cliffs and watched for the return of the canoes. After hours of watching they saw a curragh tossing in the waves as she bravely battled for home. Soon another was sighted, and so on—and all the Aran curraghs landed safely except one.

There was no trace of her and she was given up for lost, but next day we heard that she had made Middle Island after ten hours of rowing through the gale; but there were three curraghs lost on South Island strand, when trying to land. It is a very dangerous shore when a north-east gale is raging, because it is wide open to it.

The Aran curraghmen who landed on Middle Island told a strange tale. They said that in the height of the storm, as they were straining every muscle to drive the curragh ahead, a canoe flew past them, heading for the open sea, with her little sail set and drawing free. Two men were rowing while the third man sat in the stern steering her with an oar. They knew those men, they were South Islanders, and as their curragh skimmed the great waves on its way to the deep, the Aran men shouted, but the South Island men never looked towards them and never flung back a word. Soon her sail disappeared in the distance as they steered their course for another world. Yes, for, at the time that this curragh was racing to sea on top of the foaming waves, she had already been lost on South Island strand and her crew drowned.

*   *   *

We were now doing some of the group scenes of men and women looking out to sea. In one of these scenes I had a little man. It was more because he needed a few shillings than for any other reason that I had taken him. He had a very dim knowledge of English.

Mr. Flaherty, being busy with Mikeleen and Maggie, shouted to David: "You shoot these men while I carry on here."

David tried to shoot the group, but at the first click of the camera the little Firbolg man started, glanced fearfully at the camera, and then jumped quickly behind one of the bigger men from behind whose back he peered, with a frightened look on his dark bearded face. I put him into place again. He stood the clicking a little longer, but suddenly, with a yelp of fright, he leaped behind the man again, saying in Irish:

"It won't shoot me if I can help it."

I think the little Firbolg showed a fair share of courage in standing before the camera at all when he thought that it was going to shoot him. Anyhow, after some little training these groups did their work much better.

The weather had broken, and the day before Christmas was very stormy. The seas had risen rapidly, and long before dawn we heard their thunder as they smashed against the cliffs or broke on the outer reefs. One could almost feel the Island tremble, so great was their force.

I drew on my clothes, and hurried down to Kilmurvy shore, and in the dim light of dawn I looked out over the sea. It was running mountains high. Great waves smashed down and rushed madly over all the reefs, streaming behind them long, creamy-white, flying manes. On the great reef about a mile out from Kilmurvy, the breakers followed one another, line after line, furious and menacing. It was a wild, thrilling spectacle. Mr. Flaherty has often said that nowhere else in the world has he seen such marvellous seas and seascapes.

On such days as this there is a stirring of the blood, totally unlike the feeling that comes over a man when looking at a lovely summer dawn. On a beautiful summer morning one feels like singing within one's self—a hymn to beauty and to the unknown cause of all this glory, but on a real stormy day in the winter time, with the never-ceasing thunder of the seas filling the air day and night, one feels like revelling in the strength of nature by chanting unknown words and singing wild barbaric songs; and this day before Christmas was one of these days.

I hurried to the house to see Mr. Flaherty. He was already moving restlessly about, pacing up and down and looking out at the stormy sea. We talked the situation over and agreed that after a hasty breakfast we would have the sidecars take us to Bungowla. Some time before this, when preparing for the day, I had spoken to Big Patcheen and had told him to have his crew picked out and to have them always ready. He had picked them: Steve Dirrane for the middle and Patch McDonough for the stern of the curragh. The men of the Conneely and McDonough families have always been noted for their skill and daring in curragh work.

Big Patcheen is, as was his father before him, a light-house tender, and before them, I believe, the McDonoughs were doing the same work. Patcheen's brother with his crew were drowned one bad day while trying to land at Bungowla at high tide. "He was a better man than me," Big Patcheen has always said whenever people talked about that day of sorrow. Many times he has told me that he himself would never be drowned, and on asking him how he had come to that conclusion, his answer was that, once the best man was taken away by them (meaning the Good people), he himself was safe, because some member of the family must be left to carry on and keep things going—and he is the last of his line.

Tales are still told of Big Patcheen's father, who was a giant in strength. One of how he alone in his canoe beat three men in a curragh race from Rock Island to Bungowla shore. He had to run the breakers at Brannagh Island point to do it, but he won. Another tale of how, when out seeking for wreckage after a storm, there was a race between curraghs for a barrel of oil. His curragh was first, and after tying a rope around the barrel, he with his crew rowed towards Bungowla with the barrel in tow. The flood tide set in and they were being dragged to the south-east and in under the high cliffs where men and curragh would soon be dashed to pieces. On the south side is a little cove where at dead low water curraghs can land if the breakers outside can be run. With the barrel in tow, Patcheen's father had headed for the breakers, and brought up the curragh's bows to the wind. He picked up his line and measured it carefully fathom after fathom. This done he also measured the passage with his eye, and coiling the line in the stern of the canoe, with one end fastened to the barrel and the other tied to the thwart, he watched his chance. When it came he yelled to his men to row, and row they did. The line ran swiftly out, the breakers rose on the reef and rushed roaring towards him and passed by his stern. He had just enough line to let him row clear. Then with the two men rowing against the backward pull of the line, he slowly hauled the barrel through the breakers. Such a man was Patcheen's father, and with him Patcheen had been going to sea on and off since he was ten years of age.

Years ago there had been great rivalry between the Conneely and the McDonough families as to which should qualify for the Rock Island Lighthouse contract. One day, after some stormy weeks of winter weather, a flag was hoisted on Rock Island showing that a curragh was wanted out.

The Macs got ready to put to sea, as did the Conneelys. By all accounts it was a very stormy day. In Conneely's house a sheep had been killed and, when leaving, Patcheen's father seems to have been struck with a bright idea; he picked up a quarter of mutton, tucked it under his bauneen and made for the shore.

The two curraghs put out, and though they rode the seas for hours near Rock Island they found it impossible to make a landing there. Finally Conneely's curragh took a chance and came closer in, and as she topped a great wave Conneely flung the quarter of mutton on to the rocks, where it was picked up by the lightkeeper. This landing of the mutton gave the Conneelys the contract, and they have had it ever since.

Anyway, this Patch McDonough that Big Patcheen picked as his next best man is a man every inch of him, and he has always had the reputation of being a very daring curraghman. Steve Dirrane, the middle man, Patcheen himself had trained, so that Steve knew Patcheen's every move and thought when they were together in a curragh.

We started out. Mr. Flaherty, Mrs. Flaherty, Mikeleen and myself on one sidecar; John Taylor, Tiger King, Maggie and David on the other. Our car was first with Donohue driving. Pat Hernon drove the second car. Each party had a camera. We arrived at Bungowla after Donohue's horse had given us an exhibition of fast stepping, helped by Donohue's whip. Big Patcheen was there to meet us, so was McDonough and Dirrane, and what a sea!

Brannagh Island Sound was all breakers, and outside Brannagh Island point the great waves broke on seventy-five feet of water. Mr. Flaherty called me aside, saying:

"Pat, I don't think there is a chance in the world of getting a canoe out there, and it isn't fair to ask Big Patcheen and his men to try it. Plain suicide, that's what it would be."

"I will speak to Patcheen," said I.

"All right," said Mr. Flaherty. "Do as you think best; in the meantime I will set up my camera on this crag here and get some seascapes," and he set to work taking shots of the seas that were breaking and dashing up hundreds of feet into the air on the far side of Brannagh Island.

This island, one of two small ones, is to the west of Aran Island. The other is Rock Island, on which the lighthouse is built. The sound between Bungowla shore and Brannagh Island is about a half to three-quarters of a mile in width, and during great storms the seas roar through this channel with terrific force.

I called Patcheen aside and said: "Well, what do you think of it?"

"Pat," said Patcheen, "you know well enough that no curragh was ever laid on sea on such a day as this."

"I know that," said I, "but we have tried everywhere and failed, excepting the work we did in Manister, and we haven't enough of that to be of any use. Do you mean to tell me," I added, "that it can be said all over the world that Mr. Flaherty came to Aran to make a picture of us at our best and that he couldn't get men to go out in a curragh in a storm? I always told you that your time would come. It is here now, and I know you won't fail us. Surely it isn't going to be said that the Conneelys and the McDonoughs are no better men that the rest!"

I saw his eyes flash as he drew a couple of deep breaths and looked out at the breakers and the passage. Then he said in a loud voice that rang with fierce recklessness:

"My soul from the devil, we will try it. But we've got to move fast. The tide is flowing and when those rocks that partly break the strength of the sea are covered, if we are out there we will be lost in the landing. An hour and a quarter at most is all we can give you; after that, if we are still afloat, and with the help of God we shall be, we must row for the shore."

"I will give you the signal with the flag," I said. "You will be able to see me easily. I will be standing on that high boulder near where the curraghs land. I shall wave the flag when we are ready, so now in the name of God get your men, bring down your oars, and I will get some of those others who have gathered round to put down your curragh and get the net aboard her."

This scene was to be the landing of a canoe caught in a

storm after a fishing trip, so we intended putting a mackerel net aboard her. The Tiger was quite willing to go out this day, but it was impossible to let him go as it wasn't his shore, and moreover he had never rowed with these men before, so Patch McDonough had to double for him.

I turned for a last word with Patcheen, and said: "Try and manage to run to lee on to the deep spot that you tell me is in the middle of the sound. Wait there if you can till I give the signal, then face her in and make the best of it."

He gripped my hand, and looking earnestly into my eyes, he said:

"I'm depending on you. I will do my best to get something good for Mr. Flaherty, he is worthy of it; but don't you keep us waiting outside too long. We can hold the curragh's bows to the storm all right when we get on the deep, but any delay beyond what I have said and we shall be lost in the landing," and with that he hurried down to the curragh, grim but supple as a deer.

I shouted to Mr. Flaherty:

"We'd better hurry down to the sea. The curragh is going out and we have no time to spare. An hour and a quarter at most!"

"The curragh going out?" said he. "Why! Great Scott! It is impossible."

We hurried to the shore where after quickly picking out a spot that suited him, he set up his camera.

"Get John Taylor to hurry down," he shouted. "This work is going to be too important to trust it all to one camera. We will set both of them up; then if one gets blocked or runs out of film the other can carry on."

193

I looked up the beach for John Taylor; he was nowhere in sight. In the meantime Big Patcheen had put to sea; waist-deep in the water the men had held the curragh while the crew took their seats and placed their oars. The men holding the curragh retreated before the biggest seas, then pushed her well out again as each wave receded, and then at a yell from Patcheen let her go. Out she went and headed for the Sound. These men were such splendid oarsmen that it thrilled my heart to see them face bravely out with sweeping, powerful strokes into those awful seas. The tide being low gave them some advantage, and after much manœuvring and driving through heavy seas they gained deep water in the north side of the Sound; and there holding the curragh's bows to the sea, they waited and watched for the flag.

But still there was no sign of Pat Hernon's car. He should have been here long before this, even though he was usually in no hurry going anywhere. We learned later that one of the traces had parted, and he had to go into a neighbour's house for a rope to replace it. He also said that he had been in no great hurry, believing that no canoe could possibly put out that day.

Mr. Flaherty was wild because the other camera had not yet come, and he shouted: "Pat, we'd better try it with one camera. We can't leave those men out there any longer."

He was right. The tide was rising rapidly and the landing was becoming more dangerous every minute. Yet, in spite of this I waited a little while longer, for, after a year of trying, here at last was a real storm scene. It was dreadful to think that our only camera might get blocked or run out of film at a critical moment. So I hoisted no flag, though I knew that Big Patcheen was watching anxiously for it. At last Pat Hernon hove in sight driving down the hill towards the shore in an easy "God save all here" kind of a way.

I was furiously angry and rushed up to the top of the shore and with a stream of curses through the megaphone I nearly blew them all off the sidecar. My voice was heard in Bungowla village, which stands about half a mile from the shore!

John Taylor set up his camera, and Mr. Flaherty shouting "All ready, Pat!" I jumped on the high boulder and waved the flag.

Big Patcheen did not immediately run for the passage. He seemed to be biding his time. Several times, we on shore thought the time had come for him to make a run for it. We were mistaken. For after the short lull great mountainous waves came roaring around Brannagh Island point and through the Sound, in towering half-mile-long breakers. Patcheen let these frightful seas pass, and saved his curragh by rowing partly around an angle of rock that jutted out from Brannagh Island. With the tide higher there would have been no shelter here, but Patcheen knew the depth of water on every yard of Brannagh Island Sound, as he knew every bit of shelter that each hour of flood or ebb tide made safe or dangerous. So he waited, and now he began to head nearer and nearer to the passage. Then they began to stretch at their oars.

"They are running for it!" I shouted to Mr. Flaherty and John Taylor. And what a spectacle! Sometimes the canoe was completely out of sight in the waves; now only the heads of the men could be seen, as if they were swimming in the swirling foam. Then, as they rose higher, we could see that they were rowing manfully. It was obviously very difficult to make headway, for there was a strong undercurrent running against them. The curragh turned halfway about, as if the men dared come no further.

Patcheen has brought her head to a cross sea; she is around again and running for the shelter of the now almost submerged boulders that protect the landing till the tide gets too high. Down by Brannagh Point the great breakers come raging—awful to look at in their wild grandeur, as they crash hundreds of feet into the air against the far side of the little Island. They come tumbling in through the Sound, breaking from a height of fully forty or fifty feet. These great seas are not in the film. Mr. Flaherty thought that an audience. looking at this scene on the screen could never take in the fact that it was a real happening, it was so unbelievable. Yet it is true, and the canoe was there amongst those mighty waves.

But the canoe has reached the shelter of the boulders. Here they're fairly safe for about ten minutes more. They watched the seas breaking on the shore as they watched the breakers outside, and after some anxious moments in choosing the right time to make a landing, they headed for the shore. When coming closer, we noticed that they appeared a bit excited. Later we knew that the curragh's bottom had touched a flat boulder and the canvas was torn and she was making some water. And now they made the run for the shore.

Maggie and Mikeleen were down to meet them, and after much difficulty, holding the curragh to prevent her being broken up, they all managed to get her clear of the waves. They then hauled out the net. Patcheen and his

crew hoisted the curragh on their shoulders and carried her up over the rocks to a place of safety, but while they were examining the curragh's bottom the flowing tide had covered the net and it was being washed out by the sea.

Mr. Flaherty shouted to me to get them to save the net, and I in turn shouted through the megaphone. Tiger was in this scene, Patch McDonough being dropped out. They rushed down with Tiger in the lead and made several attempts to get it, but they had to run back each time from the heavy seas. Parts of the net were caught on the sharp rocks, which prevented it from being swept out immediately. At last there seemed to be a chance.

"They can get it this time!" shouted Mr. Flaherty.

The biggest of the breakers appeared to have passed, yet far out I fancied I saw another coming with its great white mane tossing even on the deep. However, they were making the attempt, and in my heart I wished them well, I also hoped that Mr. Flaherty would get something good for the film.

They rushed down to grab the net, but the great sea came roaring in and swept over them. Mikeleen, fortunately for him, was driven up a hundred feet and cast into a deep pool that was creamy-white with foam. I glanced in his direction. His head appeared through the foam. His cap was gone, and he looked like a seal as he thrashed around to get a footing, but he was left to get out of it by himself—either that or stay in! He had disappeared out of the picture for the time being, and all eyes were fixed on where the great danger lay.

Big Patcheen and Steve were also thrown up by the sea, but Tiger being farther down was overwhelmed at once by the huge wave; but he held on to the net, and it was a good thing for him that he had. Maggie had been thrown backwards and was sucked out of sight. We saw that the undertow had dragged her to the west a bit when the sea went out. I ran three steps to go to her assistance, then I stopped. There was just a chance that everything would be all right, and I knew that such work could not be done again, so I was torn both ways. About two feet to the west of Maggie there was a slope to the rock. It was smooth, slippery and covered with green moss. Had the sea taken her those two feet farther west she would have been swept out and would have been either smashed to pieces by the breakers or sucked down and out by the undertow. She tried to sit up, but she seemed to be quite helpless. Her heavy flannel clothes weighed her down; she was dazed; the next breaker was coming.

Tiger pulled himself together. He too would surely have been dragged out had he not held on to the net which was still entangled in the sharp rocks. He looked around as he got to his feet and saw Maggie sitting up but unable to get to her feet. He also saw the breaker coming. Two or three quick steps and he grabbed her by the hair.

Big Patcheen had recovered himself and was now running down to help. Between them they managed to get her on to her feet. Steve was also running down, though his hands were badly cut, and all three helped her out of danger. She was practically knocked out, but through her clearing brain ran the thought of what ought to be done. She pulled herself away from the men and ordered them down to save the net. They at once rushed down and this time managed to save it.

This day's work was over and a lucky day it was for us,

because after all, in spite of the risk that had been taken, except for Steve's hands and Mikeleen and Maggie suffering a little from shock, no harm had come to us. All through the struggle in trying to save the net, Mr. Flaherty had kept shouting:

"Pat, is there danger?" And I had answered back: "No matter. Keep on working."

There was no need for me to say that, of course, because his work always comes first with him. I do believe that if an earthquake tore up the world and sent it tumbling about his head the first words to pass his lips would be:

"What a marvellous sight! Gosh! I wish I had a camera."

That night he sent for me, and looking at me rather sharply, said:

"Pat, that was an unlooked-for accident, wasn't it? Fortunately nobody was badly injured, but anything might have happened."

"Yes," I answered, "we have been very lucky."

He gave me another sharp look, but asked no more questions, which made me think that he was wondering if I knew what was in his mind, as much as I was wondering if he knew what was on mine.

The work of that day was developed as quickly as John Taylor could do it and was shown on the screen. The work speaks for itself—it is magnificent and full of thrills, as it certainly should be.

★   ★   ★

On Christmas Day I drove around delivering Mr. Flaherty's Santa Claus presents. At night there was a dance in the Irish Cottage, where everybody was welcome.

A Christmas tree stood in a corner, lit up with electric lights. From it hung packages of candy. A swarm of children were grouped around when David Flaherty, dressed up as Santa Claus, came in and began to share out the candy amongst them.

We all had a happy Christmas-night. My father was there feeling mellow, and he insisted on dancing his favourite reel, the Bucks of Oranmore, and he cursed his lame leg when it bothered him. Big Patcheen and McDonough also danced, and Patcheen sang his Irish songs till the rafters rang again.

January 1933 came in, and we were still working, straightening out the final touches in the land sequence.

One day, while on a height overlooking Bungowla shore, Mr. Flaherty in looking through the camera fancied a place about two hundred yards in from the edge of the cliff. He took some tests of it, and after looking at them on the screen, he decided to make a garden there.

"Who owns that stretch of crags, Pat?" he asked.

"It is the last place in Aran that I would want you to pick out," I answered, "but as usual that camera of yours has the faculty of picking out the most contrary places. The man who owns that crag is a poteen man—hardly ever sober when he can lay his hands on it. We cannot put one of our own men working there unless we give *him* charge of everything. Besides, he is hard to deal with."

"No matter," said Mr. Flaherty. "Do the best you can with him, and get the spot sodded over quickly."

So I went to Tim Faherty's house, and after a talk about the weather and the health of the children and family in general, I asked him what wages he would want a day for sodding a part of the crag. We went to look at it and I showed him the spot that we wanted sodded over. He could dig the clay from clefts here and there on his adjoining crag. We arranged the terms and then he said that I must give him a man to help him. I agreed, and he mentioned a neighbour of his own as being the very man to help him hurry up the work.

"We will be here in the morning early, and we will also have a donkey to haul the clay, and of course I will be expecting a man's wages for the donkey too," were the parting words he flung after me as I left him.

We agreed that it would take five days to put soil on the little stretch of rock. As a matter of fact, it was just forty feet wide and about fifty feet in length.

Next day we went to see how they were getting on with the work. As we came near the crag we heard a chatter of voices. I hurried ahead of the rest of the party and, as I reached out to look over the stone wall, I put my arm against it and three or four stones clattered down, making a loud noise. Faherty and his neighbour were arguing as to which was the best in a heavy sea—a three-man or a four-man canoe. They were sitting down comfortably smoking their pipes, but when the stones clattered down the talking ceased, and when Mr. and Mrs. Flaherty looked over the wall the two men were working furiously. Mr. Flaherty was very pleased at the energy they showed in digging!

We stayed awhile, and Mrs. Flaherty said: "They seem to be getting on all right, but I do wish that man would not abuse the poor donkey."

This remark was caused by the neighbour having given the donkey a few smart blows with a sea-rod in his efforts to hurry the work.

"I will tell him about it," said I, and I did.

"God help her foolish head," said he, "if the lady only knew that this divil of an ass is falling off his feet with laziness, she would think different, but I know that you won't be the one to tell her," and he added: "I'm afraid that we won't ever be able to get this spot sodded over. Tim won't do a hand's turn for me or for anybody."

We then left them, still working. As we came along towards Kilmurvy we met Big Patcheen, and after we had had a few words together he turned to me and asked in Irish how Tim Faherty was getting on. I told him. He laughed and said:

"They will be lucky if they are half as good to-morrow. Tim is getting some kegs of whisky run in from Conne-mara to-night, so try and prevent Mr. Flaherty from going to that crag to-morrow."

Next morning Mr. Flaherty sent for me and asked me how far I thought the work on the crag had gone ahead and if it would be worth while getting the camera there to take what had been done. I said it wouldn't be worth while, and in any case I expected most of the day to be cloudy (as fortunately it was).

"Well," said he, "send a man over there to see how they are getting on. You stay here in case the sun comes out and then we can start on something else."

"I think I'd better go myself," says I, "because whatever hurry can be put into them there is no man can do it as well as myself. I will hurry," I added, "and be back before the sky clears." After all, there are *some* errands on which a messenger should *not* be sent, and I had an idea that this was one of them!

By taking a short cut across the crags, I arrived after an

hour's walk near to the crag where our men worked. I heard no sound as I approached the wall, and glancing over it I saw that it was empty of life with the exception of the donkey who, all straddled with baskets and ready for work, was grazing peacefully amongst the stones. I jumped over the wall and continued to look around for the men. Two spades were standing against a boulder, but there was no sign of life.

I went to the next wall and climbed on to the top of it. I looked all around, listening. I fancied I heard a voice on the breeze. Yes, it was somebody singing. Making my way towards the sound, I got quite close and looked through a hole in the wall, and there I saw them. In a grassy hollow, sheltered from the wind, were my two workmen, sitting down with a five-gallon keg of poteen whisky between them. Faherty had hold of his neighbour's hand and with tears in his eyes and voice was singing, "The Pretty Maid Milking her Cow".

I climbed over the wall, giving them the usual Aran Island salutation of "God Bless you".

"The same to you, and Cead Mile Failte,"[1] they both answered, adding in the same breath: "Sit down, sit down and make yourself comfortable, and have a drop of this."

The neighbour picked up a very rusty quart can half full of poteen, and offered me a drink. I drank a glass or two of this stuff that is supposed to be able to cure every known sickness. In reality, when taken to excess it steals away one's brain and turns a man into a beast. All drink does this, of course, but not to such an extent as poteen does.

Faherty then began to tell me of how lucky Mr.

[1] "A hundred thousand welcomes".

Flaherty was to find this particular place on his land, after all the time he had spent looking for it.

"He will make thousands of pounds out of it, and by right I should get a couple of hundred pounds for letting him into my crag," he said.

"I think we ought to try and do a little bit of work for Pat to-day or to-morrow," suggested the neighbour.

"Shut your mouth!" said Faherty. "Sure, you wouldn't have a job at all if it hadn't been for me. That's the thanks I get Pat. Me that's awake all night measuring whisky." And turning to the neighbour he added: "You were never as good a man as me, anyway."

An argument began which ended by their challenging each other, at my suggestion, as to which was best at the running hop, step and jump. No man could tell of course who was best, because as they reeled around they never jumped the same way twice. I left them there, after they had promised, with much gravity of countenance, that they would be at work next day. Their parting words were:

"Don't be afraid, Pat. We won't be long finishing the work once we make a start on it again, and be sure and tell Mr. Flaherty that we are doing well."

They sat down again, and as I headed over the crags for Kilmurvy another song floated after me on the wind.

That evening Mr. Flaherty sent for me and asked me how the work on the crag was going ahead.

"Not so bad," I answered. "They were singing as they worked, and that isn't a bad sign."

"Good, good!" said he, rubbing his hands together delightedly. "There is nothing like having men full of good spirits when they work."

"That's true!" I agreed, but as I was leaving the room Mrs. Flaherty asked:

"Pat, I hope that in their hurry to push the work ahead they are not abusing the donkey?"

"No, ma'am," I answered. "I'm sure they haven't touched the donkey with hand, foot, or sea-rod since you last saw him, and" I added "the donkey seemed to me to be quite contented and happy."

She smiled a heavenly smile as she said: "Well, Pat, this is one time that my doubts have been without foundation."

I never told Mr. Flaherty the truth about this incident, he having worry enough on his shoulders without adding any more to it. I took some men off another job, and after explaining to Faherty that his agreement with me still held good, I put them to work with him and got it finished quickly.

About this time some discussion arose between Mr. and Mrs. Flaherty and some friends who were visiting the island for a week or two, as to whether the arched fireplace was the real old kind of fireplace that had been used for centuries, or whether the small fireplace with just a lintel across it and no chimney corners was the older one of the two. Mr. Flaherty had already taken inside scenes of the cottage which we had built with the big arched chimney place.

"The old arch", says I, "is the right one, no matter what anybody tells you, and to-morrow when we pass through Creggeheran village I will prove it to you—that is if a house that has been standing for a couple of hundred years is old enough for you."

"Yes, of course it would be old enough," they said.

Next day we were passing through the village and, the driver stopping his old sidecar, I pointed out to Mr. Flaherty a roofless house built in a little hollow. On its gables tufts of grass and weeds were growing, and when we went inside we saw that the grass had found a foothold even there. The wind moaned dismally through the chimney and the few windowless spaces. It was a picture of desolation and decay, but a most beautiful arch still held over the fireplace, and on a stone in the wall above it was cut the day and year in which it was built.

I pointed it out to Mr. Flaherty.

"Yes, Pat," he said. "You are right. There can be no more doubt in the matter, but" he added "what happened to the families that through many generations must have lived here, and, judging by the exquisite finish of this arch, must at one time have been fairly prosperous, as prosperity is judged in these Islands?"

"Hard times came to them," I answered, "about the year 1867, when we had another famine in Ireland, or at least if not quite a famine the times were terribly bad—they couldn't pay their rent and they were evicted."

I went on to tell him about the horror of landlordism amongst the Irish people. It is one of the saddest chapters in our history, and so often written about that I won't say much about it, except in so far as it concerns my own Island and what I told Mr. Flaherty.

"The woman of this house was only three days confined of a child when the sheriff and bailiffs came, backed by a score or two of policemen. The day happened to be pouring with rain," I went on. "They gathered around the house and the bailiffs carried the bed with the mother and child in it, out into the rain, and left them there by the side of the road. Then they threw out the few stools, pots and so on, broke in the little windows, tore a big hole in the roof, locked the doors and departed. The people of the village had hung around, giving vent to deep sullen curses, but not daring to touch the woman or child till these so-called men who worked in the name of the law had departed. When they were gone, the people took the poor woman into a neighbour's house, to stay until another cottage could be found for her and her family. This family finally went away to America."

Mr. Flaherty listened to this terrible story.

"Who told you this, Pat?" he asked.

"My uncle," I answered.

"My God!" said Mr. Flaherty, "to think such a state of affairs could ever have existed here—evicting poor people from their little homes and from their smallholdings of land that they built and made themselves, wearing out their flesh and blood to do it. It is simply horrible to think of it." Then he asked: "Didn't the people ever try to stand up against this tyranny, or were they so beaten down through poverty that they hadn't the guts to do it?"

"Yes, there was a time," said I, "when they did stand up, and it remains like a bit of a dream in my memory; but I have often heard my father and mother talking about it. The happening came about when I was very young.

"For many years there had been some stormy scenes between the sheriff, his hirelings and the people of the Island, with the result that a couple of years passed and no sheriff could be found who would dare to venture across the Bay to Aran in order to evict people. After a time however, one spoke out and said that if he were given

bailiffs and one hundred and fifty police, he would collect
rent and pull off evictions in hell—not to talk at all of
Aran. Parnell and Davitt had put a stir in the blood of the
people all over Ireland, and whisperings of it had come to
the Islands. Anyhow, one fine day a boat sailed into
Killeany Bay and the tide being out, she dropped anchor,
and swung round to the breeze. Boats were lowered, and
the sheriff and bailiffs, or roggies as we used to call them,
with the hundred and fifty police, prepared to land. The
police came first. They formed into marching order on
the pier. The sheriff and his crew came last, and they
marched in front of the police up to the barracks which
were just across the narrow road from our house. News of
their arrival had spread quickly far and near, and the
people—men and women—were gathering.

"Now my mother was a very peaceable, though in her
day, a very powerful woman; in her young days she had
been a great horsewoman. Her brothers and father had
spent a lot of their time boating, running loads of seaweed to the mainland, and so on, so that she was most of
the time working out of doors. She often spent days hauling home the potato crop in the autumn, and was easily
able to lift a ten stone basket of potatoes on to the horse's
back, and then lift it off and walk up a plank with it when
the outhouse used to be full. A great woman to look after
a horse she was, surely. When we grew up we worked
our horse oftentimes night and day, but at whatever hour
we came home, my mother always had a mess of something waiting for it—usually half-boiled potatoes mixed
with Indian meal.

"However, as I say, she was a very peaceable and quiet
woman. She had taken our going to America tearfully, of

course, but very quietly, without any great fuss. But this day, as she stood in the doorway of her home, thoughts of what was going to happen to the two poor families in Killeany village must have come to her, and just as the police were about to march away, she stepped out and, stooping down, picked up a large stone and flung it at them with all her strength and with her curse behind it.

"It passed between two of them and broke into splinters on the barrack wall. They looked back, but it seems they had their orders, for instead of making any hostile move they swung around and marched towards Killeany. The women and men who had gathered took a short cut and joined the men and women of Killeany long before the sheriff and police had reached the foot of the big hill near Ball Alley.

"The sheriff, bailiffs and police marched up the hill, and when about halfway they were met by a volley of stones. The police drew out their batons and charged, but they were driven back down the hill in disorder. Again and again they charged, beating down everybody who came within reach of their batons. At last, the women, whether it was that they had more to lose or for some other reason, suddenly became like furies. They pushed out in front of the men, and with streaming hair and wild shrieking cries of challenge and defiance, flung stones and charged down on the policemen coming up the hill. The sheriff was knocked unconscious by a blow on the temple. The police picked him up. They staggered, then halted, but finally turned and made a rush for the shore. But the women with terrible cries were trying to get to the sheriff to tear him to pieces.

"The boats had gone back to the ship, and now police

whistles were blowing. The boats put off, and as they neared the shore the invaders of our Island rushed out into the sea, carrying their wounded with them, to get as far away as possible from the furies that still followed them with stones and wild screaming.

"It was many a long year after that happening before any sheriff came to Aran again.

"We still pay rent and rates, but Middle Island men only pay rent; they are right of course not to pay rates on an island where one has to risk one's life oftentimes in a curragh when going on board the steamer in order to make a trip to Galway; also the roads, such as they are, are not under contract. People should be paid to live on such an island, especially when it is one of the last places where the old language of the Gael is still spoken in all its purity. Our parish priest last year tried to help us by trying to get the rent and rates cut to a smaller figure. He didn't have much success. Conditions on the mainland are somewhat unsettled, and we will have to do some more waiting before we get a hearing."

CHAPTER IX

Captain Murray—"Its monstrous snout"—White-spotted Rosie—Exciting Days—"Brooding, wet and lonely"—Casabianca—A sucker Parasite

★

February came in and we began again to talk about the basking shark. The weather took a change for the better towards the end of the month. The days were getting warmer, and soon we hoped to see the great black fins cutting the water again.

Mr. Flaherty had been in touch with an old-time whaling man, Captain Murray by name. They had met in the Northland when Mr. Flaherty was making a film called *Nanook*. Murray was then master of a ship working for the Hudson Bay Company. They became great friends, and Mr. Flaherty had told us that if it were at all possible he would get Captain Murray to come over from Scotland, where his home is, in order to show us all he knew about harpooning. Word came from Murray that he was on his way to Aran, and soon after he arrived. He is a man getting well on in years—about sixty—of wonderfully powerful build, having a great, barrel-like chest, but a bit lame in one leg, his thigh having been smashed by a heavy sea years before while working his ship in a storm. He is a man we all liked.

He brought with him a harpoon gun, and also some whale and walrus harpoons. The Tiger took possession of the gun, polished and cleaned it thoroughly, the same as he had done with the gun Mr. Flaherty had brought back from 'Boffin of the wild memories. The Tiger had spent some time in the Free State Army, and he has a passion for guns. It was there he got the name "Tiger", because of his wild desire to charge the foe, it being impossible to keep him in an ambush.

March had come in with a breezy smiling face, and sentinels were now posted on the high cliffs watching out for sharks. In the meantime, Captain Murray had given us great help by showing us how to work our boat when harpooning—somewhat, but not altogether, similarly to the way he had worked his whale boats when hunting the whale. We had been doing some thinking ourselves, and we had learned a bit from the previous season, but it took Captain Murray to show us where we should have a snubbing post put in and how to use it. Near the stern of our boat, against a cross beam, an oaken post was nailed and braced. Our line of one hundred fathoms ran from the harpoon back around the post and from there to the centre of the boat, where the main part of it was neatly and very carefully coiled. We also had another hundred fathom coil ready to be attached to the second harpoon. When the shark was struck we could all lay hold of the line from bow to stern of our boat, it being the best way to use our strength in order to get the most good out of it.

Tiger was look-out man and harpooner, my part of the work at the snubbing post being to hold or slack away the line as the occasion called for, also to prevent the rope from getting snagged, and to be ready to take a half-hitch on or off, as the shark slowed down or sped on.

One day a sentinel came running in from Bungowla with the news that he had seen a shark swimming down Brannagh Island Sound. We hurried to Bungowla on the sidecars to have our first look of the season at this monster fish, but evening had fallen and it had disappeared. Next day it was not to be seen, nor did we hear any news of it again for a week.

Mr. Flaherty had sent word to Galway engaging *The Successful* for the coming hunting season. Word arrived back that she would make all speed for Kilmurvy Bay when some engine trouble had been repaired. In case the sharks began to swarm in before *The Successful* arrived, Mr. Flaherty again engaged Fitz's boat for a few days. Captain Murray mounted his gun in the bow and got his harpoons ready and his cables coiled on board. One of the reasons why Mr. Flaherty had sent for the captain was that in case we failed to harpoon the sharks from our boat he could get them with the gun.

A shark was sighted south-east from Dun Aengus, so we sailed out from Kilmurvy and headed north-west, then we sailed through Brannagh Sound. Captain Murray and Mr. Flaherty in Fitz's boat, and we in our pookawn but towed by the bigger boat. When we cleared the Sound, we headed south-east in the direction where the shark had been sighted. After about half an hour's sailing we saw two big black fins. Mr. Flaherty shouted to us that the Captain would try his hand at the gun, so in order to give Fitz's boat a chance to manœuvre we cast off from her and rowed a little distance away.

The day was not at all fine; a fairly heavy sea was rolling in from the Atlantic. Captain Murray got ready the gun; his boat came up close to the fish and then he took aim and fired. With a terrific slash of its tail the shark sent the water flying all over the boat and men, then it plunged down; fifty fathoms of line ran out, but the line suddenly stopped, so they hauled it in. The harpoon was twisted but there was no trace of the shark. The harpoon, very likely, didn't have a strong hold and the fish had broken away. Murray got ready another harpoon and they headed for the other shark.

In the meantime, we in the pookawn had made up our minds that if he missed we would make a try for it with the hand harpoon. After some manœuvring, the captain's boat came close enough for a shot. He fired and the harpoon struck under but quite close to the fin. These were heavy whale harpoons, for a hand harpoon would have bent if an attempt had been made to drive it in so high on the fish's back. After thrashing the water for a few seconds, the shark sounded. And after half an hour's rolling around on the bottom, it headed slowly westward out into the ocean, towing the boat. It had taken out a hundred fathoms of line.

The boat was rolling heavily, and soon a drizzle of rain came on. The wind began to strengthen and there seemed to be no chance of any more sunshine for the rest of the day. Mr. Flaherty and the captain made up their minds to try and get the shark alongside by shooting another harpoon into it and thereby killing it quickly—then to tow it to Kilmurvy before dark, lash it to the pier, and next day, if the sun shone, to do something with it in the way of shots for the film.

The capstan was manned, a turn of the line was taken

round it, and after much effort the fish was dragged towards the boat; or to be exact the boat was worked up to a position over the shark. Slowly the rope came in, the monster allowing itself to be hauled towards the surface. Then its tail appeared. Next came the fin; the sea was being churned into foam. Just as the captain was sighting his gun for another shot, the boat rose on a heavy sea, and the shark, as if excited at the sudden extra pulling on the line, dived down, its tail hitting the bow of the boat a terrific blow. The strong Manilla rope parted as if it were a thread, and the shark was gone, taking the harpoon with it. So we turned about and sailed for home. We were not discouraged because it was only the beginning of the hunting season.

Next day we went to sea again and sighted two sharks midway in the North Sound between Rock Island and Golem Head. Mr. Flaherty made up his mind that the first shot this time should again go to Captain Murray. So when the boat sailed up close, the captain sighted his gun on one of the sharks and fired.

The shot was a good one. The harpoon entered about two feet in front of the fin and a bit down on the side. Both sharks went down with a great splashing of water. Then, as if sensing its mate was in trouble, the other shark suddenly appeared about two hundred feet astern of our boat and came rushing through the water towards us at terrific speed. Its great tail churned the sea into foam and tossed it swirling into the air. With its horrible mouth wide open it came straight for us. Its monstrous snout was above the surface, and its evil eyes, as it came closer, glared at us savagely. For my own part, I got one of the few great starts of my life.

The first I ever had was one night in the long ago, before I had read *The Arabian Nights Entertainments*. My father was telling some neighbours and us children the story of Ali Baba and the Forty Thieves. When he had finished the story my mother sent me to bed. I had to go up through the little parlour, as we called it, in order to get to the bedroom. Both were in pitch darkness. I had no candle, and as I walked through the dark parlour I was thinking of Ali Baba; and as I neared the door of the room my mind pictured the Thieves waiting for me inside. I pushed the door open slowly and fearfully, and then I yelled out at the top of my voice "Ali Baba!" and ran shrieking down into the kitchen. I ran to my mother and buried my face in her apron. She became very much excited, and murmuring: "Oh, they cannot take you away from me, they cannot, I will not let them," she squeezed me tightly in her arms and put the sign of the cross three times on my forehead.

After a long time I quietened down, and when I got into bed I found they had put my eldest brother to sleep with me.

As I say, that was the first big startling moment of my life, and now this was another one.

Mr. Flaherty from Fitz's boat shouted to us to harpoon this awful shape, that now to my excited imagination seemed to have arisen from out of the dim past, when the world was overrun with many such gigantic forms of life—and now this monster was rushing to destroy us. We couldn't have harpooned it had we tried. It was coming dead astern of us, and our boat could not be brought about quickly enough. The shark was cutting through the water at such a rate that harpooning it was out of the question, and to tell the truth we were all so startled at the unexpectedness of this attack that we never gave a thought to the harpooning!

I grabbed my oar and held it high, having an idea that I might be able to drive it down the monster's throat and thereby gain a little time till the big boat could come to our assistance. I prepared to make the drive when it raised its snout a little higher. But when within four or five feet of the stern, with a final baleful look, it dived under. Patch Ruadh had begun to take in his steering oar, but as the shark was disappearing its tail came up with a mighty blow, and caught Patch's oar and smashed it to splinters. We all drew deep breaths of relief when this thrilling incident had passed. Somehow, after this we never gave a thought to the risk or to the danger, though I must say that I have never yet rowed up to one of those great sharks without feeling a thrill of excitement just before the harpooning.

Fitz's boat still held the other fish, and suddenly we saw it being swung around like a top. The shark had begun to rush about in circles. One could see by the action of the water that some terrific struggle was going on in the depths below. After about half an hour of this turning around, the shark changed its tactics, and as Fitz's boat swung one way, the fish rushed the other. The strain became too heavy and the harpoon was torn out. The shark was gone and we sailed back to Kilmurvy empty-handed.

Many times during the rest of the season something similar happened. Mr. Flaherty, tired of waiting for *The Successful* and realizing more than ever that Fitz's boat was most unsuitable for camera work, made a quick trip to Galway, and hired the *Johnny Summers*, a steam drifter and a fine, able boat. Both it and *The Successful* were owned by the same company.

Two days later, the *Summers*, with Mr. Flaherty on board, steamed into Kilmurvy Bay; and from her deck or rather from a platform erected on it, Mr. Flaherty has taken all the pictures of the basking shark for the film, and from our little pookawn we have done the harpooning. Many fish were harpooned from the *Summers* but most of them got away, as the boat was too heavy and didn't swing easily enough to the movements of the shark.

With our boat, small and light in comparison, it was different. She swung easily. The shark, when fighting, usually made a mad rush straight ahead, but by paying out a few fathoms of line gradually the boat was got gently in motion, so that the strain on line or harpoon was seldom too great. The sharks were now becoming more plentiful, the weather had settled, and in high spirits we steamed through the North Sound with the pookawn in tow. Sharks were swimming around in great numbers. This was the first time this season that we saw Rosie, a monster shark well over thirty feet in length with a white spot on its fin.

During the spring, on Sundays, we had taken excursions in Fitz's boat in order to find out if the sharks gathered in greater numbers in certain bays and inlets rather than others.

On these trips Mrs. Flaherty and her family came with us. One day we sighted a school of sharks off Hag's Head, near the Clare land. As we sailed amongst them, we noticed that one of the fish had a large white spot on its fin. We singled it out and sailed closer. This shark was the largest of the school. Great white spots were all over its dark grey body, looking like scars from healed wounds. It looked a regular old warrior of the deep.

As we sailed past, this fish turned and swam after us, and always keeping dead astern it followed the boat for the best part of a mile.

When on another trip, we sighted several sharks near Skerrick Rocks, and there amongst them was the spotted giant of the deep. This time it followed us just as before. We saw it again outside Kilmurvy Bay. After this, whenever we sailed towards a lone shark or a school of them, the girls were always on the look-out for the spotted monster.

One Sunday we were approaching a school some miles off Gregory's Sound when Barbara Flaherty sang out: "Oh, there's Rosie!" She had sighted the spotted shark.

It will pass my understanding forever why she should call this villainous looking, battle-scarred pirate of the deep by such a fancy name, but my surprise was great indeed when on this day she turned to me and said:

"Pat, you must never kill Rosie."

I spoke to the other men and we all agreed that we would never interfere with Rosie, and we never did.

This day on the *Summers* was the first time this year that we had seen it. I called Captain Murray aside and pointed out the shark with the white spot on its fin.

"A great big fellow, Pat, isn't he?" said the captain.

"You must never sight your gun on that shark," I told him. "Its name is Rosie, and it is a friend of the family," and I told him the story.

"Well, Pat," he said, "it is the first time in my life that I have ever heard of one of them ugly-looking monsters being a friend to anybody; however," he added with a smile, "there is no accounting for the notions young ladies take sometimes, and of course whatever else we harpoon we cannot touch a friend of the family!"

On this day Mr. Flaherty was ready with his camera as we sailed amongst them. Captain Murray had the gun loaded with a harpoon sticking out of its barrel, but Mr. Flaherty said that we in our boat should do the harpooning. So we hauled our boat alongside the *Summers*, jumped in and cast off. We singled out one of the biggest sharks and rowed across the circle it made in feeding, in order to come nearly bow on to it when passing. This we believed to be the safest and best way to attack the fish, and this course we always followed except in breezy weather, when the sharks became restless and swam in all directions with the fin just showing above the surface. At such times we often had to row after them for long distances before being able to come close enough for a throw. In hoarse voices we spoke as we rowed, and gradually closed the distance between ourselves and the shark. Closer still—its snout was past our bows. Then, as if seeing us, it began to sink slowly deeper in the water.

Tiger stood in the bow, harpoon held high, waiting, and now the great fin was within reach, but going ever deeper.

The Tiger struck, and with a furious lashing of its tail that drenched us with water, the shark went down. The line ran out so swiftly that it smoked on the post and burned my hands as I tried to let it run clear. The Tiger had his axe in hand and a Barber knife between his teeth ready to cut away all, if the line fouled. The shark reached the bottom, and the rope slackened or became taut, and

we had to haul in or give out line according to the movements of the fish. Unfortunately after about half an hour clouds began to gather. Mr. Flaherty said we had better haul in and try to get the shark to the surface while the sun shone. We hauled away, and as we heaved we every once in a while looked over the side watching for air bubbles and movements of the water, which would give us an idea of how near the shark had come to the surface, so that we could be ready to drive in another harpoon.

We had taken in a considerable length of line when suddenly the shark tore away sideways from us. I had taken a couple of turns on the post. Hauling in an eight ton shark whose strength is not spent is no child's play, and we were badly in need of a few minutes' rest, this being my reason for taking the couple of turns on the post. We were taken by surprise and, before I could get the hitches off, the boat had heeled over, almost gunwale under, and now the shark changed its course and was rushing past our stern.

The line slipped off the bollard in the bow, slid over and broke the thole pins along the boat's side, and now the boat was being towed astern at a furious rate. I had cleared the turns off the post to let the line run free, but now the shark went off at a slant downward, and whether our line was being dragged under a sunken ledge of rock or not I cannot say, but fathom after fathom of the line ran out. Still it went downward at a slanting angle. Tiger had flung his axe to me, and I picked it up and prepared to cut the line if the need arose.

"You have the end of the line," shouted the Tiger, "and the others get ready to cut away!"

The end had been tied to the thwart. Hoping against

hope that even now the line would stop running out, I waited a few seconds longer, but now our boat was being pulled under. I raised the axe and was about to sever the line, when it parted—harpoon, line and shark were gone. This was the line that had been used the year before when it had been entangled in the rocks outside Dun Aengus. We thought it was almost as good as new, though it was somewhat frayed.

We finished the day tired and somewhat discouraged. Mr. Flaherty worked his camera to the limit, but even so it was very hard to get much good work done. The *Summers* had to be bow or stern to the swell unless the day was flat calm, in order that good camera work could be done. Side on to the swell she rolled a bit, so that the camera often pointed to the sky instead of at the shark. On the other hand, the fish often swam in different directions, and many times it happened that when the *Summers* was in position, our boat was between it and the shark. In spite of everything, Mr. Flaherty was bit by bit getting material for his film.

Next day we steamed out about a mile and sighted a number of sharks swimming in a very small circle. There was a roll in the sea, but when we came close up to the sharks we manned our pookawn and rowed into the middle of the school. They numbered about a dozen. The *Summers* manœuvred into position, and all was ready, but the sharks took another turn, and we had an idea that they were going to scatter, so we rowed after them. The *Summers* swung around a bit as a huge shark swam across our bows. It was too good a chance to miss, and I shouted to the Tiger to strike home.

He drove his harpoon in with all his force, leaning far

out after the thrust. The shark thrashed the water, but instead of going down it sped along the surface; at the same moment, all the other sharks rushed on in the same direction as if startled. The sea for a hundred yards around us was a tossing smother of foam and spray, then they all went down.

It was a most thrilling sight, and I hoped Mr. Flaherty had taken it, but the *Summers* having no headway had fallen off from being bows on to the sea, and when she rolled it was only the action of the crew in grabbing hold of Mr. Flaherty that had prevented him and his camera from going off the platform over the side and into the water. After several hours fighting, we killed the shark, and the *Summers* towed it into Kilmurvy.

A few days later, Pat Gill, who owns a fishing boat, sent us word that when sailing through Costelloe Bay he had seen a great school of sharks. He had seen them leaping clear out of the water to a height of fifteen or twenty feet, and the sound of their vast bulk striking the sea as they fell back again could be heard far away.

We sailed for the bay next day, but unluckily the sharks had moved on, so we headed for South Island, and kept a sharp look-out. As we rounded the Island, sailing out of the South Sound, several of us on board suddenly saw a great dark body rise clear of the water about half a mile away, towards the cliffs of Moher. As it fell back again we could hear the sound of the crash as it struck the water, and the foam flew high in the air. However, it was too far away for us to be able to tell whether it was a basking shark of monstrous size, or a whale. But believing as we do that spring and early summer is the mating season of these fish, there is no reason whatever to doubt Pat Gill's story.

David Flaherty told us that on one of his trips back from Samoa, he had seen a whale leap up several yards clear of the water.

About a mile from Hag's Head, we sighted a black fin low down in the water and cutting through it swiftly. Mr. Flaherty suggested that I gave the Tiger a hand on the harpoon. He wanted a shot of two men doing the harpooning. We manned our boat and rowed towards the shark. As we came closer I prepared for the quick run to the bow to help the Tiger, and then to jump back again to my place at the snubbing post.

It headed directly for us, swimming fast, and before we could swing our boat into what we now knew to be the right position, it swam right down by our side with its horrible mouth wide open, gleaming whitely in the green water. Rows of small sharp teeth showed, and its wicked eyes seemed to be watching us, when with a final lifting of its snout over the water, for a last awe-inspiring look, it sank slowly down and disappeared from sight.

One of the *Summers* crew shouted, asking us why we had not harpooned it, and I shouted back: "Oh, go to blazes!"

The reason we had not tried was because a shark swimming along from bow to stern could not be harpooned directly from the bow. The harpooner would have to move back at least as far as the shoulder of the boat, and then wait till the big fin was directly opposite him before he struck with his harpoon. While striking, a man must often lean far out over the side of the boat in order to reach the vital spot. Then comes the terrific thrashing of the giant tail and the harpooner is directly in line with it, as is for that matter every man in the boat. Our boat was lying low in the water. The tail of one of these sharks measures from six to eight feet across and a downward blow from it would either smash our boat to pieces or, if coming with a fierce sweeping stroke from bow to stern, would crush us all to death.

I have read accounts here and there lately about these basking sharks, some of which say that they are harmless and inoffensive. This may be true, but I don't think that it mattered a great deal to us whether a shark meant it or not, when a sweep of his tail was able to smash our boat or knock us into Kingdom Come at a moment's notice! Boats ten tons bigger than ours had been lost with their crews that way in the old shark-hunting days.

On the other hand, rowing as we used to bow on, and a few feet ahead of the fin, the narrowest and strongest part of the boat was towards it, and as the great fish went ahead on its downward course the first furious blows from its tail struck the stem or strongest part of the boat; and when it came up over the bows the harpooner always had a chance to throw himself backward—and I believe now that it was due to this foresight on our part that we are all alive to tell the tale.

The shark soon appeared again some distance ahead, and we rowed hard to head it off. As it was crossing our bows, I unshipped my oar quickly and jumped to the Tiger's assistance. When passing Tommy O'Rourke I grabbed his cap and hair with my right hand and yanked it behind me, so that I could put on additional speed. Tommy's remark was unprintable! Tiger raised his harpoon, and as he thrust I threw my weight on the haft to drive it home.

With a furious thrashing of its tail the shark went down,

and in that first plunge it very nearly took our boat under head first, a part of the line having fouled under a thwart.

Tiger raised his axe, but the line had been cleared and the boat righted herself. This shark towed us about six miles, and we were continually hauling in or paying out line, as the rushing or the slowing up of the fish demanded.

At nightfall we got it alongside, drove in another harpoon, and after another hour's fighting we towed it into Kilmurvy, and the tide being low we anchored it. Next morning we rowed in to the shore with the fish lashed alongside.

Mike and Maggie took part in the next scene. Getting a huge boiler on props with the help of some men, they built a fire under it. They poured some water into the boiler in order to keep the liver of the shark from burning, the liver being treated in this way so as to get the oil from it. Then Maggie, when the oil was ready, poured some of it into a tankard, and she and Mike took it home.

Sunshine, west winds and low passing clouds favoured this part of the story, and Mr. Flaherty's work on it is, I think, as beautiful as any ever shown on the screen.

*   *   *

In the first days of May there was a swell in the sea, a forerunner of the big seas and stormy weather that usually come in this month, and wash ashore the biggest seaweed crop of the year, which is most anxiously waited for. It was during these early days of May that for the first time in my life I made up my mind to try and save a pound or two and put it away for a rainy day.

I had been a master kelpman—nice words enough, one would think, yet how empty sounding if one only knew

the truth, especially as regards a man who has worked alone as I have. In order to be a master kelpman one must have the best material, which means having the pick of the shores' best seaweed and sea-rods. Ten or fifteen families had been coming to my shore, and in each family there were two or three men, say two sons and the father—all intent on having the honour of being the best kelpman, and all of them hardy men and good workers.

The sea-rod is, above all other sea growths, the best for making iodine, but it is never torn from its roots on the bottom of the sea until the big winter storms rage. Then they are thrown up by the sea in scores of tons. Night and day we watch for them, meeting every flood tide, each family gathering what it can, each intent on having the best kelp. The following season the stuff is burned into ash.

The men have to be well looked after, always having a dry change of clothes to put on when they come home, and always in the early morning, after a hard night's work, having plenty of hot tea, with bread and butter, brought to them on the shore. Dinner and supper was brought the same way, because nearly all the kelpmakers' homes have a woman in them, and maybe a couple of young girls. Yet in spite of all this I had become a master kelpman, and I alone, no one to dry my clothes, nobody to cook me a meal.

P.J. was too young, and he was going to school, and my father was too old. Yet I stuck to the shore night and day, until finally the time came when, if a great storm was raging, the other kelpmen would turn in their beds and say:

"Oh, well, what business have I getting up and going

to the shore when I know that that big devil is there ahead of me!"

They had to be made to think that way, before I could become a top hand at the business. For five successive years I had taken by far and away the highest price for kelp. Still, as I say again, what empty words they were so far as I was concerned. Many a time, when coming home, I have unconsciously cast my eyes up to the chimney, expecting to see the blue curling smoke that warms one's heart, because it nearly always means on our Island that there is life within, life in the shape of a bustling woman, who is ready to enquire how well one has fared on the shore, while she gets ready the dry change of clothes and prepares a hot meal. In my case it could not be, and many, many times I have sat by my cold hearthstone, too tired to put down a fire, and there, brooding, wet and lonely, I have with my mind's eye looked upon the dead ashes of my dreams. I shall make kelp no more.

★　　★　　★

The swell in the sea making camera work on board the *Summers* impossible, Mr. Flaherty asked me to get some sentinels on the stretch of cliff near Dun Aengus in order that he might get some connecting shark shots. I got the men together and, taking the cameras with us, we all climbed up the slope to the ancient dun. I had placed the sentinels on the high points looking out over the sea, when Mr. Flaherty decided, on looking through his camera, that Gortnagapple village should come into the scene and, as a connecting link, one of the sentinels must stand on a high point of cliff outside but some distance to the west of, the village. This sentinel would be a good distance from us, with a bight of sea between, where the cliffs had been eaten away, so I had to be particular when I gave this sentinel, whose name was Steve, his orders. The others would be within reach of my voice so that they were safe enough to do the right thing.

The first sentinel to sight a shark was to shout to the nearest man, and he in his turn to pass the word along. Then they were all to hurry down towards Kilmurvy village and the shore, all but Steve who was to run for Gortnagapple village when he saw the other sentinels running.

"Steve," said I, "you are to stand on that far point and keep a look-out for sharks. These other men are going to do the same thing on these points around here. You can see them if they run, and when they start, then you run for Gortnagapple. The fish" I added "are westward from here and one of these men will see them before you do, but in case you see a shark *before* the men start running, you head for Gortnagapple. I shall have my eye on you and I shall start the others at the same time."

"What about the camera?" said Steve. "Won't it see me looking towards ye, and won't I spoil the picture?"

"Don't bother about that," I answered. "You will be so far away that you can quite safely look our way."

A dozen times I went over his part with him, and with a final "It is time for me to know my business", he ran away over the rough rocks, as sure-footed as a goat. He hopped over the walls and made for the point. It was about eleven o'clock in the morning. The sun was shining for the time being, but the south-western sky looked like rain and I could see we were going to have showers later.

The sentinels were standing at their different points, or

pacing slowly back and forth to ease the strain of watching. They looked eagerly out to sea. Suddenly the cry of: "Levawn, Levawn Mor, see it!" rang out—one look, and they ran down the slope. But Steve held his ground. He stood as firm as a rock, looking fixedly out to sea.

"Make Steve move," shouted Mr. Flaherty.

"Make the devil move," says I, Steve being too far away from me for him to hear my voice, which was drowned by the noise of the sea beating against the cliff. However, I jumped up on the wall of the dun, and kept on shouting through the megaphone; then I waved it to and fro through the air, to attract his attention. But Steve did not move. Again and again we tried this scene with the same result. Then the day turned to rain, and we went to shelter, all but Steve, who still stood looking out to sea.

"What in heaven's name is the matter with that man?" asked Mr. Flaherty. "Did you tell him, Pat, what he was to do?"

"Of course I did," I answered.

"Why didn't he do it, then?"

"I couldn't tell you," says I, "but I hope he sticks there. I hope he dies there, and anyway," I added, "how the blazes was I to know that he was a relation of Casabianca's?"

The day cleared up a bit after lunch, two sentinels were placed on points further west, for another "tie-up" shot. At four o'clock there came another shower. Later, when the evening had cleared, Mr. Flaherty decided that he would like a shot of Gortnagapple village in the soft evening sunlight.

He looked through the camera and said: "I wish we had a man stationed at that far point. But look," he continued, "there is a man there already—a fisherman, I suppose. I hope he doesn't move till I take this shot."

"Move, no," I assured him, "that man will stay there until the last trumpet call, unless somebody goes and drags him away."

"What!" said Mr. Flaherty. "Is that Steve there still?"

"Still Steve is the name," I answered. "And Still Steve is the man."

"Why didn't you tell him to come away from there?" asked Mr. Flaherty.

"You didn't need him, and he seemed to be enjoying the scenery so much that it was a shame to move him," I answered.

I felt angry with Steve. I sent a man out after him to drag him away from his post, and I asked him why he hadn't headed for Gortnagapple, or had he forgotten what I had told him.

"I remembered everything," said Steve, "but at the last minute I said to myself in my own mind that if I looked over to where you all were, the devil of a camera would catch me looking. Right enough," he went on, "I heard your voice, but I wasn't sure of what you were saying. Just the same, I think that I did pretty well to stand out there all day in case that I'd be needed."

I said no more about it—there was nothing left to be said.

A few days later we went to work again. We decided to work on the land sequence. On the hill overlooking Bungowla, Mr. Flaherty got Tiger and Maggie building a house. It was a wild, storm-swept spot. A Bungowla man was preparing to build a house on this same crag. I told Mr. Flaherty about it, and went on to explain that later, when the house was finished, little gardens would begin to be made around it, because of the good bottom on the crag.

"What!" said he. "A garden here? Impossible!"

I explained to him that we of Aran considered a stretch of rock from which the upper layer could be lifted, leaving a level stretch of rotten ledge underneath, a good bottom on which to make a garden. The rotten ledge, full of tiny fissures, lets the rain seep through, and the small pieces of yellow clay deep down in those fissures hold the moisture. A man making a garden on such rock is considered to be very lucky. He is fairly sure of a crop even when dry weather comes, because the sun only dries up the soil gradually, and the moisture takes a long time to come up from the fissures, thus keeping the thin top layer of soil damp for a couple of weeks or more. Or, as we say here, such a garden has great standing of dry weather.

Mr. Flaherty looked at me, only half believing, saying again:

"Do you really mean to tell me that sometime a garden shall appear on that waste?"

"We can make sure by asking the owner," I answered.

I sent for him. He was a lean, tall man, six feet four in height, and I asked him about his garden.

"Yes," he said. "With the help of God, I will have the house built this year, and there to the west of it next year I will make a little garden. The next year after that, if God leaves us our health, we may be able to make another little one. We can get sand in the shore, but it is hard to get clay any more, because most of it has already been picked out of the clefts; but anyway," he added, and a faint gleam of joy lit up his countenance as he surveyed the Godforsaken stretch of waste rock, "there's plenty of time, and my son comes after me. There is room here to work forever."

The Tiger and Maggie went to work building the house. Later they hauled some seaweed. From this craggy height there is a most magnificent view of the North Sound and beyond it the Connemara Mountains, with the Twelve Pins that look so softly blue in the distance. Also the north-western Islands that, on a fine summer evening, look like fairy isles suspended by invisible threads hanging over the sea, and to the west the Atlantic Ocean stretching away to the horizon. But I doubt if the six-foot-four man sees much of its beauty. His house has to be built, and there before him lies this barren stretch that has to be made into land. I believe that all his thoughts are centred joyously on this soul-killing labour.

*　　*　　*

The weather settled down a bit. The sea had fallen somewhat, and we again went shark-hunting. We steamed well to the west of Rock Island and sighted a school of eight or ten scattered out over a wide area. Captain Murray harpooned one with his gun off the *Summers*, and while they were trying to play it we got into our boat and rowed away to harpoon another. We crossed in front of it and, as it neared us, Tiger sunk his harpoon in the water until it touched the grey streak; then with all his weight on it he drove it in with great force. The shark slashed some barrels of water over our rail and sounded. After about an hour it headed towards the west, towing us along at a good speed. The shark that towed the *Summers* headed north-east and with ours heading west, the boats drifted apart, until some miles separated them. Suddenly in the distance we saw the *Summers* put up steam, and she began to go ahead at a fast clip. We knew she had lost her shark and was going after another.

After a quarter of an hour we heard the boom of the gun, and saw the *Summers* slowing down; we knew that she was fast in another. Our boat was still being towed westward, and it wasn't long before we completely lost sight of the *Summers*. We wanted several sharks at this time, Mr. Flaherty having an idea that if we rendered all the livers of the fish into oil and had many barrels of it to show, he could get outside buyers interested in the work, and thereby get an industry started which would be of great benefit to the Islanders. We did get many barrels of very fine oil, but nothing ever came of it. I have heard since that the work wouldn't pay because the oil would now only sell at a very low price. After about an hour and a half, we saw the *Summers* steaming in our direction. We knew immediately that she had lost her second shark.

Mrs. Flaherty was on board her on this trip, taking still photographs as they are called, and I noticed that as the *Summers* swung up close alongside us Mrs. Flaherty looked a bit anxious. It seems that the last shark they had harpooned had struck the *Summers* a blow with its tail that had shaken her from stem to stern. Mrs. Flaherty had been anxious about us. She always said after this that when dealing with such monsters anything might happen, and had the blow of the shark's tail been struck on our boat instead of the *Summers*, it would have smashed it to splinters.

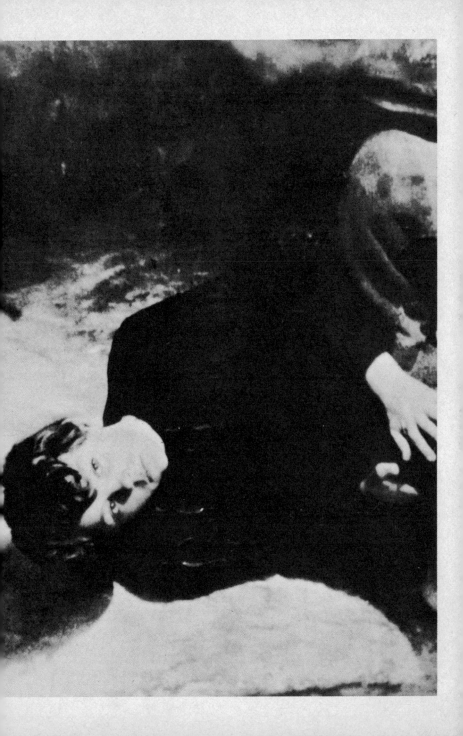

About thirty years ago, my father had been telling us, as we had sat around the fire, about a strange fish that they had taken on board while mackerel fishing, about ten miles to the west of Rock Island. This fish was about three feet long and eel-shaped. The fish was thrown on the deck of the boat, which it immediately caught with its teeth, and it then stuck its tail straight up in the air. It had taken a strong pull to get it to loosen its grip. He had said that no man aboard the boat had ever seen the like before, nor since as far as he knew. I had often thought about this strange fish when other men were talking of their fishing experiences. I didn't know whether to believe my father or not, for though I had taken his every word for Gospel truth when I was young, I have long since learned that he was subject to little flights of fancy when he felt inclined that way.

Now, however, as we got this shark close alongside, and it heaved itself over on its side, we were much surprised to see sticking out of its hide several eel-shaped fish, some of them appearing to have sunk themselves half their length into the body of the shark. Suddenly, as if sensing that something was wrong, a couple of them dropped off into the deep, but Tommy O'Rourke caught hold of one that still stuck on, and it took a strong pull to drag it away. Where it had been fastened on the shark was a red spot, giving blood. We caught half a dozen of them, and when we threw them down on the bottom of the boat, they stuck on to anything. Their mouths were formed like circles, and they fastened on to one's hand as easily as to the boat. They measured from about a foot and a half to three feet in length. We thought at first that they might be young sharks who fed thus on the female of the species, but later we came to the conclusion that they were some sucker parasite fish who fed on these monsters by sucking their blood.

However, we killed our shark, and it was towed into Kilmurvy Bay. These great fish have now become a pest to fishermen when mackerel fishing in the spring, because they tear through the nets, or get entangled in them, thereby carrying sometimes as many as eight or ten nets away with them in their efforts to get free.

Soon after this Mr. Flaherty received a telegram stating that two publicity men from the Gainsborough Company were coming. So the *Summers* was sent to pick them up at Great Man's Bay. Mrs. Flaherty was on board this trip. The men were met and we steamed for Kilmurvy.

On our way in we saw a monster shark; so we got into our boat and after rowing after it for a short time succeeded in harpooning it. It dived down and headed straight under the *Summers'* keel. Tiger and the other men wanted me to slack away, but as Mr. Flaherty was working his camera, I held on. Our boat ran full tilt into the *Summers* and her stem was smashed. I cursed loudly. The shock tore the harpoon out, so we boarded the *Summers* and headed for home. I had forgotten in the excitement that Mrs. Flaherty was on board, and I hurriedly asked the crew if they had heard me very plainly when I was cursing.

"Why, man," said they, "you could be heard in Galway."

I was much ashamed. After a while I plucked up courage to go to Mrs. Flaherty and beg her pardon.

"I'm sorry, Mrs. Flaherty," says I, "that I cursed in your hearing. But in the excitement of the moment I had forgotten you were on board. Please forgive me."

I fancied that the corners of her mouth trembled as if back in her mind somewhere a smile was lurking, but her eyes were quite innocent of any devilment as she looked at me straight and said:

"Pat, did you curse, really, did you? Why," she went on, "I never heard you."

"Oh, I'm so glad you didn't," I answered. Of course, I couldn't say anything else. All of which shows how fine and good a woman can be when she wants to.

The publicity men said that before they left England they had been thinking what a pity it was that no sound outfit had been sent to Aran to take the dialogue, but since hearing me swear they thought it was a good job one hadn't been sent! I don't curse much as a rule, but I couldn't help letting myself go sometimes when we were making the film.

A carpenter was put to work and repaired our boat. The following Sunday sharks appeared in the mouth of Kilmurvy Bay. We were doing no hunting, it being Sunday, besides the day was cloudy. I asked Mrs. Flaherty if she would like to come out in a curragh to get some close-up views of the fish. She readily consented.

"I may be able to get some good stills of them, Pat," she said, "if the sun only breaks out for a minute."

I got two other men to come, and we put down a curragh, got into her and rowed to the pier, where we picked up Mrs. Flaherty and put her sitting in the stern. Though one wouldn't think it to look at her, she must have been a pretty hefty weight, for the curragh's stern sank deep in the water.

We rowed out in fine style to where the sharks were

swimming around. As we were drawing close to them, one huge monster turned and swam swiftly towards us. It was Rosie, terrible to look at with the big white spot on her fin, and the great scars on her body showing as usual. With her huge mouth wide open, she didn't look very friendly, especially when approaching at great speed a frail canvas canoe weighed down very much in the stern by Mrs. Flaherty! Rosie swam right up close astern, stuck her snout out of the water and glared in an awful manner at Mrs. Flaherty, who was only about three feet away and about six inches above the water.

She let out a little scream and said: "Pat, Pat, what is it going to do?"

We were all a bit startled, but I spoke coolly enough: "It's all right, ma'am. That's Rosie. That's the one the girls have taken a fancy to. She's supposed to be a friend of the family!"

"I don't care whose friend she is," said Mrs. Flaherty. "It doesn't look to be any friend of mine. Do please hurry and row ashore as fast as you can before the awful beast swallows us all up."

We did row, but we might just as well have taken it easy, because Rosie followed us and kept the same distance, and always, it seemed to us, keeping a wicked eye on Mrs. Flaherty. However, as we neared the pier, she turned about and swam away to join her mates. Mrs. Flaherty drew several long deep breaths of relief when she got out on to the pier.

"Pat, never again for me. It has been the most awful experience I have ever been through," she said.

Soon after this the sharks began to gather in large schools, and seemed to be moving more swiftly through the water as they fed, gathering into their great jaws all the food possible, preparatory to swimming away from our coast on their migration. We killed many more and had some exciting times. One day that was more exciting than the others was when a huge shark tore the braced oaken post out of our boat, and with a clout of its tail nearly sent us all to the bottom of the sea.

Luckily, before they disappeared Mr. Flaherty had taken enough pictures to finish the basking shark sequence for the film.

CHAPTER X

Greased Lightning—A Wedding—The Duke—
"Hundreds of years ago"—Danger, Sweat and
Brine—The Last Shot

★

Later on Mr. Flaherty decided to get some more shots of groups, and also of men and women running towards the shore at Bungowla.

"Pat," he said, "you know what we want done, so pick the characters yourself."

So next morning I started out and picked as my first man Shauneen Tom, an old friend of mine—a man who had done me many a good turn. Shauneen is getting on in years, he is about sixty-two. In his youth he was a fine specimen of an Aran Islander and an artist painted him on canvas as such a type. He has always been a leader in his own community. When he speaks he does it with a curl of the lip and a twist of the tongue that brings with it an air of great finality, as much as to say: "You have heard me talk, so there is no more to be said!"

In his youth he had fallen in love with a beautiful young girl from his own village, as she did with him.

They had no way of settling down, there being too many brothers and sisters in each family; this may seem strange to one who doesn't know Aran, but the reason is this, the land holdings are very small, averaging only about sixteen acres, of what is mostly rock, to each house-holder; consequently there is room for only one member of each family to settle on each little holding. Nearly always the eldest son inherits the land, but he never marries until practically all his younger brothers and sisters have gone away to America.

They agreed that the best way was for her to send for passage money to friends in America. She did this and after some months of waiting she received the money to pay her fare, with the understanding between them that as soon as possible she would send him the money that she had earned for his passage. She sailed away. Shauneen was very despondent—he couldn't do much work. His thoughts were always flying over the sea to the girl he loved. Some letters went back and forth between them.

In the last letter Shauneen received, she said that she was in very poor health, having caught a cold on the boat going out, and that now it had developed into something more serious. He was terribly upset, so much so that he shipped his horse to Galway and sold it at the fair, and with the money he paid his passage to America; but he was too late, for on arriving there he found that the girl he loved was dead and buried. He only stayed a short time in that country, as he couldn't make himself con-tented. And soon, still grieving, he made his way back home.

Years afterwards, his brothers and sisters having gone to America, Shauneen married, but it is doubtful if he ever loved so deeply as he did at first. But a man *must* marry on Aran if he wants to live, and that's all there is to be said about it.

Shauneen, since he came home from America, holds the opinion that man is the superior of woman. There may be something to be said in favour of this view when looking at life on Aran, where the man is always the provider. A lone woman in a house by herself on these Islands is a very very helpless creature.

Anyway, to shorten the story, I took Shauneen with me, and on our way to Bungowla we picked up several men and women, and finally as we went through the village I picked up a tall yellow-haired slip of a girl, who was full of life and wild as a hare. We all headed for the shore. Shauneen, after looking at the slip of a girl with a sarcastic smile on his lips, said to me:

"What the hell business have you bringing that long-legged thing down to work alongside of men? The other women aren't so bad; they look sensible enough, but this thing with the long legs, well, 'tis the devil entirely. I'd like to know what the world is coming to."

Mr. Flaherty picked out the place he fancied for the scene. It was on a stretch of broken rock which led in from some low cliffs to the south of Bungowla shore. The men and women were to hurry singly and in pairs across the stretch of rock and then to stand on the low cliff looking out to sea as if watching for a curragh; but the last pair were to stand by a boulder about a hundred yards back from the cliff, from which point they too were to look out to sea with every appearance of excitement. I had put them all in place with the exception of the last pair, which somehow happened to be Shauneen and the slip of a girl. They were the two who were to run to the boulder, stand there and show excitement. They would have to run fast to reach this spot in order to tally their time with those who had to stand on the cliff's edge, because they had farther to go. As I was placing them in position, Shauneen spat in disgust, saying:

"Am I to run with this thing?"

"Well, not exactly," says I, "she is to start out ahead of you, but you being a man will gain on her, and when about halfway to the boulder you are to pass her in order to reach your place several yards ahead of her. Doing it that way," I added, "will show that there is real need to hurry."

"Oh, that's all right," says Shauneen. "I thought you were going to have that thing ahead of me all the way."

He stretched himself and spat out some tobacco juice, with a very satisfied look on his face. The yellow-haired slip looked at him strangely, and though I told her time and time again about her part, I'd have given my oath that she was only half listening. Above all things, I tried to impress on her mind that Shauneen had to pass her halfway to the boulder.

All now being ready, I gave the signal to Mr. Flaherty, then I shouted my orders through the megaphone, and the crowd started running.

The first group did all right, and then in the distance appeared Shauneen and his yellow-haired sparring partner. They had started all right, the girl well in advance, and Shauneen running along pretty lively for a man of his age. He gained on the girl and shouted some words at her. I was too far away to understand what he had said. Halfway to the boulder he reached her side. This stretch of rock was awfully rough to run on, with big loose sharp-pointed stones everywhere and great clefts in the solid rock underneath. Side by side they ran for a

243

little way, then Shauneen went ahead for a yard, then the girl with a little spurt passed him. They raced *past* the boulder and never stopped until they reached the edge of the cliff.

I went over to them all and told them that their work was very good with the exception of the parts Shauneen and the girl had played. To these I gave a piece of my mind. Shauneen sat on a rock with his back to the crowd. He was a trifle pale and breathing heavily. Then to finish my talk and to take the harm out of it, I asked him how he thought he had got on.

"I'd have got on all right," he said, "if you had put me with any woman with a spark of sense in her. But with that cracked devil. . . ." He turned and looked at her, saying: "Bad luck to ye over there—trying to run a poor man off his feet, but I shall be dead entirely before I shall ever let a woman beat me at anything."

The girl stood with the other women, apparently indifferent to what Shauneen was saying. So I took Shauneen over to her.

"You both ran a good race," I said, feeling my way.

The girl smiled at Shauneen, the smile of Youth against the world.

Then her face grew hard again as she said:

"Sure, you don't call that a race, do you? I was only making fun with him."

Shauneen fumed and cursed, and ended up by saying the blame was hers for not stopping at the boulder.

"Why didn't *you* stop at it?" she asked. "The trouble with you", she added, "is that you think there is no woman as good as a man."

I stopped their argument and went to Mr. Flaherty,

who asked me what had happened, and why hadn't the last pair stopped midway to the cliff.

"Shauneen doesn't like to be beaten by a woman, old as he is," I said, "and the only thing I can do is to start them all over again, and to impress on their minds, if I can, that it is *your* work that counts and that they're not running a race."

There was no time to regroup the crowd because clouds were coming up, so I put the first group in position and then spoke earnestly to Shauneen; but I saw a flash in his eyes as he tightened his criss.

Aran men are queer in some ways, for in spite of being very independent, they can be handled easily when the handling is done in a friendly way. On the other hand, when they are stirred, they get very stubborn and it is almost impossible to do anything with them at all.

I then spoke to the girl, and begged her to try and understand a man of Shauneen's temperament.

"I had nothing against him", she answered, "till he shouted behind me and said that it was a bad day surely when he had to be running after me."

She looked very wild as she said this, and I saw that she was angry, though she was trying to conceal it.

" 'Tis all over now," I told her. "Next time both do your best and do it right," I added.

"We will see if it is all over!" she answered, and now I began to realize that she cared nothing for what I'd said or about the film—she seemed to have made up her mind as to what she was about to do. Anyhow, there was no time for any more talk. Shauneen was to come into view, appearing from behind a great boulder, with the girl well in advance until halfway to the mark, when he was to pass her and continue to gain ground until the spot where they were to stand was reached.

Mr. Flaherty signalled that he was ready, and I shouted at the parties to get going as before. The first group got into place in good order, but at my shout Shauneen leapt out from behind the boulder, and with his black felt hat in his hand was racing over the ground like a born runner. Yellow Hair must have been taken by surprise, because she was to have started first, but he had beaten her to it and was now going like an Alfred Shrubb, leaping up and down over the rocks at great speed. However, she soon got started—and couldn't she run!

Both of them had apparently forgotten that we were making a film. Shauneen's one idea was to win the race like a man, and it began to look as if he were about to do it. But by now the girl was letting herself out, and her pampooties beat a tattoo on the rocks as she flew over them. Sometimes a stone, evenly balanced, went over as her shoe touched it, but she was away to another in the twinkling of an eye. Then up and down she flew over the sharp rocks. Shauneen looked behind and stumbled, and before he had fully recovered, the girl had sped past him and kept straight on for the edge of the cliff. Shauneen also passed the stopping place close in her wake, but suddenly realizing that he was being hopelessly beaten, a bright thought came to him. He hesitated, then stopped and turned back quickly. With two springs he reached the stopping place, where he stood and looked out to sea, looking very excited.

There wasn't much acting needed, for he was excited anyway!

"Good man, Shauneen!" I shouted. "You have saved

the day and made the picture! Keep it up! That's great work you're doing!"

Shauneen is really a born actor anyway, when he gets started right.

This scene was now over, and as clouds were coming up we had to call it a day. I came up to Shauneen. He looked at me searchingly, trying to see if I had noticed what had been passing through his mind. I must have looked pretty innocent, because he said:

"You see, Pat, I was taking my time getting my second wind when long spindle-shanks passed me out. I could have beaten her easily because I had her measure in my pocket." But, he added, with every appearance of sincerity: "It was God himself that put it into my heart to think of that gentleman down there and his picture, so I said to myself that whatever I'd lose I'd turn back and try to do something for him; but", he added, and a glint of admiration lit up his eyes as he looked over at the girl, "I never saw anything on two legs yet that could make such headway, unless it's myself. She is a great runner entirely."

Then we all went down towards the road in the sidecars, all except the girl. She skipped over the crags towards a short cut that led to Bungowla.

*　　*　　*

A wedding was coming off, and we were all invited. Everybody on these Islands gets excited when a couple are going to be married; it is always a big event. We have such few pleasures in our lives that we make the most of a wedding and, besides, we are easily made happy and we are all great lovers of music.

My father still tries to dance, although he is eighty-five.

My grandmother, who was born on the same day as Queen Victoria, won a prize for step-dancing. We had heard that the Queen always danced on her birthday. So not to be outdone, my grandmother danced also. I don't remember now which of these two dancing-hearted queens lived the longest on this earth, but I do know that my grandmother danced when she was ninety-seven years old.

There would be at a wedding in the old days about two hundred people. Nowadays, unless the families are middling well-to-do, there would not be so many. However, this wedding was sure to be fairly big, because, as they say here, both these families always had full and plenty of everything.

There was an old couple in the young man's house, his father and mother, and a fine old couple they were. The woman saintly and toil-worn; and the man, who was a great curraghman in his day, was still powerful despite his seventy-five years. Of great bone, with a huge round body like a bull, well over six feet in height, with hair as white as snow and a great golden beard thickly streaked with grey—one of the old timers, who had red blood enough in him to be a sinner. Aran people are about the most moral in the whole world. By sinner I mean a man who has always worked hard and who at fair time or kelp-burning takes a few drinks and then on his way home hurls out his challenge of superiority to all who are within hearing. This man was one of the old stock, and many a time long ago, we, as boys, would hang around the roads till the public house closed, in order to see him go home. Always for a start when coming out of the pub, he looked around and wiped his great beard with the back of his

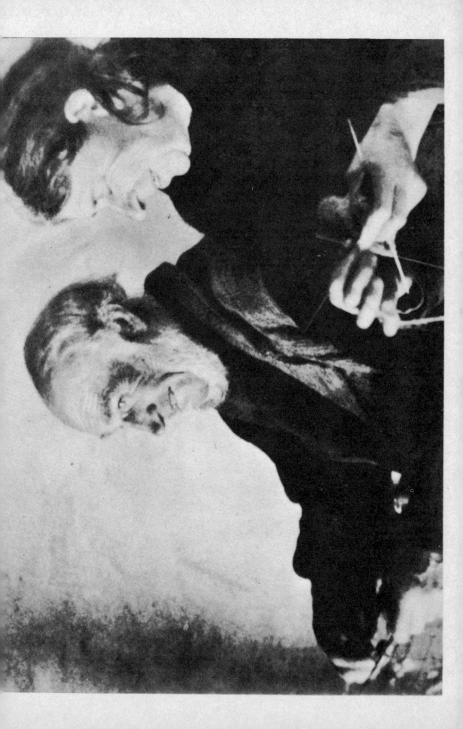

hand. He tilted his black felt hat at a rakish angle over his left ear and tightened his criss; then he cursed and damned his way up and down through the village a couple of times. We had always taken an unholy delight in this part of the performance, but when he turned around every once in a while and glared at us, we ran away like so many frightened rabbits, only to steal back again immediately. He finally stood on the top of Jobber's Hill, stripped himself to his shirt and walked back and forth for half an hour, nobody bothering him or willing to take a chance of getting within reach of his great hands. Then he would calmly put on his clothes again and after a furious glare in our direction would head for home, making the echoes ring with his wild singing.

A first class Aran Island wedding done in the old style is a great affair, usually taking place between eleven and one o'clock in the day. Most of the weddings in Kilronan are horribly civilized things, being entirely lifeless, but in the other villages they are splendid.

Mr. and Mrs. Flaherty got ready, as also did Frances and Monica. I hitched up my big white horse, who was full of fire after a long much-needed rest. We drove to the house of the bride to be. There were already seven or eight sidecars there ahead of us. There had been a party in her house all night, consisting of the bridegroom, his father and their relations, also relations and friends of the bride. About thirty horses were tied here and there to the wall along the road, all mettlesome, and all seeming to be full of the spirit of the wedding. Many men had left to go and fetch their horses, which grazed in little fields amongst the crags.

We went inside; Mr. Flaherty and I drank a glass of

poteen. Mrs. Flaherty and the girls had some tea. Then, after a short time, we prepared to start on the wild six mile race to the chapel. The young couple got on the first sidecar and the rest of the sidecars lined up behind, packed with women and young girls, who were all ready to start singing. A few of them had accordions and these were also ready to rend the air with their music. The men leaped on their horses. They are all splendid bare-back riders, and they were all three sheets in the wind. As many as three people were mounted on some of the horses.

Then away we started at a furious gallop with women singing, accordions screaming, wild yells, ear-splitting whistles and songs from the men on horseback. Coming from every road and every boreen, fully another score of horsemen, all on the dead run and with their horses covered with foam, joined us, and the wild thrilling cries of these men now mingled with our own.

On we tore towards the chapel, never stopping in our gallop. Every now and then a wild rider, mounted on a wilder horse, raced past our sidecars—with the single-rope halter caught between the rider's teeth, his arms spread wide and his bauneen flying.

We reached the chapel and all of us crowded in to see the ceremony. This soon being over, we again got under way and quickly made the short run to the bridegroom's house, where the saintly old woman stood at the door, with her giant of a man, who had left the chapel before us. They welcomed us all with a Cead Mile Failte. The horsemen, after a glass of poteen, went out to put their horses in the little fields of the village. Though jealously careful of every little bit of grass, at these weddings every man's horse is free to graze anywhere. All these horsemen then

came back to the wedding house and joined the others, who had come from every village on the Island. They all danced and sang till late the next day, when they went home, tired and happy.

Thrilling affairs indeed, these old-time weddings! I have read in the newspapers now and again about famous weddings that have been done with great ceremony, in Dublin and in St. Paul's in London, where scores of yards of lace and silk have floated around light and airy, like cobwebs, with bouquets of flowers and all that kind of thing. A grand sight, so the papers say. I suppose it all depends upon one's viewpoint. For my own part, I don't think they can compare with our weddings.

Mr. Flaherty has never tired of talking about the great hoary-headed old sinner, who had tossed off tumbler after tumbler of powerful poteen whiskey and still remained the same kingly looking courteous host. As we were leaving, he came out on the road with us, and bid us good night and God speed, looking calmly grave and full of kindness.

*　　*　　*

The weather now began to look threatening and the great rollers to rise on the reefs—a sure sign that at last the big break was coming which would fill the shores with May seaweed and make all kelpmen happy.

Mr. Flaherty, after many days and nights of running his storm scenes on the screen, came to the conclusion that the Manister curragh film and the Brannagh Island Sound film would not match, so that they could not be put together. He therefore decided to try and pull off another storm scene. So we began to get ready for the heavy weather which we now knew was coming at any moment.

One of the oldest men in Kilmurvy village is a man called the Duke—it is not his proper name, of course. About eighty years ago a duke—it might have been the Duke of Connaught, or of Edinburgh—paid a visit to Aran Island. On the day of his arrival, a woman named Mrs. Joyce gave birth to a baby boy. The Duke, when passing along the road, had heard about the happy event, and he went into the house to see the young hopeful. When leaving, he bent down over the baby and left a birthday gift beside him on the pillow.

Now I cannot say whether it was because of this child breathing in the ducal atmosphere so early in life, or for some other reason, but the boy grew up with an insatiable thirst for knowledge. On reaching manhood he was possessed of a fine brain, but unfortunately it was more or less wasted on Aran, there being no outlet for his talents. Of hardy stock, he became a splendid curraghman. He was low-sized, stockily built and had a strong face in which glittered the most piercing pair of black eyes that I have ever seen.

Once I had a heated argument with this man, over our donkey having got into his potato garden. He vanquished me easily. It happened years ago, but I shall never forget the snapping fury of those black eyes, and how they burned through me. He was a great scholar and always read everything that he could lay his hands on. Now he is very old and losing his grip on things. During the past ten years, every now and again, we used to meet on the road, and the Duke and I had many a long talk. We talked about the world and of the past and present conditions of the races of men who live in it. We talked of mines of gold, and indeed of nearly every known subject worth talking about! He was a regular store of knowledge, but we always finished our talks by coming back to our own Island; talking of our land-making, fishing, our curraghs and curraghmen. He had often told me that a curragh is the best boat of her size in the world—but of course she only goes as long as man-power lasts. In order to get her at her absolute best, when she could live when a seagull could hardly fly, the crew must be fearless and understand how to conserve their strength, never wasting one atom of energy and giving only just what is needed; but above all there must be absolute rhythm in thought and move-ment, as though the entire crew was controlled by one brain. Three such men in a good curragh can and have outlived the most furious gales, but such crews are rare. Most curraghmen are good, but the Duke told me that in his fifty years of going to sea in curraghs he had only met two curragh crews who could reach the high standard that he had described. One of these crews consisted of his father and two others who, when hauling long lines in their curragh about six miles off the mouth of Gregory's Sound, were caught in a southerly gale.

Theirs was the only curragh that had put to sea that day, the weather being broken and the morning looking bad. They could only hold her bow on to the sea, but every once in a while when the chance offered, they would bring her off a little and with a few swift powerful strokes endeavour to gain a little on their course to safety.

She was driven down Gregory's Sound, and the Glassin Rock cliffs were lined with people watching the curragh which was bravely trying to edge in bit by bit towards the land. Nothing could be done to help them, and the onlookers feared that at any moment she would be swamped by the great waves. The curraghmen tried their best to make the beach at Iararna, from where they had left in the morning, but try as they might she was blown past it and down into Galway Bay, and finally with her bows still held to sea and wind, she landed at Salt Hill, near the town of Galway.

The curragh had been blown across thirty-six miles of raging seas—the men had fought every yard of the way and had lived to tell their story.

Now, rare as it is, according to the Duke—and I believe him—to find such absolutely perfect curraghmen working together in the same canoe, I *do* believe that in the case of Big Patcheen and his men we had an absolutely perfect crew, and I consider it most fortunate that we managed to get them. Otherwise those storm scenes in the *Man of Aran* would never have been done without loss of life, or perhaps never done at all.

About the middle of May the shores were full of sea-weed. The seas ran high, and on all the reefs around our Island they rushed tumbling white for miles. We were all ready to try for our final storm scenes, but unfortunately the weather was cloudy and wet.

One Friday it poured with rain, and Patch Bawn, an old blind man from Onaght village, who had walked six miles to Kilronan for his old age pension, came into our cottage on his way home to dry himself by the big turf fire, which we always kept burning on such days. There were about a dozen of us, and we were talking about the weather and also about kelp. Getting tired of these never ending conversations about the same things, I turned to

Patch Bawn, who had by this time been pretty well steamed and dried, as he sat in the chimney corner, and I asked him to tell us a story.

Like all good story-tellers, he coughed a lot of small coughs before he got ready to start, and kept saying in between, in a modest kind of way, that he wasn't much good at storytelling. We waited patiently, but at the same time we kept making all kinds of encouraging remarks, such as: "Go ahead, Patch," "Put it out from your heart." "Sure, storytelling runs in your family—look how your father used to tell them; and they say that your grandfather wasn't a bad hand at telling them."

At last, with a final cough and a great clearing of his throat, he began, and this is the story he told.

★   ★   ★

Hundreds of years ago in a far away land across the seas, a strange child was born to a woman, and people who saw it at its birth had whispered that it had been put on this world for some awful purpose, because on its back was a birthmark, a black hand grasping a three-pronged fork— a fork shaped, we are told, like those the devils use in hell. This far away land was the country of the Jews, and the boy's name was Judas. The boy grew up full of mean tricks and devilment, which, however, he always tried to conceal and keep people from finding out.

In the meantime another child had been born in a stable, whose name was Jesus. This child had on its breast a birthmark in the shape of a cross, and we all know that he was the Saviour of Mankind—The Son of God. When Jesus grew up to manhood, he was preaching one day about His Father who was in Heaven, the Kingdom of Bliss, and of the best way for men to act in this world in order after death to get to Heaven.

Now Judas happened to be one of the crowd who was listening, and when Jesus stopped preaching, Judas came to him and said: "Oh Lord, I will follow you and go with you everywhere, because you are the Truth and the Light."

But even as he said these words there must have been evil in his heart, for we know there is an account of what happened afterwards; but Jesus took him as one of His disciples.

A few more years passed and the Jews, especially the rich ones, had begun to hate Jesus, because He was continually preaching that, in order to please God and go to Heaven, they would have to give their money away to charity and turn their hands from money-making to the doing of good deeds.

It isn't any great wonder that they hated Him, for when a man in any country preaches too much of the truth and tells the rich that, in order to reach a state of perfect happiness in this world and the next, they must give away most of their wealth to charities and spend the rest of their lives in the performing of good deeds, he too is hated and laughed at.

There came a day when the Jews were looking for Jesus, in order to try him before some kind of a court for preaching against law and order. Jesus was hiding in a garden, and Judas made up his mind to betray Him and sell Him to the soldiers who were looking for Him. He would betray Him by a kiss, and for this terrible treachery he was to get thirty pieces of silver.

He did betray Him, and Our Saviour was crucified.

The devils in hell had a grip on Judas, but in order to make sure of him they tempted him to hang himself. He was found dead, hanging to the limb of a tree, and he went down to hell forever.

At least, that is what nearly everybody has always believed; they also believe that the story of Judas ended there. But in reality, continued Patch Bawn, it is only the beginning. Patch Bawn went on with the story.

Some years ago there were three Aran men fishing in a curragh about five miles to the south-west of Rock Island. The day was very warm and a light breeze blew from the south-east. They were stripped to their shirts because of the fineness of the day.

About one o'clock the wind veered around to the south-west and brought with it, from the western ocean, a chill that made them shiver. They hurriedly put on their bauneens and vests, but still they shivered. They looked over the ocean wondering what had come over the weather, and saw what they believed to be a white-looking island, and they thought it might be Hy Brazil, a phantom island, the Isle of the Blest, the Land of perpetual youth for the men of Ancient Aran. Only the chosen few ever see this Isle, and then it is seen well to the south-west of Dun Aengus, when the sun is about to sink into the sea at the end of a lovely summer day. They rowed toward the island and, though they rowed hard, still they shivered. On coming closer they saw that it was an island of ice that rose up high out of the water, and from one corner of it torrents of water were rushing down, foaming into the sea. A kind of steam also hung over this corner of the island.

The men of Aran wondered at this, and they rowed

quite close up to the island, and to their amazement they saw a naked man sitting on it. From all around him the water ran down in torrents and rivers to the sea, and clouds of steam went up into the air; but they were dumbfounded entirely when they saw this man jump up and run to another part of the island, and when he sat down again the water begin to run in torrents as the ice melted rapidly around him, and steam to rise and float away once again.

At last one of the curragh men found his voice and shouted: "Who, in God's name, are you? What are you doing there?"

And with a wild shriek of agony the man answered back: "I am Judas!"

"We always thought you were in hell," shouted back the man of Aran.

"So I am," shrieked the doomed man, "but once in every hundred years I am allowed out for a day in order to cool the heat and fire that burns my soul," and he added wildly: "I wouldn't have got this one day in a hundred years had I not done one good turn in my life."

"What good turn was it?" asked the man of Aran, "because to tell you the truth, we've never heard a good word said about you."

"The one good turn I did," said Judas, "was before I hanged myself I divided the thirty pieces of silver among the poor, but many people don't know that I did this. Row around to the other side of the island," he added in an agonized voice, "and I will be over there in a minute. I don't want to lose your company yet, but I must keep moving around, otherwise the heat from me would melt a hole through the island down to the sea underneath, and if I fell in the sea I'd make the water so hot that I'd be boiled alive."

Then, with another shriek of agony, he hopped over to the other side of the island. This part of the island was higher than the rest, and Judas was out of sight of the curraghmen for a little while, but the steam began to float up and torrents of water began to flow down, and he soon melted this higher part down to the level of the rest of the island, and the curraghmen saw him.

"You are melting it fast," says the Aran man.

"I am," answered Judas. "It will soon be all melted. It will only last me for the day, and when the sun goes down I must go back again to hell for another hundred years."

"Begob! You are having a hell of a time right enough," says the man of Aran. "But God is good, and maybe by and by after a while He might take pity on you and at the day of judgment He may take you up to Heaven entirely, along with ourselves. Or," he added, "is the Heaven where Aran men go the kind of a heaven you would like?"

"Indeed it isn't," said Judas, "because I saw one of ye in hell, but only one, and he was always shouting and screaming for poteen whisky to drink, and the divils have a hard time to do anything at all with him. Now if I went to Heaven with ye, and ye ever got hold of any drink, think what would happen when ye knew me to be Judas: my life wouldn't be worth a grain of tobacco."

"Well, you'd better move again or you will soon be in the water," said the man of Aran, "but anyhow, I believe it isn't any harm to ask you what kind of a heaven you would like to be in."

"Oh, the heaven I want", moaned Judas, "would be one where I'd have a world all to myself—a whole world filled up with great islands and continents of ice; so much ice that the heat from my burning soul couldn't have it melted till long after the end of forever."

"Faith! You can have that kind of a heaven for all I care," said the man of Aran. Then, as an afterthought, he asked: "What time will theirselves be coming after ye, because when they do come I would like to be a little bit out of the way myself."

"Not long now," said Judas, and he began to shriek again. He then howled: "My island is nearly melted and I'm soon going back to hell!"

"Yes, and we'll be rowing home," said the curraghmen. "I hope you will have plenty of ice to sit and cool yourself on, after the Day of Judgment, and tell the Aran man who is in hell that we asked after him, but that we aren't in any great hurry to go to see him."

After bidding Judas good-bye, they rowed for home, and as the sun was going down they could hear his wild screams come floating over the water. They were near home as night fell, but they kept looking in the direction where the island had been, and suddenly they saw a great streak of fire go flying over the sea towards the west. Judas was on his way.

. We all drew deep breaths when Patch Bawn at last finished his story. We then began to speculate on who the Aran man could be who was doing time in the fiery regions. Stephen O'Rourke, Tommy's father, said that he was absolutely sure he knew who it was. Some of us also had an idea who the man was, but of course I'm not going to give his name here.

I asked Patch how it was that the Aran curraghman and Judas understood one another so easily.

"Mullen," said Patch, "you must have forgotten your early teaching. Didn't you know that all the Saviour's disciples could talk in any language and in any way they liked, and on the day that the curraghmen saw Judas on the island of ice Judas spoke Irish like an Aran man."

*   *   *

Next morning, although the sky was clear the weather was unsettled, so we could not tell what fortune the day was going to bring to us as regards sunshine. Everything else looked favourable, for a strong gale blew from the west and a terrific sea was running. This was surely the day for us to get our final storm scene. It was important that we should, because Mr. Flaherty had got word that he must hurry to England with the *Man of Aran* film.

So getting everything ready, we made for Bungowla shore. A little to the south of it is the cove where we intended to take the storm scene and the landing. It was the place I have referred to before, when mentioning Big Patcheen's father and his barrel of oil; the place where a landing could be made at low tide provided that one could get through the breakers outside. It seemed doubtful on this day, for when we got there and surveyed it the breakers were coming clear across the entrance, and it was only at long intervals that a chance could be taken of running the passage.

I had a long earnest talk with Big Patcheen and his men, and explained to them that this was the day of all days when the work must be done, because any day now this annual week of rough weather would be over, and no more storm scenes could then be taken, as Mr. Flaherty had to leave Aran soon.

They agreed with me, and said that they would do their best, but they went on to say that the day looked very threatening, and if the wind veered out to the south-west later on, which it looked like doing, we were sure to have showers of rain with squalls.

That I knew, of course, but looking Big Patcheen in the eye, I said: "We will finish the picture to-day, rain or shine, by hook or by crook."

He was much stirred, and he smiled. "Mullen," he said, "if I can get out there I am not coming in till you give the signal, that is, if there is a chance of a bit of sun at all."

In about an hour's time the tide would be at its lowest ebb. We had some further talk and decided that the safest way was to leave Bungowla shore, dodge the seas there by rowing down around the north side of Brannagh Island, then out through the Sound between it and Rock Island, turn south-east and come up into the wind outside the breakers in the mouth of the cove, there to wait till they got the signal from me to make a try for the passage. The long row around we deemed safest; we didn't like the idea of having the curragh run the breakers twice, going out from as well as coming into the cove. As they tightened their crisses securely, Big Patcheen was all fire and energy, Steve Dirrane was calm and steady, believing always that when with Patcheen nothing could ever happen to him, and McDonough's blue eyes were lit up with indomitable courage and resolution.

We carried down the curragh and, while some other men held her, Patcheen and his crew jumped in, caught their oars and, after a final prayer and wish of "God strengthen your arms this day" from us on shore, Big Patcheen gave the word, the curragh was shoved off and they were away. These words from McDonough and Patcheen came back to me over the water:

"Don't be afraid for us, Mullen!"

Then they began to battle their way through the seas and soon gained deep water. They swung around the north point of Brannagh Island and disappeared from our sight. We hurried out to the Cove, and there Mr. Flaherty set up his camera. David Flaherty set up the other.

After about three-quarters of an hour we sighted the curragh to the south of Brannagh Island. She was already having heavy weather, and I began to get uneasy. Cloud banks had begun to appear low down in the south-western sky, and the wind gradually began to haul out there—it had begun to strengthen if anything—and I could see that our hopes of continuous sunshine for the day were shattered, and that we would be very lucky if we managed to get our storm scene without any serious accident occurring. Finally, the curragh came into position outside the breakers.

It was now low tide, and the right time for our landing scene because the canoe had the best chance of running the breakers and coming ashore before the turn of the tide. At dead low water the tide is at its slackest; even the great waves seem to rest a bit before beginning their on-slaught anew; at low tide this cove was somewhat shel-tered and once a curragh was inside the breakers she was safe, but after the first half hour of flood tide it began to get dangerous, because Brannagh Island Sound breaks across and into it in two places. Great sharp rocks are piled up here and there in between these two channels, so that as the flood tide gets higher, the sea runs into the cove from the south-east, and also from the south-west and north, and on a stormy day for ten hours. During the last five hours of the flood and the first five hours of the ebb tide, the cove becomes a veritable whirlpool of clashing seas; three different lines of breakers meeting together in its centre, only to be thrown back again and caught by the next oncoming seas. Sometimes all three breakers, after clashing, seem to recede each into its own respective channel, at other times the breakers from Brannagh Sound overpower the others, beat them down and rush over them out into the deep towards the south-east.

Amidst all this turmoil of water, the sharp-pointed rocks become exposed for an instant as a breaker rushes over them; then they are submerged again, and woe betide a curragh if one of those treacherous rocks grips her bottom: her whole framework is ripped to pieces as easily as one would tear a sheet of paper. Nor would there be much hope for the crew. The currents run so strongly that even a good swimmer would be helpless, assuredly being swept out to sea and dragged under. So that a landing is practically impossible unless done at the last hour of the ebb or the first hour of the flood tide.

"It will be an in and out day, Pat," said Mr. Flaherty, as heavy dark clouds were driven over the face of the sun. "We are lucky if we can do anything. I don't like it. That curragh out there is standing up against heavy weather enough as it is, yet we can't do anything without sun-shine."

"The sun will soon be out again," said I hopefully, but to tell the truth I was becoming more and more uneasy. The clouds were banking more heavily and, though the sun shone brightly in flashes, it wasn't staying out long enough for Mr. Flaherty to get his camera going.

Suddenly Mr. Flaherty would shout: "All ready, Pat. Will we signal her to come in?"

But before anything could be done the clouds had covered the sun again, and another spell of waiting took place.

I had the signal flag ready in my hand. When I raised it on high it meant that we were ready for the canoe to make a try for the passage, but it was understood between us that Big Patcheen was to use his own judgment absolutely in the running of the breakers. Time was passing and Mrs. Flaherty became very anxious.

"When is the turn of the tide, Pat?" she asked.

A heavy rain squall swept in from the sea and we had to seek shelter behind a high boulder.

"The tide has turned long ago, ma'am," I answered, adding: "I know the men out there are in a bad position, but they are the pick of the best men, and with God's help the day may clear yet, so that Mr. Flaherty may finish his picture."

"Oh, Pat, I don't know," said she. "Not for the world, as I have told you many a time before, would we have anything happen to anybody engaged in working for us. At the same time, of course, you know more about those men and what they are able to do than I, so if you think the sun *will* come out and that there is not much danger as yet, then do as you think best. But just the same," she went on, "it looks simply awful out there to me."

Still Big Patcheen and his crew kept their curragh's bows to the sea, waiting and watching for the sun and the flag. At about half past one a rift appeared in the clouds, and we knew the sun would break through.

"All ready!" said Mr. Flaherty.

"A few seconds more," said I, "and we might as well venture it. You might get something done before the clouds come again."

As the last wisp of flying cloud was passing over the sun, I raised the flag, and the curragh headed for the passage; and being eager to get some good work done while the sun shone, they came on bravely. Glancing ahead, and on each side at the lines of breakers, Big Patcheen thought he would chance the run through. Half a dozen more strokes, eager though watchful as a hawk, he saw on the western reef a great sea rise up in a monstrous menacing black wall; a moment it towered, then it broke and raced towards them. Quick as a flash of light, six oars dipped as one. The curragh was turned out; a few strong stretching strokes and she was clear again.

The breaker tore across the passage with a roar as if of rage at being cheated of its prey. The curragh went farther out on the deep.

"Was there danger then, Pat?" asked Mrs. Flaherty.

"Plenty of it," I answered. "Any other men in that boat would never get through."

She looked at me with one of those strange looks she sometimes gave me, as if trying to find out whether I had not become quite heartless and cared not a jot whether men lost their lives or whether they didn't, provided the film was finished. I do admit that at this time I did have very strange thoughts, and like Mrs. Flaherty I too have sometimes wondered. But indeed the making of *Man of Aran* was enough to make any man think strangely.

We had another long spell of waiting, and Mr. Flaherty spoke many times of signalling the curragh to come in, sun or no sun. The narrow channel inside the passage had by this time become a hell of tossing tumbling seas, coming from all directions at once. Now there was no landing possible, at least there was none such as we had ever seen a curragh make before.

When Mr. Flaherty spoke about getting the curragh in without the sun shining, disappointment was written so largely over his face that I knew that even he was hoping against hope that the curragh might be able to hold out for a while longer, so that after all these long months of waiting this scene that was to finish the film might be completed. There came another rain squall but, as I gazed anxiously into the south-western sky, I spied a patch of blue.

"All ready after the shower," I shouted. "The sun will be out when the rain passes."

The curraghmen were also watching. The rain passed, and as the last shadow sailed past the sun I hoisted my flag. The curragh came in closer, but now the great seas broke clean across the passage, the rush through could not be made, and the blue patch of sky was being pushed away hurriedly by heavy black clouds. It seemed to be an entirely hopeless situation, and yet if those breakers just lowered for only a few minutes, Big Patcheen might make a try for it.

"Ready! Ready!" I shouted, as I saw the oars snap forward. On the reef the breakers still reared high, but not so high it seemed as they did a few seconds before. Yes, they were trying, these great picked men of the west. On they came through those mighty seas, rowing strongly, yet finding it difficult to make much headway because of the terrific undertow. They disappeared down into the trough of the sea. My heart stood still, and through our minds on shore the same thoughts flashed: will she ever be seen again, will she win through? Yes, we see her again, and the superb skill shown in her handling by Big Patcheen and his men bring wild cries of admiration from Shauneen Tom and some other men who had by this time gathered on the shore.

A great wall of water lifted its length on the reef. It was the first of three great breakers. Higher it rose as it gathered its strength for destruction, and from the men on shore the cry arose: "Ah, God! Give them strength, it is coming! It is down on top of them. They are lost!"

But they weren't lost. The curragh had come through the worst of the passage and now as this monster sea came raging towards them there was a chance to fight it, and this Patcheen and his men, with superhuman effort, prepared to do. I shall never forget the thrill it gave me, when I saw Big Patcheen with a left-hand stroke, his men timing their strokes instinctively with his, get ready to meet the crest of the wave, and how McDonough flashed up his right-hand oar to let the cap of the sea go by.

A dozen more strokes and they were inside and in safety, that is they would have been safe had the sun been shining continuously all day. The delay caused by having to wait for the clouds and rain to pass had now made a landing frightfully dangerous. It was blowing hard, and the sea had been getting up since the first of the flood tide. Through the three channels the great seas came breaching, storm-tossed and angry, smashing each against the other. Channels and passage were now in one continuous turmoil, while here and there as the seas drove in or receded, sharp-spiked treacherous rocks hid their heads, only to

lift them up cruelly through the waters, as if waiting and watching to deliver a death blow to the gallant little craft that was now fighting for its life.

It was not a question with us on shore now as to whether the sun shone or not. To have the curragh land as quickly as possible was the first thought in our minds. Mike and Maggie were on the shore; I had pointed out to them the place where the curragh must land—that is if it ever landed—and all through the curragh's battling with the waves they shouted and signalled to the crew, pointing to the only spot where as a last chance a curragh might make a run for it.

Mrs. Flaherty hurried to where I stood, and looking at me beseechingly, said: "Oh, Pat, Pat, can they ever land?"

"I will tell you something, Mrs. Flaherty," I answered. "They cannot land, that is come ashore in any way that a curragh ever landed before, as far as *I* know. The day has turned out so terribly bad that they cannot go back out again through the passage, and I'm afraid after another hour and a half the curragh will be lost in this channel, because the high tide will come breaching over that ledge of rock. That is the only protection they now have from the whole force of the western ocean."

As the curragh topped a gigantic wave, and then disappeared out of sight, Mrs. Flaherty cried out: "Oh, my God!" She turned away and covered her eyes with her hands. "What shall we ever do if anything happens to those brave men?"

"I wouldn't take on as bad as that," I said, "because there is still hope. Patcheen believes he will never be drowned, and when a man believes that and knows his business besides, 'tis hard to lose him!" I told her some more about how I had impressed on his mind the dire necessity of doing the work this day, and what it meant to Aran and to the Flaherty family.

She looked at me very reproachfully, and said: "May God forgive you."

Now and again a spot of blue appeared, but Mr. Flaherty was working his camera in sunshine and in cloud, all the time shouting: "Can they make it, Pat? Can they make it?"

Such work as these peerless curraghmen were doing could never be done again. Time and time again they tried to make a landing when the great seas were not coming through all three channels at once, but they were driven out again and again to continue fighting what now seemed to be a losing battle.

Shauneen Tom turned on me, his face white and his eyes blazing, saying: "Oh, you ruffian! You have the men lost! There is no blame coming to the Flahertys, but *you* know what kind of a sea ran here with a high tide and a storm."

"You are right, Shauneen," I answered, "but even so, I have hopes yet that Patcheen will make one big try and he will either live or die in the doing of it."

"I know," said Shauneen wildly, "that they are three as good men as ever caught an oar. But there is no curragh that was ever laid on sea can last there much longer."

By this time other men had appeared, some coming from their gardens, while others had run from Bungowla shore and village on hearing that Big Patcheen was out on the south side on this wild and stormy day, trying to run the passage of the breakers there.

These men kept shouting to one another and to the

curraghmen, though of course the latter couldn't hear them. They were wild with excitement, as they asked God to give strength and help to the men in the canoe. Still Big Patcheen, with his chances lessening more and more because of the rising tide, watched all three channels with eagle eyes. This was the biggest moment in his life, and he meant to combine brain, skill and muscle into a final effort—do or die!

Once again they had to row out. A heavy sea had broken on the reef, and rushing in against the ledge to the west, it was thrown back and caused such a dangerous cross sea that Patcheen for the first time put into execution the most difficult, muscle-straining stroke of a master curraghman, and only used on occasions of desperate need. Ordinarily, when a curragh is to be brought about, the three oars on one side make a forward stroke, the other three are held with ends resting in the water, or at most with a light backward pressure. But in Big Patcheen's case this couldn't be done. They had the curragh's bows facing out as they rowed, when suddenly this sea broke on the ledge and was thrown back on them in a second, leaping, as it seemed, in its fury to reach the curragh and take her unawares before her bows could be brought on to it. It was on her, she was doomed—so it looked to us on shore, and we all yelled wildly:

"Ah! Bring her up to it, Patcheen, or you are lost! You are lost!"

Patcheen and his men in a flash saw their danger. It was a matter of only a couple of seconds in which to save their curragh. But look at him—this man of iron strength and reckless courage! The curragh could not go forward, as the sea was coming so swiftly on her. She had to face it

271

without moving ahead one inch. Quick as thought Patcheen's right hand went forward for a powerful stroke, while his left hand came back for a backward drive. Thus one side of the man was exerting every muscle for a forward pull, while the other side was tensed for a backward push. Lower he bent, straining, lower still till his head almost reached as low as the curragh's gunwale.

The sea struck her. But Patcheen had won. His two men had helped all they could, but we on shore knew that it was that great stroke of Patcheen's that had really saved her, and we drew deep breaths of relief when we saw that once more she had come clear, out from the jaws of death.

The curragh was now being tossed and buffeted here and there by the force of the seas, Patcheen and his men trying fiercely to hold her in a favourable position so that if the chance came they might be able to run for the shore. Three times we could see they almost fancied that their chance had come, but with lightning strokes they had driven their curragh out again. Great monster seas tore through the Brannagh Sound channels. This last time, that they rowed out, there came in front of them a giant wave, bellowing in through the south passage, and, though we on shore had thought that it was from the seas in the Brannagh Sound channels that Big Patcheen had expected the danger to come, we soon saw that this was not so, for by far and away the biggest sea of all that had come up to this time came rushing in through the south passage. This was where the real danger lay. It might have caught and driven the curragh against the Brannagh Sound breakers, and, had such a thing happened, nothing could have saved either men or curragh.

We didn't know that when Patcheen saw this giant wave coming that at last he had sensed his opportunity, and he prepared to take advantage of it. He rowed out to meet this wave before it broke. The curragh topped its crest and disappeared from sight down the other side. The great sea broke and came raging into and through the channel and on to meet the other breakers racing in from Brannagh Sound.

We looked and could hardly believe our eyes, for the curragh had turned in after it had let the great wave pass, and now here they were rowing with all their power for the shore, putting into their work the last atom of their strength. Patcheen had taken the slender and only chance of the giant wave being able to overpower and hold in check the seas from Brannagh Sound long enough to enable him to reach the shore. It was a long chance but it was the only one, and he was taking it. Would they come through? They should now be able to hear our shouts of encouragement, but our shouting suddenly turned to cries of dismay, because farther in and directly in front of them, sometimes clear of the foaming water, sometimes hidden under it, were those treacherous rocks.

I shouted through the megaphone, telling Patcheen to beware, especially of one that was in the centre of the channel. My voice grew hoarse with excitement, but still the canoe came on, seemingly paying no heed to any warning; her crew were glancing swiftly on every side as they rowed, and now for the first time real fear for their safety struck my heart. If they failed to judge to the inch the position of the submerged rocks and should the receding sea suddenly leave the fangs exposed, then Patcheen and his men would be seen no more, except for the few seconds before they would be sucked under by the current and swept away.

Though the great wave had smashed the force of the other breakers, they still struggled onward on their course towards the curragh. The rocks were now entirely sub-merged. The curragh is amongst them—she has now almost passed the spot where we knew the most dangerous one to be.

"Run her in, Patcheen! Run her in!" was shouted from the shore; but it was almost impossible to drive the canoe against the current, and before Patcheen could head the curragh for the straight short run to the shore, another sea came roaring in from the South Channel, and he had to swing his curragh's bows to meet it. The current dragged her relentlessly toward where death lay lurking. As the curragh swung around, those rocky fangs came up drip-ping white and seemed to reach out for her, but death missed Patcheen and his crew by a foot; with superhuman strength and uncanny skill they had managed to hold the curragh about a foot from the cruel toothed rock as she met the next sea bows on, while the next breakers came foaming in; she was turned in again in the flash of an eye, and was now running straight for the shore.

Shauneen Tom and some others were for rushing down, but I cursed them back, for here was the chance to finish the film, as Mr. Flaherty had planned, and I now depended on Big Patcheen and his men being able to save themelves without any assistance from us.

As the canoe was driven up on the rocks, Patcheen and his men leaped out of her. A great sea was rushing in, and after one glance at it, to judge its power, they ran up over the rocks to safety. The oncoming sea caught the curragh, dragged it out and smashed it to pieces, and this last sea finished the *Man of Aran*.

Patcheen and his men were drenched with sweat and brine, but their blue eyes were lit up with fire, and a great thrill of wild pride shot through me as I looked at them, for here had been a trial of some of the old, old stock, and the blood still ran true.

CHAPTER XI

We sail from Aran—The Greatest City—The
Opening Night—My Curragh's ready

★

Shortly after this, Mr. Flaherty took the film to London, and after a few months he sent me word to
have the shark-boat crew, with Mike, Maggie and
Big Patcheen, all in readiness to sail for London in order
to add some dialogue to the film.

I didn't have such an easy time with Maggie, because
rumours were flying around that we were going to a
pagan country, consequently she was a bit shaky about
going. However, she finally consented.

David Flaherty arrived in Aran at the beginning of
December. He had come to do some checking up on
material that had been left over after our film work, and
also to give to us much-needed moral support, to what
to most of us was a more or less terrifying journey.

We sailed from Aran, and in due course, not having
stopped overnight in Galway, we arrived in Dublin,
where we put up for the night at the Hotel Russell. We
all felt a bit strange in the big room as we sat down to
have our first good meal after leaving Aran. The room
had been reserved for us, so we were alone and soon felt
quite at home. Next morning we sailed for Holyhead,

and during the short trip across in the boat most of us talked about the adventures that lay before us, but Patch Ruadh never seemed to tire of examining the ship; he paced back and forth and every once in a while he asked me what her length was. He expressed a wish time and time again that he would like to pace her from bow to stern so that he could make sure for himself how many feet long this great ship was. We landed at Holyhead and took the train for London, and on the journey we kept looking out of the windows at the country we were passing through, and when we got into the flat country, where there were no crags, we said:

"Ah! What fine land it is, sure it isn't any wonder the English people are the richest in the world when they have land like this."

We talked on and on until nightfall, and then we watched the lights as they flew past, and at last we drew into Euston station.

None of us, with the exception of David Flaherty and myself, had ever set eyes on this great magnificent city of London. A city full of wealth and beautiful kindly women. A city full of joy, sorrow and pride, the greatest city that the world has ever known.

Mr. and Mrs. Flaherty and Miss Barbara Flaherty and John Goldman and a lot of newspaper men, and also some friends of mine, met us as we stepped off the train. The kindly reception we received from them took some of the feeling of strangeness away from us. They had some refreshments waiting, which we partook of, and after some flashlight pictures we were taken in taxis to an hotel near Earl's Court.

We were taken around to see the sights of the city for

a week before we began work. The members of the National University of Ireland Club had heard of our coming and they soon got into touch with us. They staged a great party in our honour and we were overwhelmed with kindness. I tried to speak a few words of thanks, but I made a poor job of it, because so much kindness and hospitality had knocked the wind out of me and I felt as if I was in a kind of fairyland. All this friendship made us feel more and more at home, so much so that later on when we went to all kinds of fine houses where we were entertained royally, we felt at our ease, as if we were at home in Aran working in our little gardens!

The Zoo was Mikeleen's favourite place of pastime. Maggie liked to visit the stores and look at the lovely clothes for women. But beyond admiring them she showed no great interest, saying they would be no good to her in Aran. She and Mikeleen had gone to stay with Tommy O'Rourke's sister, who is married and lives in London. Mrs. Flaherty knew they would be more at home there than anywhere else. The rest of us knocked about with a guide.

We visited art galleries, museums, the Tower of London and lots of other places including, of course, Madame Tussaud's. Most of us would have given our oaths that the Sleeping Beauty was alive—she is a waxen figure of a woman who seems to breathe most naturally. In the Chamber of Horrors I wasn't a bit surprised to see a waxen figure of a man whose name was Mullen; maybe he was a relation of mine, but indeed if he was, he was no relation to be proud of!

Tiger paid much attention to the suits of armour when we visited the British Museum. At all the places that we

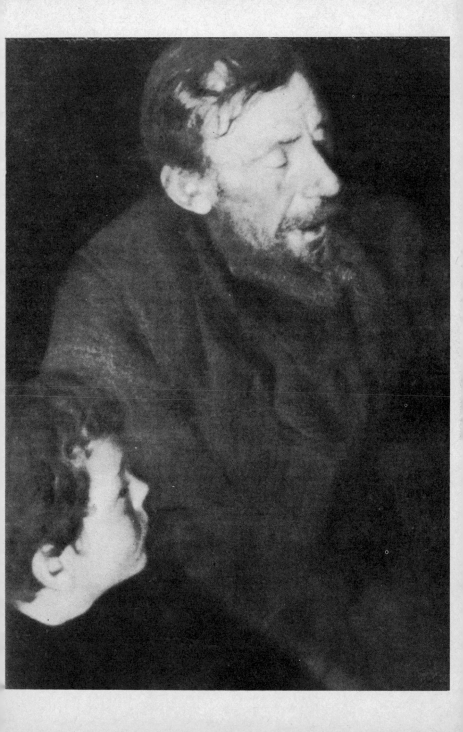

visited we were treated by the attendants with the greatest kindness and consideration.

After a little over a week we got ready to go to work at the Gainsborough Studios. We found it terribly stuffy after the free breezes of the Isles. We didn't have much bother in putting the dialogue in because we all remembered, more or less, what we said when working on the different scenes in Aran. But of course nearly all of my cursing had to be left out, which seems a pity because most of it was very brilliant and flowery! Mr. Flaherty took Tiger, Maggie, Mike and myself to the British Broadcasting Corporation building, where, as was usual with us now, we were treated very kindly. We broadcasted a little bit from there, and then we were taken to see the latest thing in television, which was truly wonderful. The Tiger, however, was not impressed; he said that he had visioned television fifteen years ago! Later on, Mr. Flaherty took us to see the circus. Patch Ruadh, when asked what he thought about it, said he believed the horses were real live animals, but that he had strong doubts about the girl riders being of this world, because they kept flying through the air most of the time.

We went to many parties and dinners, luncheons and some kind of thing they called high tea; we didn't know if they were really called dinners or lunches or suppers, nor did we care a hang, for we enjoyed them all thoroughly and met many splendid people, to all of whom we owe a great deal for their kindness to us.

While working in the studio, Evelyn Laye, who was starring in a new film called *Princess Charming*, invited us to have tea with her. We did, and a Princess Charming she proved herself to be, and we shall ever remember her kindness. I had the great honour of meeting her once more before she sailed on a trip to America. When leaving, she promised to come to Aran to see us all some day. I know she will come because she has a splendid character and the light in her great blue eyes shone true.

London wouldn't be right of course without Shauneen Tom putting in his appearance, and sure enough he dropped in on us one night at the house where we were staying.

He looked us over condescendingly with the same curl of the lip and twist of the tongue. He was starring in a little film of his own called *The Story Teller*. Mr. Flaherty had been asked to make it by the Irish Government, and Shauneen being wonderfully dramatic on the screen as well as off it, had come to London to tell the story because the sound had to be taken over here. He had no trouble telling his story, and I expect it will be liked by the school-children in Ireland.

We all had great trouble dodging the trams, buses and motor cars which fill the streets of this great city. These vehicles seem to be nearly always on murder bent, the way they crisscross everywhere and keep tearing to and fro. Some of us got tumbled upside down. I myself was driven sliding on one ear for yards, but being a bit hardy we are all still on our feet!

After nine weeks of London the time came for us to go back home, or at least for all but me. Some friends of mine had kindly invited me to stay with them for some weeks longer, and I accepted their invitation. A crowd of us saw the others off at Euston station; it was a sad going away, for the men of Aran had been kindly treated and had made many friends, so that their songs were mingled with tears, because at that time they thought they would never meet again those friends that they were now leaving behind. The train pulled out and they were on their way.

I stayed on in London and kept in touch with Mr. Flaherty who always had an idea that the cast would be needed for the opening night of the film. He was right; for after some weeks he sent for me and told me to get ready to go home to Aran and bring the cast back. I was to bring Tiger, Mikeleen and Maggie to London. He also told me to bring Patch Ruadh, and I, believing that the film was going to be a good one, made up my mind to bring my father as well. I left for Aran, and arriving there gathered them together with the exception of the Tiger, whom I had met in Galway and who promised to meet me in Dublin. We sailed from Aran in great form, my father being the noisiest of the lot. He sang a song as the boat left Kilronan pier, he told me afterwards that he did it more for spite than for anything else, just to show them— meaning neighbours and some men of Aran that he doesn't like—that he was going to London where none of them old devils had ever been! We stayed at Bailey's Hotel in Galway for the night. It was a fine place, be- cause the people who run it are finely Irish and very big- hearted. Next day we took the train for Dublin, where we were joined by the Tiger, and at Kingstown we went on board the Holyhead boat.

My father and Maggie had the time of their lives on this trip; they held one another's hands, as is the West of Ireland custom when singing, and their Irish songs floated through the ship and out over the Irish sea all the way to Holyhead. We were well known along the route by this time, and people gathered to see us on our way and send us God speed and good luck.

Once more we got out at Euston station and I took them all to where I had been staying. After a few days knocking about, talking to old friends whom we visited and having a good time generally, we showed the sights of London to my father, who showed no surprise at anything he saw or heard, whether he felt it or not. He wanted to talk to everybody, and as usual his theme was horseracing. I was taking him and Patch Ruadh home late one night, and we had to change in a hurry at Baker Street tube station. They were both pretty well under the weather and I had some trouble in hurrying them along; at last, and just as the train was about to start, we scrambled in and threw ourselves into the seats. A man and a woman were sitting together and my father sat down beside the man and I sat down beside the woman. Patch sat opposite us, his eyes looking beautifully vacant. As soon as my father got settled properly he leaned towards the gentleman and said:

"What's your fancy for the Derby?"

The gentleman looked at him and smiled. My father gave him no time to draw a breath, but went on talking:

"Take my tip, now, so-and-so, and so-and-so, but when all is said and done watch out for such-and-such a horse."

The gentleman said nothing but just nodded and smiled with a look of great toleration in his eyes and on his face; every once in a while my father threw me a look of prideful knowledge as much as to say: "Do you see me? Now here is an English gentleman and he agrees with everything I say about the horses, that shows you that I must know what I'm talking about. Can't you see now that your father is a great man?" After a while I became very much ashamed as he continued to shout about jockeys and horses at the top of his voice, so I turned to the woman and said:

"I'm sorry, ma'am, that my father is annoying your friend, as a matter of fact he has just come from a land where everybody talks to everybody else, and he thinks he should be allowed to do the same thing here."

She looked at me with a kind of a bright little smile, and said: "It is quite all right, your father can talk and shout all he wants to. This man is my husband, and he is stone deaf!"

"Thank God for that!" I answered fervently, and she gave me a startled look, but said nothing.

A few days later came the private showing of the film. It was shown at the Tivoli, to friends of the Gainsborough Company and newspaper men. Everyone pronounced it a great success. Then came the big dinner in the Savoy Hotel. My father says he is King of Aran for some reason or other. I think he says it is by virtue of his age, and he is the oldest man on Aran. I don't think it is vanity that prompts him to say it, but just sheer devilment with a view to making angry some of his neighbours that he doesn't like. At this big dinner he was toasted as King of Aran, all of which he took as a matter of course; here too he drank his first champagne. I asked him what he thought of this famous drink, and his answer was:

"Faith, it isn't so bad at all, but you think the divil a much strength there is in it, 'pon me soul I'd rather have a good glass of whisky."

This night was also fixed for the big opening at the

New Gallery Theatre. I went there with very mixed feelings. Here at last, after about two years of effort, made up of joyful moments, when some good work had been done, and of days, weeks and months of disappointments, when it seemed impossible ever to get anything to go right, here at last was the final test; for though everybody who had seen it had thought it good, yet this opening night was the real trial. We were all there in film costume, sitting up in one of the wings of the theatre. My father was with us, and to look at him one would imagine that it was he who had made the *Man of Aran* film instead of Robert J. Flaherty. The Irish Guards band was there and they played beautiful Irish airs for some time before the picture was shown.

The theatre was packed full with well dressed men and lovely women, beautifully gowned. The picture was put on the screen; it was run through, and then, as we of Aran stood up in our seats, the house rang with applause. Handclapping and cheering filled the air. My father, though a little man, felt as big as a giant. Maggie was very pleased and had a wonderful expression of happiness on her face. Mikeleen was very proud, but the Tiger maintained his stoic expression, and Patch Ruadh said simply in Irish:

"They seem to be making a lot of us; they are giving us a lot of praise and credit for working on the picture and helping to make it what it is; all of them seem to be happy." Then he turned to me and said earnestly: "And, Pat, God knows to-night that I'm glad they are happy."

A lot of pictures were taken of us as we left the theatre, and here and there one could hear remarks passed.

"The men of Aran—yes, that's Maggie." "That's Tiger; no, there!" and so on.

We were a bit shy and got away as quickly as we could. I was very happy that night, because we had been through a lot of heartbreaking work in the making of the film, and it was a joy to know that our work had not been in vain.

The last invitation we had in London was to a little treat by the National University of Ireland Club; that was as it should be, I think.

At last the time came when we had to say good-bye, and once again we crossed the Irish sea to our homes on the sea-girt stormy little Isles in the west. We had a quiet time on the boat crossing to Kingstown.

We had reached the highest peak in our simple lives, and now we were already sending our thoughts on to Aran. We stayed in Dublin for a week, and we were present at the opening night of the film at the Grafton Theatre. Here too it was a great success and I was much thrilled when I heard some women say during the great storm scene: "Oh, God, bring them safe in!"

Mikeleen, Tiger and Maggie got a wonderful reception as they appeared in the doorway after the show. Mikeleen and Tiger returned to England to travel around the cities there in the interests of the film. Maggie, Patch Ruadh, my father and I returned home to Aran, to live again the lives we lived before we went to work on the film.

Most of us have saved some money. Maggie, who really needed a few pounds more than anybody else, is now fairly well to do, and she can look ahead without fear while her family grows up. Patch Ruadh has some money put away, as also has Patch McDonough and Steve Dirrane. Mikeleen has placed his family on Easy Street for years to come. There never was a better son than Mikeleen, and while he has been away in England he has sent his mother practically all his earnings. Tiger also, I'm sure, has a bit of change put away. Tommy O'Rourke didn't save much, and Patcheen Faherty only saved very little.

There now remain of the *Man of Aran* film-crowd Big Patcheen of the west and myself. No, we didn't save anything; there must always be fools in every big family! Big Patcheen couldn't hold gold even if he were digging it, and I'm afraid that where money is concerned there must be a big hole in my hand somewhere; it just flies away somehow, but it really doesn't matter a bit, for we can begin again where we left off, Big Patcheen and I.

You might ask if we have been spoiled by our trips to London and by the wonderful receptions we have had. No, why should we be spoiled? We have been finely treated and we can look back to our days in London with very great pleasure. On the other hand I am convinced that nothing could spoil a Man of Aran.

*   *   *

My curragh and my nets are ready, and any day now we shall see the shoals of mackerel turning the surface of the sea into dark ripples as they sink down and rise again. The winter supply of fish must be got in and there is no time to lose.

Now as I finish I give my sincerest thoughts in thankfulness to the friend who throughout the writing of this book has always given me the greatest inspiration, and also encouraged me to persevere to the end.

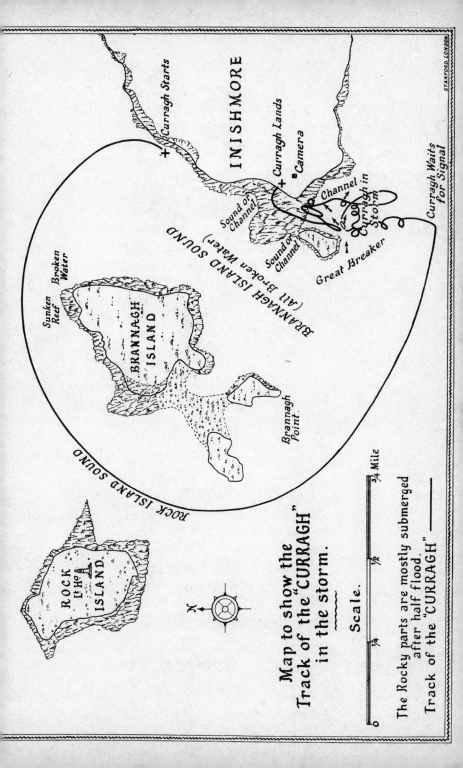

INISHMORE

Curragh Starts

Curragh Lands

+ Camera

Channel

Curragh in Storm

Sound or Channel

Sound or Channel

BRANNAGH ISLAND SOUND
(All Broken Water)

Great Breaker

Curragh Waits for Signal

Broken Water

Sunken Reef

BRANNAGH ISLAND

Brannagh Point

ROCK ISLAND SOUND

ROCK ISLAND
Lt. Ho.

STANFORD LONDON

Map to show the
Track of the "CURRAGH"
in the storm.

N

Scale.

0   ¼   ½   ¾ Mile

The Rocky parts are mostly submerged
after half flood.
Track of the "CURRAGH" ──────

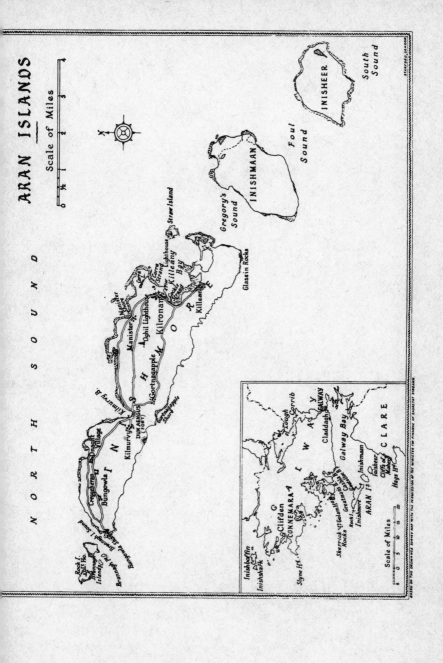

ARAN ISLANDS

Scale of Miles

NORTH SOUND

INISHMORE

INISHMAAN

INISHEER

Gregory's Sound

Foul Sound

South Sound

Killeany Bay

Glassin Rocks

Straw Island

Lighthouse

Killeany

Kilronan

Oghil Lighthouse

Gorthnagapple

Kilmurvy

DUN AENGUS (FORT)

Bungowla

Onaght Village

Creggarugh

Brannock Islands

Rock I.

Bill Rks.

Kilronan B.

STANFORD, LONDON

Inishboffin

Inishshark

Slyne Hd.

Clifden

CONNEMARA

GALWAY

Corrib

Lough

Claddagh GALWAY

Galway Bay

Skerrick

Golam Hd.

Rocks

Greatman's Bay

Casla

Costelloe

Inishmaan

Inishmore

Inishmaan

ARAN IS.

Inisheer

Cliffs of Moher

Hags Hd.

CLARE

Scale of Miles

BASED ON THE ORDNANCE SURVEY MAP WITH THE PERMISSION OF THE MINISTER FOR FINANCE OF EIREANN.